SCHOOLCRAFT COLLEGE LIBRARY
D1545927

THE TALMUD

THE TALMUD

An Analytical Guide
to its
History and Teachings

by
ISAAC UNTERMAN

BLOCH PUBLISHING COMPANY
New York

Third Printing 1971

ISBN: 0-8197-0189-0

Printed in the United States of America

Library of Congress Catalog Card Number 73-148291

Dedicated to
My Grandchildren

CONTENTS

FOREWORD

IT IS CLEAR THAT THOSE OF US WHO ARE STILL LINKED TO THE past and continue to weave the threads of our ancient culture, must also bring back to life its creators and builders.

If we truly try to imbibe the spirit of generations gone by, if we truly cherish those who have carried on the process of Jewish cultural creation, if we are still infused by Jewish lore and thought, Jewish ideals and culture, then we must first of all try to understand the inner essence of these creators and their achievements.

We have had, comparatively speaking, many spiritual giants, many commentators, savants and scholars, who by their profound knowledge and creativeness have become the very life strength of our people. We have had many thinkers and philosophers, martyrs and saints, teachers and leaders, who paved a path for our people and became the driving force in our history. We have also had our revolutionists and utopians, ascetics and materialists, militants and pacifists. And all of them together, each one in his own particular way, have given color and content to our life.

What, indeed, has sustained the Jew in his long life in the Diaspora? What, indeed, has given the Jew the strength to keep on existing, if not this ancient culture, these spiritual treasures to which we are still indissolubly linked?

Indeed, wherein lies this great strength which has molded all of us in a similar spiritual pattern and has welded together the disparate parts of a people scattered throughout the earth?

This is nothing else but the Jewish faith, this strong and powerful belief which is part of our very being. On this there is absolute unanimity. Every scholar, if he only wishes to be honest and objective, must reach this conclusion.

And what intellectual fruit did this faith nourish and yield?

Certainly this is nothing else but the Talmud!

States sprang up and states vanished. But the Jew has always preserved his Talmud and from it drew the strength to overcome all the tragedies of his history. The inner world of the Jew has always remained whole and untouched; no outside influence, no danger and no whirlwind had sufficient power to destroy this world.

Not every Jew was a Talmudic scholar and not every Jew was a sage, but every Jew drew his spiritual nourishment from the Talmud and made it a part of his very life. Every Jew, even the very simplest, was spiritual heir of the Talmud. If he had no knowledge of the Law, he nevertheless had access to the Talmud; he knew many stories from the Gemara, was able to relate a tale from the Midrash, recite a famous sermon, tell an aphorism or wise saying so abundantly found in the Talmud.

And the Jew maintained the heritage scrupulously! He was inseparably bound to it, and it to him. The Jew, as well as the Talmud, had to suffer many slanders and calumnies, many bans and persecutions. Historical fate has dealt with both alike, and both have continued to exist, although esoteric in nature and not always understood.

Even the Bible, the Book of Books, is a sealed book for many, closed with a thousand locks, but still worse is the general attitude towards the Talmud. It is not only a negative attitude, but an antagonistic, hostile, contrary attitude. For this, there are surely many causes. But the main cause—and there is no shame in saying it—is certainly the lack of knowledge of the Talmud, the ill-comprehension of its great achievements.

The Talmud has always been a book solely for scholars, savants, and researchers. The necessity for popularizing the Talmud was often seen, and new interpretations were made. However, these attempts helped little. The interpretations were often more difficult, and more arid that it demanded greater expertness and dialectical understanding than the original text itself.

Generally, our generation has not become fully infused with the Jewish lore and knowledge of the Talmud. The research and interpretation of our cultural heritage has become increasingly monopolized by Christian scholars, and the results bear a purely Christian stamp. In most cases, even our friends are liable to be misled in ideas of the Talmud derived from such sources.

Christian scholars often have a peculiar viewpoint: The Talmud spreads hatred; the Talmud is not a work that can be included among the world's scientific works; the Talmud is filled with foolish fantastic tales and superstitions. What uninformed ideas have not been spread about the Talmud?

But the truth is that the Talmud is a significant part of our very life. It embraces the creativeness of many hundreds of years. It is an efflorescence which has substantially helped to mold and form our very essence.

The Talmud is the cornerstone of Jewish culture, the creative strength of the Jewish people, the backbone of Jewish history.

The Talmud is filled with the contents of Jewish life, with the treasures of Jewish culture and knowledge. Our Talmudic scholars were themselves poets and lyricists, doctors and sociologists, botanists and geologists, philosophers and theologians. In the schools of Beth Shamai and Beth Hillel, the methods of Greek philosophy were studied. Our laws are partially built upon their logical foundations.

Throughout all generations and all countries, the Talmud has been the guide and main nerve center of the Jewish people. In the Talmud, we find sayings of profound meaning and great literary quality. The words of our spiritual giants, the Talmudic scholars, molded our fate. The style and completeness of the Mishna is of great artistry, rich and profound in thought. The words, infused by faith, are simple and pure.

Even our indigenous speech, our Yiddish language, whose continued existence we attempt to maintain with so much effort, is linked by a thousand threads to the language of the Talmud and the Midrash. The nuances, idiomatic expressions, aphorisms and wise sayings which adorn our Yiddish, are a living part of this great work.

Yet, how many of us are really acquainted with this great and rich source of culture? How many of us really know the decisive role which the Talmud played in the development and maintenance of the Jewish people? How many of us really comprehend the great power and influence of Talmudic law upon our folk-ways?

And when, at the present time, we speak with so much

enthusiasm about building our life only upon the basis of Jewish culture, why any estrangement from this original source?

Many have translated parts of the Talmud in order to show the non-Jewish world and our own assimilated Jewish youth the treasures of Jewish thought and feeling, the profound work in which the Jewish creative spirit is embodied, the Jewish soul and the secrets of Jewish eternity. This is, of course, a great cultural contribution. Nevertheless, it is not of very great usefulness.

One who has not had the opportunity to study the original will not, despite all these translations, be able to comprehend the real meaning. The real Jew is linked to the Talmud not only through its contents, but through its very letters and form. They are like the reflection of the sea which cannot be separated and divorced from the sea.

The Jew who has not studied the Gemara and has not heard the sweet chant of Abaye and Rabba, will not derive any pleasure from the translation, not even from the translation of the Scriptures. It will neither nourish nor influence him.

My present work does not seek to explain, interpret or translate. It is not even a monograph about the creators of the Talmud. Such has been done before, and with great erudition and devotion. The contents and significance of the Talmud, the achievements and gains through the Talmud, the fecundity and spirituality in the Talmud, its origin and development, methods and systems, causes and results—discussions of all this, are the modest aims of my work.

CHAPTER ONE

THE TALMUDIC CONSTRUCTION OF A RELIGIO-NATIONAL LIFE

THE INTUITIVE COGNITION. THE PROPHETIC TENDENCY. THE TALMUDIC CONCEPTION AND ACHIEVEMENTS. ESSENCE AND SPIRITUALITY.

FROM EARLIEST TIMES THE JEW WAS THE ONLY ONE TO GRASP intuitively the concept of monotheism, of a God who is basically without corporeality and without form, without beginning and without end.

The national-historical imagination of the divine revelation and relationship to the Jewish people pictures Abraham intuitively perceiving God and making an eternal covenant with Him, binding the Jews to Him and making them His Chosen People. Because of this spontaneous cognition, God promised Abraham, and later reaffirmed it to Isaac and Jacob, that from among all the peoples of the earth He would choose Abraham's children as His own beloved people, as a holy and consecrated people.

Since the divine part of the covenant is eternal and unbroken, so therefore is the Jew also forever bound to this covenant. The fact that on Mount Sinai the Jews said that they would first do and then listen shows that there had existed between the two parties a previous understanding.

The act of cognition itself came to the Jews purely intuitively, with little searching or seeking, negotiation or bargaining. The Jew perceived God primarily emotionally and intellectually, through his feelings and his thoughts, and the covenant came into being as a result. As soon as the Jew apprehended himself, grasped his own inner essence and being, he also apprehended the Divine Power. Both God and Jew then became a single unity, and their relations became personal and filial: God is the father and the Jew is His chosen child.

The relation has not always remained the same. In times of human corruption, God became a God of revenge. He became the implacable ruler, and the Jew His slave. When a formalized morality and ethics evolved, God became a God of mercy and sympathy. He is still the ruler, but His rule is paternal, full of love and compassion.

It was possible for the Jew to develop this relationship, because the Deity and Judaism were never conceived as a dogma, but as a vital necessity for the unique existence of the people. That is why the Torah and its regulations of daily life are of such great moment for Judaism.

The sages of the Talmud, they who gave the Jew his perfect form of uniqueness and divergence from other peoples, have more fully and deeply developed this conception. The Gemara declares: God is different from man. When a man mints coins from a pattern, they are all alike. But the Deity has molded man from one pattern and yet they are all dissimilar.

And according to the Talmud differences are physical and external, spiritual and innate. Difference is individuality and exists in an individual as well as in a people. Only when there is consciousness of disparity do the people possess individuality and integrity. When the consciousness of difference is destroyed, then the people cease to exist.

The Jew spontaneously apprehended the idea of the Deity and espoused it emotionally and intellectually. What was lacking, however, was the link with the national instinct. This crystallization came later, at first through the Prophets, and later in more complete form through the sages of the Talmud. Although the Biblical religio-ethical idea, as well as the Bible itself, later became the spiritual possession of most civilized nations, only the Jewish people became historically indissolubly linked with it. Again, this was made possible only by the Talmud. To remain at the level of the Prophets, with its spiritualism, was virtually impossible for a people possessing a healthy national instinct for survival. We might have evolved into a sort of super-national group, but certainly not into a living nation.

A profound allegory in the Midrash relates:

Moses had intended to inscribe also the Unwritten Law, but since he perceived with divine instinct that the other nations of the world would claim that they are the true believers, the true Sons of Israel with whom God made a covenant, God gave him an unmistakable sign: Whoever possesses my secret is the true Jew. The Talmud, expounding the Written Law, is this secret which distinguishes the Jews from all other peoples.

This also makes it clear why all tendencies in the direction of divorcing the Talmud from Jewish life were bound to suffer an ignominious defeat. The healthy national instinct has always, without much difficulty, severely liquidated these processes of separation.

A false view of the Talmud and its significance has been pressed on us by the Gentiles. To them, the Talmudists were legalists and dry pedants, who would not perceive real life nor understand it. This view has its source in the beginning of Christianity, and has since stood in open conflict with the Jewish way of life. The Talmudic affirmations have firmly distinguished Christianity from Judaism and have since incurred attacks.

The instinct of the Jewish people has always been healthy and has always clearly perceived that by seeking to create a gap between them and the Talmud, their religio-spiritual life, an attempt is made on their very existence, on their national continuity. When the Talmud was burned in Rome or in Spain, in Germany or in Poland, the object was not to burn books but to destroy the Jewish spiritual creative processes and thus undermine the very existence of the Jewish people.

The Talmudic, and this is to say the Jewish, attitude towards faith was never abstract. According to the Jewish conception, truth can never be abstract, and an abstract view can never be the absolute truth. Truth is life.

Truth and faith were for the Jews always a living reality. The Talmud fully comprehended this objective truth, the truth which leads to life, to a moral and just life.

The wise men of the Talmud, who profoundly analyzed the essence of Judaism, have revealed to us the cause of Jewish eternity. It is in the maxim of "we will do and we will hear," first act and then listen, that the meaning and quintessence of the eternal existence of Judaism are expressed.

Judaism is a philosophy of life, an ideology, as profound and as wide as the Jewish people themselves. But its inner strength lies in a way of life expressed in a specific and unique mode. The old and renowned Chassidic Rabbi, the "Sephath Emeth," interpreted the Biblical verse: "Keep therefore and do them: for this is your wisdom and your understanding before the eyes of the nations," as follows: Science and knowledge are expressed through our deeds. The deed is the most important, and the theory is merely a result of the deed.

It is this concept of the vital significance of action which distinguishes Judaism from Christianity. We did not stop at monotheism, nor even at abstract faith. We have linked our faith from the very beginning to the deed, with action of a high moral character, with justice and fairness, kindness and compassion, humanism and divinity. Every high ideal, every noble feeling has been raised to the service of God. To honor one's parents, to make a loan to someone in need, to be hospitable to strangers, to fit out an impecunious bride, to pay honor to the deceased—all these ethical precepts have been raised to the level of a good deed favored by God.

The Talmud combats mythology, and seeks instead cognition and devotion. Cognition, and not abstract belief, is the source of Judaism. The apprehension of one God has led to the apprehension of an ethical unity. The Talmud even rejects the metaphysical view, and concentrates instead upon the human being, his needs and way of life.

Maimonides asks (More Nebukim, chapters 26 and 48): Of what concern are the secrets of God and nature to me? Of prime interests to me are human deeds, the canons and precepts of human conduct.

According to the Talmud, the shell, the outer garment, the form, has the same value as the seed, the essence, the nucleus. More, the shell, the form, is often capable of offering far greater resistance to change than the contents. Talmudic law, which crystallized and constructed a Jewish way of life and endowed it with its own specific national form, is the shell in which the Jewish core is clothed.

According to the conventional and time-worn Christian view, the history of the Jews and of the Jewish religion is divided into two epochs. The first epoch is grandiose and creative. This is the epoch of the Decalogue and the Prophets, when ethical monotheism, the belief in one absolute God whose essence is justice and charity, germinated. With the end of this period, so argue the Christians, the creative spirit of the Jews ends and the creativeness of the Christians begins as the completion and fulfillment of ethical monotheism. The Christian God is not only a God of truth, justice, and charity, but also—and most importantly—a God of love.

And what, according to this Christian view, was the essence of the second phase in the history of Judaism and the Jews?

It is, so this view runs, a concentration upon the externals of faith, upon its outer shell. This later period lays the foundation of Talmudic Judaism, which is preoccupied with dry laws and regulations, with a barren formalism. The Talmud, say the Christians, buried the sacred flame of the prophets and their lofty vision in a mountain of legalism. This constituted the second epoch of the Jewish religion, an epoch of lowering and degrading Jewish creativity.

This view is not limited to the severely orthodox and pious Christian interpreter; we find the same view among the liberal and friendly Christian scholars. Moreover, very often the liberal scholar is more prone to exaggeration than the orthodox and religious Christian, and he does it sometimes precisely because of his deep desire to free the Christian faith from its dogmatic shackles.

The truth, however, is that in Judaism there is no such division, there is no first or second epoch. It is one continuous flow, one unified creative period. The division is a fictitious one and most certainly unjustified, because there is only one historic Judaism whose golden thread leads from Mount Sinai to the Prophets, to the Kneseth Hagdolah, to the Tanaim and Amoraim, on through to Saddia Gaon and Maimonides, and so on to our own days. This fact even such Christian scholars as Moore, Herford and Parks have understood.

The picture which the New Testament gives us of the Pharisees is not even a caricature; it is a good deal worse and there is not an iota of truth in it. The picture is dark and ugly, because of a definite aim: because the Pharisees represented a democratic, religiously inspired, and extraordinarily sensitive group of Jews. The greatness of the creators of the Talmud resides in the fact that they did not separate practice from theory, built no wall between faith and daily life. They would not even consider the question whether the miracles of Jesus were true or not, since they could not see any practical value for Jewish life in such speculation. The creators of the Talmud had before them only one object: to achieve an equilibrium between faith and life and to clothe the beautiful vision of Judaism in the skin and flesh of practical life. They therefore knew that no matter how intriguing and wonderful miracles may be, they cannot lead to a moral and spiritual transformation of human life. They understood that the road which leads to such a transformation is difficult indeed and full of pitfalls. They realized the danger which exists that because miracles are by their very nature so dramatic and attractive, the difficult but correct road may be left unseen and bypassed. No, the Pharisees did not base their faith upon miracles. For them there existed no doubt that the miracles of the Messiah will become revealed through justice and charity, outweighing hatred and injustice throughout the world.

There is no Hebrew word for religion, such as exists among other peoples. This is so because for the Jews the "religious" experience is not something separate, but is profoundly interwoven with the warp and woof of life. The longing for salvation is, according to Jewish thought, impossible outside the limits of the people and society as a whole. The Messianic salvation of the Jewish people is always linked to the salvation of the entire humanity. Man, society, and God—this is the "trinity" of the Jews.

The Hellenic element in Western civilization is very evident in Christianity. It constitutes the metaphysics of Christianity and is the very reverse of Judaism. To the extent that Christianity is differentiated from Judaism, it is based upon the mystery religions of Egypt, Babylonia, Greece—more particularly Greece. According to these mystery religions—and this, of course, is their very essence—man is himself incapable of achieving salvation and can do it only through the belief in a god that was born, died, became resurrected, and is now the god in the "other" world. Whether good deeds are important or not is not relevant here. Only through him, through the god that was also a man, and through belief in him is salvation of the individual possible. In the last analysis the life of the individual and the individual achievement of his soul's salvation have very little relation to society and its morality. Perhaps they are even a hindrance and the less the individual has any dealings with society the smoother his path to salvation will be. Jewish faith, on the other hand, staunchly maintains that somewhere in our world the morality of the individual must intersect the morality of society and this is the true beacon light for a seeking mankind.

The Talmud never asks what is God and what is morality. But with the power and influence of life itself, it investigated and determined these things. The essential question was: how to serve God and how to carry out God's will in actual life. The explorations of the Talmud purported only to investigate how the real and the actual may be linked with the absolute consciousness of God and Man into one force.

The Talmudic scholars conceived faith as an intimate, psychological, actual and spiritual phenomenon and physical need. The road of the Talmud led not to philosophy and theology, but to law and justice; it pursued not the abstract, but the concrete.

It is perhaps not surprising that the Talmudic scholars sought to base every rule of life upon the authority of some text in the Bible. Thereby they attempted to strengthen the law and its harmonious relation to the life of the people. Without this authority, every regulation would have remained congealed and without living vitality.

Above all and everything stands the Pentateuch, the Law of Moses, this ancient creation which first laid down the elementary principles of law and morality. Then come the

Prophets, they who raised Jewish spirituality to new heights and laid the basis for universalism. Next comes the Talmud, which linked all of it together and integrated it with actual Jewish life.

From the very beginning the Talmud was concerned with the problem that the Jews should be able to exist in a strange and often hostile environment, and at the same time not lose their identity and spirituality. Jewish life must therefore be linked to the Deity. God, the highest human concept of fullness and completeness, must become the aim of life.

Although the Talmud is based firmly on faith, it considers the Bible in its broad aspects merely as a guide to life, something which serves to sustain the life of the individual and of the people. "Obey my laws which man must carry out and live with—I am God."

Through the Talmud, the Bible became a practical religio-national guide to life, a life-giving lore which combines within itself God and man, heaven and earth, spirituality and materiality. The religious character and motive which were appended to purely human affairs, certainly immeasurably strengthened the unity and consistency of personality and life. The Bible became an inseparable part of Jewish life. One became dependent upon the other. One without the other could under no circumstances have survived the many years of history.

Through the Talmud, the Bible became a vital principle clothed always in a national garment. When the essence sometimes becomes weakened or lost, there remains to the people the forms, the outer garments, which then receive a national-cultural sanction.

The Talmudic scholars, the various commentators, interpreters and savants did not constitute a clergy. They were the representatives of our community life; they were the leaders, elected and sanctioned by the people, of our miniature state in the Diaspora. The Jewish people have always accepted this leadership with love and devotion.

Whoever wishes may deplore the fact that the essence of Jewish nationality has become embodied in the Jewish faith. But no one can change this fact. Religion was the great force able to sustain the Jew, and this was made possible because the Talmudic scholars took the long view. They virtually created the Jewish way of life, which sustained the integrity of the Jewish people. Again, a people without a unique way of life is an impossibility ethnically.

Even our Bible is different. Our Bible is first of all an expression of Jewish history, a history created by God and which therefore has no need of the motive forces and elements so necessary for other nations. Others must have territory and government. And when political independence is lost, the nation itself declines. This has not held true for the Jew, however. The Jews were a nation even before they had a country and they have remained a nation even when they lost their country.

Even while they were still in the desert receiving the Decalogue, the Jews were already a unique people with well defined historical objectives and customs. Jewish national consciousness, however, arose only when the Jews had begun to form that religio-national life based on Talmudic laws.

The Talmudic scholars, living as they did in the tragic years of the destruction of the Jewish state, adopted a practical course. Upon the ruins of the destruction they laid down a useful foundation for a new national edifice. Not the ethical ideals of the Prophets, but Talmudic law, the law which took the form of an entire state-constitution and which established a juridical framework for the Jewish people, proved capable of sustaining this edifice.

Of course, many of the Talmudic injunctions became invalid after the decline of the Jewish state, but in general the constitutional framework remained in force and was elaborated through further regulation and interpretation. And so long as the Jews remained under the direct influence of these regulations, so long was the Jewish spiritual state unified on a high level. We did not observe foreign holidays and rest-days, we did not seek foreign judges, but held to our own.

The Talmud erected a solid wall, and behind that wall existed a Jewish state, a state within a state. Even the adoption of foreign languages was incapable of assimilating us nationally and culturally. On the contrary, the assimilation of languages, to the degree that this process went on, rapidly aided us in more clearly defining our national mold and unique way of life.

Through the barriers it had set up, the Talmud virtually realized the right of the Jews to self-determination and made possible a kind of self-earned and fully-blown national cultural autonomy. Only Hebrew law and the Hebrew court prevailed among us. We did not appeal to government courts, and did not recognize them in our own Jewish life. Even state laws recognized Jewish de facto autonomy, while attempting to destroy it.

We are not merely a religious group or religious community, but a people—a people with its own way of life, history and culture.

Why did the Jews so readily accept strict isolation?

Many try to explain this isolation as the result of continual persecution. But that is not true. We began to isolate ourselves from the very start and subsequent history inevitably determined our fate. We entered the Diaspora with an already ancient, divergent and different culture and folkways. Hatred and persecution certainly strengthened this isolation, but did not cause it.

Even the fundamental development of the Talmudic law was also never dependent upon our political and economic status. The Talmudic upswing took place precisely at a time when the Jews were politically protected and enjoyed economic well-being.

It is true that the Jews were always under the shadow of persecution and because of this fear, the closing of the Talmud was hastened. But the great creative powers were revealed precisely when conditions were favorable. It was then that the Yeshivas in Babylonia blossomed forth, that the Jews freely accepted the Talmudic restraints. In periods of great persecutions, it is true that some Jews repudiated the Talmud and participated in treason.

Our uniqueness is determined by our historical fate and the will of God, and it is precisely because of this uniqueness that our history has universal meaning and cultural value.

CHAPTER TWO

THE TALMUD AS A UNIQUE CULTURAL PHENOMENON

THE EXTENSIVE THEMATIC AND UNIVERSAL SIGNIFICANCE. THE SOCIAL AND PRACTICAL VALUES. CULTURE IN STRUGGLE AGAINST EXTERNAL GLAMOUR. THE STUDY OF THE BIBLE AND HIGHER CRITICISM.

THE CREATIVE PROCESS AND TRADITION OF OUR CULTURE RUNS like a golden thread through our life, a thread which runs right from Mt. Sinai to the present, and which has never been torn asunder. With immense pride the Jew is able to look back upon the historical development of his glorious culture. From the very beginning the Jew has always been subject to an atmosphere of foreign intellectual currents, and yet has always been able to emerge with his own unique temper. Beginning with Egypt, Babylonia, Assyria, Persia, Greece, Rome, and reaching down to the greatest European culture in all its rich manifestations, ancient Jewish culture has always glowed with its own unique character and spirituality.

In the very center of this Jewish culture is the Bible, which has had the greatest influence on the political and intellectual development of the entire world. The Bible is the oldest written legal monument still in use. Even the Hammurabi codex, the Assyrian code, and the laws of the Hittites are historically linked to the Law of Moses.

From the moment that the Jews received the Decalogue, the foundation was laid for the development of Jewish culture. Subsequently the Jews have undergone many vicissitudes so that they have delayed on the road and even strayed from the chosen path. Nevertheless, they have always created new cultural values and have always carried forward their historical tradition.

All Jewish creation, beginning with the Bible and continuing through Chassidism, is a part of Jewish culture, uniquely Jewish and nationally Jewish, and in no sense similar to the form and contents of the great world culture. Jews have always pursued their own chosen path in the creation of their culture, their customs, and national character. The source from which the Jew drew his nourishment was original, and even the role which he played in world culture was a specifically Jewish role and uniquely determined.

Historically, one may look upon the receiving of the Law of Moses in his own way. Analytically speaking, one may regard the principle of "first do, then hear" according to his own scientific conceptions and ideas. One thing is certain, however, this principle found expression in our socio-ethical life. The very fact that the socio-ethical and cultural-ethical ideals of the Bible became an integral part of our lives is a direct result of this fundamental principle. The receiving of the Torah has, in our case, created an historically true culture.

And this is true also of the Talmud. The Talmud, the second greatest creation of the Jewish genius, is a national cultural creation. Perhaps that is why the Talmud could never become a part of the non-Jewish world. Its unique national cultural stamp is probably the cause.

Many of us still complain why the Jews did not assimilate the Greek philosophy and art. Many of us—even those who have long lost every vestige of religious feeling—still have a hankering for Apollo and Venus. But the truth is that Jewish thought never disregarded the spiritual creations of the Greeks and other peoples. On the contrary, it admits that they possess much wisdom and significance. But this wisdom is insufficient if we wish to achieve a fruitful life, a life of high morality, spirituality and purity. The Jewish Torah, Jewish ethics and Jewish spiritual values are indispensable for such a life.

Certainly, the Jew seeks a healthy physical life. But at the same time he strives for a life full of inner enthusiasm, inner spiritual fervor which shall redirect him from this rational world with its practical wisdom to the world of nobility, to the higher spheres of feeling and ethereality, of inspiration and purification, of divinity and integration.

The struggle of the Maccabeans against the powerful Syrian king, as depicted in the story of Chanukah, was not an ordinary struggle. It was not a question of the loss or gain of Jewish territory; nor was it a question of political power and aggrandizement. It was a struggle for an all-encompassing philosophy. The Jewish system of thought clashed with paganism, glamour, desire, physical strength, and carnal profanity. Had the Maccabeans been defeated in that struggle, all Jewish spiritual values and cultural riches would have been totally destroyed.

Greek culture was from the very beginning based primarily on outward allure, and was considerably removed from the justice, truth and morality which the Jews studied and practiced. Furthermore, the Jews realized that a people which assimilates foreign cultures can no longer hope to continue an independent existence.

Other peoples adopted Greek rule and culture without the slightest struggle. Greek armies were victorious, and conquered inhabitants assimilated the dominant culture, made it their own, and later themselves became the bearers and fighters for the advancement of this once foreign culture. The result was that these peoples later declined historically and lost every vestige of their own independent culture.

Here and there Greek armies met resistance. But this came about not because of a desire to preserve the native cultural riches, but because of a desire to save the golden treasures which existed in many pagan temples. Whenever the conquerors promised not to touch the golden treasures, or when they even occasionally promised to leave some vestige of political liberty, the opposition to them immediately subsided.

The situation was totally different, however, in the tiny country on the Mediterranean, in the Land of Judah. Here there was also a group of aristocrats and government officials who adopted Greek culture. But the majority of the people, the common folk, had a far healthier sense, and fought bitterly and stubbornly. Jewish stubbornness always came to the fore in the struggle for a free and independent spirit. It is necessary only to give a cursory glance at Jewish history to see this clearly and sharply.

And this stubbornness was not illogical or unjustified. It is always expressed in thinking through to the ultimate and inner significance of things and events. Jewish stubbornness, as illustrated in the epic struggle of the Maccabeans, came to the surface only because of the spurious Greek culture.

True Greek culture, receiving its highest expression in the philosophy of Aristotle, Socrates and Plato, finds no difficulty in harmonizing with the philosophy of the Rambam and other Jewish intellectual giants. The Jewish spirit absorbed the foreign ideas that had true value and gave them a Jewish form, clothed them in a Jewish mantle, and thereby enriched Jewish culture.

And yet, how can even this higher form of Greek culture be compared with our ancient Jewish culture? Our part in world civilization and in world culture is still greater than that of the Greeks or that of the modern period. Compare Greek philosophy, and with it also modern European literature, with the Bible and the Talmud and it will be easily perceived which will outweigh the other in the balance. The cultures of the ancient and modern world certainly contain many colorful and fragrant flowers, but cannot be compared with the fertile and rich Jewish culture.

It has been the fate of the Jews—a good as well as evil fate—that we have always come into contact with cultured peoples. Even as early as during the period of the first Temple we have come into contact with such highly civilized countries as Egypt, Assyria, Canaan, Babylonia, and Persia. Undoubtedly their influence upon us has been very great. According to the Bible, the House of Judah and the House of Samaria assimilated the foreign culture with its paganism and its complex religious rites, and although the thread of Jewish culture remained unbroken, it served as a warning to later generations.

Almost as if by miracle, whenever the Jews were seized by foreign influences, an inner awakening took place and an upswing of new determination to live in accordance with the unique Jewish character. The result was always an enrichment of our own culture, a creation of new ethical philosophical works, and a crystallization and purification of our own inner life.

The picture which our enemies paint of the Talmud and the later commentators as a degeneration of the Jewish spirit is completely false. The truth is that the Talmud, including the entire Rabbinical literature, has created a higher cultural life, a greater store of cultural values than, let us say, modern Hebrew or even Yiddish literature. It is precisely the Talmudic-Rabbinical literature, and later also the Chassidic literature, which has saved us from backwardness and congealment.

It is this literature which aids in imparting to the Jew his uniqueness and his wholeness. And although this fact may sometimes become blurred in historical extremes, it is crystal clear in Jewish consciousness.

The bare study of the Talmud itself has evoked within the Jew the very highest ideals. Through this study the Jew has relived all the solemn moments in the history of his people and its aspirations. Drawing nourishment from the Talmudic spring, the Jew fortified himself with the living creative power of his great masters. The study of the Talmud has also served to concentrate thought, deepen the understanding, and teach not to accept anything as axiomatic. The student was able to look at things in all their various aspects and ramifications, and with his own mind and knowledge to analyze and synthesize.

Even the Jewish child was able, through the Talmud, to enter an endless forest of deeply rooted wisdom and become entranced with its colorfulness and vibrant freshness. The Talmud has refined the senses, developed the abilities of the Jewish child, and has filled his heart with the ever-growing desire to rise spiritually. The child has instinctively sensed here a field which has the power to engross his entire being and to satisfy his intellectual hunger. The study of the Talmud developed the thinking capacity and made it possible for him to integrate and differentiate.

The Talmud has thus created the freshness and the vitality of the Jewish spirit, and throughout the long years of the Diaspora has been transformed into a widely ramified culture. Because of the Talmud the Jew has never ceased to be culturally active and creative, and everywhere, in all countries and in all his wanderings, he has left his mark.

The Talmud is a cultural creation of human brotherhood; a religious literature, in the etymological sense of the word, which should be unique among all religious creeds. Yet it strives towards complete unity of all peoples and not towards isolation and the sowing of hatreds.

It may seem that the Talmud is exclusively Jewish. In reality, however, the Talmud never ceases to have universal meaning. We never encounter in it the degrading and insulting views of other cultural peoples, and certainly not the exaggerated attitude towards our own national heroes, who are, as is wont, always perfect, good and honorable. The

Talmud does not scruple to find faults and sins even in Moses, David, and in many of the sages.

The Talmud embodies everything that concerns mankind. The most far-reaching human problems are treated in it. It is difficult to realize how much expression, emotion and unseen vistas of morals, knowledge and social justice are incorporated in the Talmud. A true love of mankind—a love which is simple, healthy and defeats all obstacles—is most clearly expressed. People of all races, colors and beliefs can study the Talmud with joy and profit.

And because the Talmud is so objective and universal it has been able to unite the scattered Jewish people throughout the world.

The Talmud is primarily the purely Jewish monument, marked by Jewish creative power, scope, content and significance. It is the written expression of an organic form which in the course of many generations has become welded to the very essence of the Jewish people.

The Talmud is a part of Jewish literature and comprises within itself everything that concerns our cultural life and folkways. The Talmud has given the Jew his homogeneity and wholeness, and although this may not be apparent in the extremes of history, it clearly exists in Jewish consciousness.

Some people believe that by our isolation from other cultures and their philosophical trends we became spiritually backward. It is, however, an incontrovertible fact that precisely through this isolation was the purity of the Jewish people maintained. And the continuation of a people and a culture is, after all, the primary necessity and justification. Without this isolation a Jewish consciousness might have been maintained, a kind of subjective Judaism expressing itself in nostalgia; a Judaism sustaining a comfortable existence amidst a non-Jewish environment.

It is perhaps also possible to probe the depths of the Platonic philosophy and marvel and admire the great luxuriance of its thoughts. But the Talmud speaks of a world of eternal verities and reveals to us the most profound and the most beautiful truths. The books of the Talmud are the greatest creations in the cultural history of mankind.

The Talmud embodies the profound yearning of the soul of the Jew and weaves the triple-strong strand of eternity which links and knits every Jew to his people.

Such is the peculiar character of Jewish life. It is always articulated to our long road which starts in the past and moves forward to the future and oscillates like the eternally capricious sea that alternately sends its waves to the shore and recalls them to its bosom.

And at times when the Jewish spirit is in a state of listlessness, when dark autumn clouds oppress the body as if with iron chains, when the spirit is laden with the weight of a dreary winter that is like an eternity, when it is immersed in a melancholy mood and clothed in gross materiality, then the Jew seeks to free himself from these confining influences—from the gray routine—to break all barriers and reach the summit of spirituality.

It is then that the nostalgia for the past—for the splendor of the Temple, the pageantry of the Service, the glory of the House of David—begins to smolder. And within the people the dream of a new future—a happier and more beautiful future, kindled by the warm reflections of God's kindness and sympathy—glows anew.

The Talmud, like the Scriptures, is animated by this immense potential power to excite the ideal of the coming joyful world order and to provide in moments of national tragedy and sadness fresh hope and consolation.

The Talmud is essentially as universal as thought itself. The Talmudic literature, as well as the Bible, is imbued with the highest of universal ideals, full of the love of mankind and human brotherhood.

The Talmud creates a broad ethical world, and it is from this that the Jew has drawn his universal conception of morality and responsibility. The desire for and aspiration to human decency, which are so clearly discerned in the voice of our conscience, are part of the divine power, and through the Talmud became identified with the source of all the divine attributes.

The universalism and ethical precepts of the Prophets are embodied in the Talmud and in the later writings, and there they find their complete fulfillment. The Talmudic conception is always the socio-ethical conception, and is linked indissolubly with the liberation of all mankind, with the abolition of evil government, and with the establishment of divine rule permeated by social justice and the Brotherhood of Man, irrespective of race or color, caste or class.

The Jewish concept of the Bible concerns itself little with sin or virtue, divinity or religiosity, although there is a world of beauty and morality, spirituality and dignity in those qualities. But the Bible in the broader sense means culture, moral and ethical precepts and restraints; a social outlook, human and universal ideals, which are contained in practically every word of the Bible and the Talmudic-Rabbinical literature, and are an integral part of it.

Even the modern apostles have in this respect created nothing new. The ethical precept which was formulated in the Bible, and then renewed and strengthened by the wise and tolerant Hillel, is still the leading ideal of social justice.

The rule, "Do not unto others what you would not have others do unto you," which expresses the ideal ascribed to Christianity with so much sacredness without crediting the original source, has always been and remains the keystone of the arch of Judaic culture. Christianity proclaimed it and embodied it in a beautiful phrase. But Judaism first created it and realized it in actual life.

Truth, justice and equity—wasn't this what Moses demanded and the Talmud preached? The fine attitude to the weak and to the oppressed has its primary source in human Judaism and in Jewish humanism.

That is why, perhaps, this healthy outlook is expressed so directly and so clearly even in our communal Jewish life in this country. The various societies and charity institutions, the foundations of our social life in the Diaspora, are nothing else but the expression of our ancient culture and ethics. Even our bitterest enemies here and elsewhere must admit those aspects of spiritual greatness and beauty and admire our morality and charitable activity.

Can anyone point to any other people in the entire world, even among the greatest, richest and oldest, which has a larger proportion of democratic, social and charitable organizations? Can anyone point to any other national group in the United States, even among the oldest and richest, which is as outstanding in its philanthropy?

Certainly many evils and weaknesses, even in charitable work, may be pointed out. Certainly such must be exposed and improved. But this very fact, this desire to see our institutions perfected, is itself part of Judaism, part of our cultural traditions, which lives in all of us almost against our wills and knowledge.

The first Jewish immigrants to the shores of America were strangers to us and even hateful to us who came later. They were assimilationists and Reform Jews, with a foreign culture and foreign ideals, foreign language and way of living. And yet there glowed in them the centuries-old feeling of responsibility and charity. No one in the United States forced them to build Jewish institutions—just as other national groups were not forced. No one could have complained if they had not done so, and yet the unique Jewish spirit expressed itself so clearly in their accomplishments.

In what, then, does our great strength lie, if not in our ancient ethical culture? If not in the finest precepts of behavior and in the ideals of justice so solemnly prescribed in the Bible and in the Talmud? If not in the fact that the Jewish mode of life is a continuation of our culture, the Talmudic culture, which is realistic as well as spiritual, national as well as universal?

Like every other true cultural creation, the Talmud propagandized for progress and social equality, and in great measure actually realized it in Jewish life. But the objectives and fundamental aim were totally different; they were more, much more, profound and far deeper than those of the modern era which are so much misunderstood. Progress and civilization without moral, ethical and spiritual development, are valueless and even harmful. A generation may develop the most far-flung sciences and elaborate its economic and political theories to their highest point, but they will remain useless if the conscience is besmirched and the hands sullied. Such a generation is perhaps more reactionary than progressive. Progress does not mean physical or material gain, but the fulfillment of a world-goal, the achievement of a moral and ethical, a spiritually heightened, humanity.

The Talmudic concept is thus fully a progressive concept, one which looks to the future. Jewish conscience has always looked into the distant future, always lived with hope and expectation, always held the ideal of a new era, a happier age for all mankind.

The Talmud is therefore a guide for every person who honestly seeks to unite with God and man, with the love of God as well as with the love of man.

The Talmudic concept is that not man's desire alone, but the will of God is supreme. Not man's justified or unjustified passions and caprices must be fulfilled, but the eternal law of God, which is the law of morality and justice, of truth and fairness, of peace and love.

The Torah, says the Gemara, was given in the desert, in order thereby to indicate that just like the desert belongs to no one and whoever wishes may possess it, so the Torah belongs to no one and whoever wishes may have it.

Even the Messianic concept, which once more is an idea which looks to the future, is also a universal concept. When the Messiah will come, all peoples will gather together and unite in one single nation. That is why, perhaps, the Talmud, the highest expression of purity and sacredness, fought so bitterly the belief of the early Christians that the Messiah had already arrived. The Talmudic scholars, like the Jews generally, linked the Messianic concept to the concept of a life of justice and rectitude. The Jew was always certain in his belief that so long as man rules over man, the stronger over the weaker, the rich over the poor, the Messiah cannot have arrived.

The secular view that morality is not the result of faith has placed the accent on man and has thereby prepared the soil for uncontrolled individualism and absolute ego. Man became the only creator of the world, the foundation and the essence of being. The world exists only in and through man. It is his own concept and idea, and only as such does it have a place in existence. Even political absolutism drew nourishment from these false concepts, and the present totalitarian governments are perhaps the result of this idea of absolute ego.

The cultural values which the Talmud created as a direct continuation of the Torah and the Prophets therefore lie much more in the social sphere than in the religious sphere. The Talmud, like ancient Hebrew literature generally, is strictly objective and full of humanitarian motivation and social ideals. The social laws do not smack of the sort of liberal reforms introduced by the democratic countries, but go much further. They are the bases of a definite social program for the real and actual life of an ethical-minded and just people and even contain such radical aspects as are characteristic of an extreme revolutionary social order.

If culture really means spiritual uplifting and social justice, then the Talmud is the most unique cultural phenomenon. The Talmud is not, even by the wildest comparison, a kind of compendium or encyclopedia of articles. The Talmud is much more than that; it contains all these things but with this important addition: The Talmud is the living Jewish power in the process of creativity, the national laboratory in which the Jewish intellectual creation has taken shape.

For generations Jewish minds have worked in this laboratory, each one with his own specific and peculiar stamp, each one with his original ideas and emotional expression. Each one has expressed his own essence and linked it with the Jewish community-at-large, dreamed about God and thought about man, saw the contradictions in life and preached and practiced truth. The entire creativeness turned about the one and only central pivot, the only motive: the Jew and his relations to God and to the universe.

Our culture, the creation of many thinkers, scholars and commentators, has been built up into a gigantic monument, has grown into a colossal literature, and has become the unique written expression of the Jewish organism; and in the course of many generations it has become a very living part of our being.

CHAPTER THREE

THE JEWISH PROPENSITY FOR LEARNING

CRITERION OF EDUCATION, CULTURE AND CIVILIZATION. "PILPUL" AND DIALECTICAL ACUMEN. KEENNESS AND ERUDITION IN HALACHA AND AGADA.

THE JEWISH PEOPLE HAVE CONTINUED TO EXIST BECAUSE OF the fact that they have always been a people of students, of learners and of scholars. As soon as we finished studying one thing, we began all over again. The folk saying "Repeat over and over again" reveals in a flash the entire Jewish world ethos, which is based upon learning. We have thereby maintained our faith, our books, and the people themselves. Only a people of scholars can conquer all its enemies. A people of mere readers could not do it. The greatest enemies of the Jewish people have disappeared from the face of the earth because they were readers and not learners, because they had no Torah.

The Jewish people have their own criterion of education, of culture and of civilization. An educated person is not one who has merely read many books superficially. An educated person is one who has read and studied the same books over and over again. It is not the number of books that one has read which is the important thing, but the extent to which these books have entered his consciousness and become a part of him and he a part of them. And this can be achieved only through deep study. We have never heard a Jew celebrating the conclusion of *reading* a book. A celebration is made only after concluding *studying* a book, only at a "siyum." This is because reading by itself means very little. One reads and then quickly forgets. But when one studies a book it is entirely a different matter. One then acquires the knowledge of the book, one imbibes the contents of the book. Hence the celebration, the "siyum." The student has now entered a higher phase. And there is another reason why a celebration is made at the conclusion of one's study, and this is the more important reason. "Siyum" means beginning, starting all over again. The joy therefore consists not only in having achieved, but in beginning a new achievement, in beginning the study of the book all over again.

There has never been a more inspiring picture than that of a group of adult people—workers, store keepers, merchants, rich and poor—gathering in a synagogue in the evening hours, and sitting down at the table to study the Mishna, Ein Jacob, Chaye Odom or Mesilath Yeshorim. These books they would study either by themselves or with a rabbi, study them with all the commentaries and interpretations.

What a truly noble scene it was, when tailors and cobblers would leave their work benches for the synagogue and sit down to study the sacred words of the books. They would call their synagogue by some name of a book, such as: Chevra

Mishnayoth, because the Mishna was being studied there; or Chevra Ein Jacob, because the Ein Jacob was studied there, etc. These were the universities of the eternal people, universities which do not have a counterpart among other nations. Here the study was for its own sake, and here the thoughts of the great books sank into every consciousness.

When a Jew goes to the synagogue, he goes there not because it is a club for reading some fascinating story, but in order to study. "A Jew must study the Torah." The holy thoughts contained in it are not merely to be glanced at, but to be studied thoroughly in order to find in them the secret of the world, the mystery of our existence. What Rabbi Akiba has said is not to be read, but to be studied constantly. "Turn the Torah, and turn it over again, for everything is contained therein." And what Rabbi Meir said is not merely some clever saying to be heard or read superficially, but to be studied thoroughly. And the more one studies the more one finds. The more one studies, the more one grows, and the more one grows, the better can one understand what Rabbi Akiba and Rabbi Meir, and all the other scholars, have taught. One must study and not merely read. Even the ordinary words of a scholar must be studied, the Gemara teaches us. And if this is true of his ordinary words, how much more true is it of the words contained in the Torah!

Was there ever a Jew who did not have on the tip of his tongue some saying of the Torah, some aphorism of a scholar, or some example from the Talmud?

To this day, even in the United States, when one enters an orthodox synagogue one always sees a dozen or more Jews sitting around a table and studying. One's heart then expands, one's joy increases. The Jewish people have not died. So long as there are Jews in a synagogue around a table studying these ancient texts that we have preserved through the ages, through all extremities and perils, so long as Jews still express themselves in these books, so long can we hope to remain an eternal people and withstand all dangers.

Yes, ten Jews sitting around a table and studying weigh much in the scales of history. Ten Jews, or nine or eight, or fewer, sitting down at a few pages of the Torah, or some book of the Talmud, are the backbone of the Jewish community. They are the quintessence of Judaism. There are even American-born Jews who have acquired this excellent habit of study. They have discovered the eternal truth that in study they will find the pith of Jewish life, the essence of the Jewish religion and the Jewish people. A Jewish community glories not in its rich men nor in its high officials, but in those few individuals sitting around in a synagogue immersed in study. We Jews have also been known as a bookish people.

Paradoxical as this may sound, we have always been drawn to the study of the Torah by both of the chief human qualities—good and evil spirit. We are capable of dragging even our evil spirit down to a synagogue and sit him down to study a book of the Gemara, and it would thereby fully realize itself. If the essence of the evil spirit is to seek pleasure, then it would surely derive utmost satisfaction from study. Other nations, on the contrary, often invoked their good spirit to the aid of wars, crusades, or cruel sports.

The wonderful romance between the Jew and his book; the widespread recognition of the scholar as the highest authority ("a bastard scholar is to be preferred to an illiterate High Priest"); the complete emotional and spiritual absorption and self-expression in one's study; the beautiful and uplifting scene of a group of Jews in the synagogue enwrapped in their books; the complete and full divesting of oneself from earthly cares, and one's transformation into an intellectual being whose soul imbibes courage, rejuvenation, strength and vigor—all this is a specifically Jewish phenomenon. It is a result of a spiritual prophylaxis of an entire people, a unique achievement of will power on an all-encompassing and eternal scale, to which all philosophers and psychologists must pay homage.

The choice of a book for study was usually dictated not by objective criteria, but by individual predilection. Whatever book gave most pleasure and attracted most, was loved most. A Jew who had time, ability and learning, could not indulge his evil spirit—if we may thus express it—merely by the study of the Pentateuch and Rashi. He derived far greater pleasure from a chapter in the Mishna, a page in the Gemara, or some philosophical argument. There can be no comparison on the level of intellectual sport between understanding some passage in the Pentateuch, even including the commentaries of Rashi, and the logical repartees of the Talmudic scholars.

The exuberant temperament of the Jew, his intellectual fleetness and verve, the sharpness of his mind, which sometimes borders on diffusion, his characteristic flights of imagination, his buoyant optimism and excited movements, his enthusiasm not unmixed with levity, which sometimes issues in lack of constancy and system—these are the spiritual foundations upon which were built the classic arguments and the occasionally slovenly sophistry.

"Now, you just give me your thesis and I will immediately destroy it"—this is the characteristic essence of the Talmudic intellectual sport, a sport which requires keenness and logical precision.

The eagerness for this intellectual sport and the desire to gain the admiration of one's fellows have brought about the habit on the part of many students and scholars of avoiding the study of the Talmud in ordinary and regular succession, and of choosing special subjects or hypotheses under the new interpretation of Rabbi Akiba Eiger, and the authors of Urim V'Tumim and Ktzoth Ha'Choschen.

Whoever has not observed two rabbis or scholars conducting a discussion on some subject never saw a mental game between two intellectual-artists played on the highest logical level.

"The Torah is learned through the intellectual exercise of the scholars" (Aboth, Chapter VI, Mishna 5). "Whoever is able to manipulate logic, whoever has a keen mind and can bring forth a new interpretation or new reasons for an old interpretation may be compared to a rich man who has all sorts of money, silver and gold, copper and paper money; he may also be compared to one who sells only the best of oil and never lacks for a customer."

The Hebrew word for argument is "Pilpul" and stems from the word for pepper. And, indeed, the Talmudic arguments are as pungent and strong as pepper. The chief method is to take a sentence or some subject, analyze it into its many parts, and then to compare these parts with other analogous sentences or subjects on the basis of language, content, logic, etc. Thus the argument continues until the assertion is indisputably established.

Such a method of argumentation does not admit of dealing with a subject in a dilettante or superficial manner. A subject must be thoroughly fathomed and plumbed. This method of study is quite old. According to the Gemara, immediately after the death of Moses, Othniel ben Kenaz was able to establish by his keen argumentative powers 1,700 principles and regulations of the Law of the Torah which had already been forgotten. The Talmudic scholars believed that this dialectical system of argumentation is an absolute must and that whoever eschews it in the study of the Torah will have to account for it after his death (Sabbath, 31a).

Nevertheless, many of the Talmudic scholars were very much dissatisfied with this method of arriving at conclusions. They believed that this method often misled the Tanaim and Amoraim. Thus Rabbi Jeremiah, in the fourth century of our era, was for a long time excluded from the Yeshiva only because he annoyed the scholars with his excess of argumentation (Baba Bathra, 23b). Thus also in later generations a controversy arose about the usefulness of this dialectical method. (See, Yelinek, Levinson, Gideman, and Weiss.)

Keenness and erudition are two qualities which characterize the scholar. Keenness or sharpness refers to the ability to penetrate into the depths of a matter, the ability to analyze every law and regulation in order to be able to make logical comparisons and distinguish various elements which on the surface seem to be similar. Erudition or knowledge is the ability to have at hand all the sources of the law and to know where this or that saying may be found. Whoever has studied the Gemara has undoubtedly observed on every turn keenness and erudition working hand in hand and creating the substance of the Talmud. Whenever the Gemara wishes to support or expound a certain thesis in the law, it makes use of erudition and cites evidence from the Mishna, Tosephta and Baraitha. Then keenness comes into play, and with the words, "these things are not analogous," or "this is digressing from the subject"; it explains that although at first blush the cited evidence may have relevance to the disputed thesis, upon closer examination of the foundations of the law it is seen that the given evidence contains elements which distinguish it from the disputed regulation. This deeper analysis is of utmost significance for every scholar, and even more so for everyone who is in a position to make decisions. Not every question which arises in life can find a ready-made answer in the recipes of the Shulchan Aruch. The judge must bring his originality to bear upon the question and must use his analytical power to interpret the law by a proper comparison of the written laws. He must therefore possess, first, the necessary learning, that is to say, the erudition of the Talmudic Commentaries; secondly, the keenness of understanding in order not to draw false analogies and in order to understand the various bases of the law.

The Gemara (Horayoth, 2b) discusses which of the two, keenness or erudition, is more valuable. The answer is that every scholar must rely on his memory for the various traditional decisions and sayings. In olden times the laurels went to erudition, because teaching was then done without books, since there were no written decisions and laws. But today, when we have all the various commentaries on the Talmud, when every branch of the law has its place in books and can easily be found, the relative merits of keenness and erudition are more and more nearly in proportion. Let us give the following illustration. If the Law is compared to a building, erudition may be said to be the materials for the house: wood, iron, bricks, etc. But keenness may be compared to the knowledge requisite to use these materials in actually constructing the edifice. Without the sources of the Law, as without the bricks and wood, no structure can be erected. But, on the other hand, without the requisite knowledge these materials are of no use.

The Jews possess an enormous literature dealing with the Law, consisting of books giving the written opinions of the outstanding Hebrew scholars of every generation concerning the Law. These scholars are noted some for their erudition, and others for their keenness of mind.

It is worthy of notice that although these terms, Charifoth and Bkioth—keenness and erudition—are Hebrew terms, used in relation to the Law, they are also widely used in international jurisprudence. There are, of course, jurists who are especially noted for their erudition; that is to say, for the knowledge of all the written opinions and judgments of the Law. Others, on the other hand, are more noted for their sharpness, their analytical powers, their ability to dissect a given question into its component elements.

The decisions of the Law are based upon the sources of the Law (Halacha). The greater the erudition the greater the evidence one is able to cite. This is true concerning the interpretation of the Law. But in the Agada the situation is reversed. There, keenness is of greater importance. The proper knowledge of the Agada requires a lightning-like mind, the profound ability to interpret a saying, and the acumen to extract from an old saying an original interpretation which can be applied to modern times. The Agada does not render any decisions and that is why no great erudition is required for its understanding. It is, therefore, also clear why all the books of the Agada have been written with subtlety of understanding, keenness of mind, and crispness of style.

CHAPTER FOUR

THE TALMUD AS A SPIRITUAL CREATIVE PROCESS IN JUDAISM

THE UNWRITTEN TORAH. INTERPRETATION AND PERMANENT PROCESS. EZRA AND THE GREAT SYNOD. THE EDITORIAL PRINCIPLES OF THE TORAH'S PROHIBITIONS. THE BABYLONIAN TALMUD AND THE JERUSALEM TALMUD.

THE TALMUD, IN ITS BROADER ASPECTS AND AS UNDERSTOOD here, embodies within itself the entire creative process, begun traditionally in the period of Ezra the Scribe and ending not earlier than the close of the Middle Ages.

This creative process and development always continued in a single, definite direction; and as widespread as this process was, it represented in essence only a single unity. It was the verbal interpretation of the Written Law in order to adapt it to the continually changing forms of national, social and individual life.

The Torah, the Written Law, was the complete expression of ancient Jewish law, customs and folkways. But in their own independent state, and later under foreign rule, the life of the Jews evoked new needs, new cultural norms, new social rules and a new way of life, continually changing under the impact of internal and external forces.

These new needs, the various influences of political and historical transformations and events, the contact with foreign peoples and cultures, foreign drifts and trends, unfolded new tendencies in the spiritual creative process.

It is this process which is called the Unwritten or Oral Law, the Talmud.

In the narrower sense the Talmud was closed in the fifth century C.E. But the Oral Torah—the Talmud in its broader meaning—was continued by later generations, and included the early and later interpreters, the later savants and the whole sum of Rabbinical literature.

The various epochs in this permanent creative process may be briefly summarized as follows:

The Bible: The Written Law, which includes the Five Books of Moses, the Prophets and the Writings.

The Mishna: The interpretation of the Bible and its adaptation to new conditions; the final canonization of the oral doctrine as developed from the period of the earliest Halachic exegesis down to that of the fixed and crystallized Halachoth of the early third century.

The Gemara (in the narrower sense: the Talmud): The continued teachings and exegesis of the Amoraim, the generation of scholars which begins with Abba Areca, himself still a student of Rabbi Judah Hanasi, the codifier and organizer of the Mishna, and ends with the last Amora, who formally and definitively closed the Gemara in the fifth century.

The Saboraim and Geonim: Those who continued this spiritual creation through new interpretations, but did not in the least thereby deviate from the previously laid-down lines.

The Expositors: Rashi, Tosaphists, Alfasi, Rambam, Rosh, Rashba, etc.

Now, all this interpretation by the various categories of Talmudic scholars laid the foundation for the establishment of a Jewish religio-national way of life and transformed the Jewish religion into a purely national affair. Even God, as it were, was metamorphosed into a guardian of the Jewish people.

One cannot find in the entire history of the world another such work representing a process of intellectual, cultural, and at the same time, secular juridical creation of more than a thousand years. Nowhere can we find a book or even a series of books which encompasses such a vast field, including as it does the thoughts and regulations, the folklore and erudition of thousands and thousands of scholars. It is also impossible to find another literary creation which is so closely identified with a whole people as the Talmud is identified with the Jewish people.

Practically all nations have laws, science and cultural treasures. But none of them possesses such a creation as the Talmud. As the Talmud says, if you are told that other people possess a Torah, do not believe it.

It is perhaps not without significance that the Agada relates that God revealed to Moses the entire creative process of the Unwritten Law. This legend was, apparently, the result of the will of the Jewish people, the result of this desire which ardently declared: First do and then hear. Instinctively and intuitively the soul of the Jewish people perceived the necessity and the great value of the Talmud and intended that it should belong to the Jewish people and to no one else.

The fate of history from the very beginning linked the Jews to the Talmud, linked them both together so indissolubly and inseparably that it was never possible to separate them. This was the fate of a people that had lost its political independence and that began to reach for a meaning which should sustain it spiritually and nationally through all storms and stresses. The Talmud is thus the spiritual territory which the Jew created for himself after he lost his earthly territory.

No other people underwent such a process. The historical fate of the Jewish people is completely unique in the entire world. It therefore follows that the process of its intellectual creation was also unique and unequalled.

Scholars and critics may point out foreign sources of our spiritual creation. But even if that be true, the Jewish spirit first completely transformed them, and this Jewish spirit is unique and has never changed or lost its continuity in the slightest degree.

The beginning of the creation of the Unwritten Law is much older than the Written Torah. Such is always the natural process of the intellectual creation of a people. But this is even more true of the Jewish people. The Unwritten Torah, the Talmud in its broader sense, was the regulator of the life of the Jewish people. Such regulations are always first created by life itself, and then canonized and written down.

Life never stands still, it is never stagnant and static. Life always changes and moves forward, and is always transforming its outer and inner essence.

Our ancient teachers, therefore, did not want the Jewish folkways to remain simply an echo of the distant past—of ancient times—without relation to the present life of the individual Jew. They therefore made every attempt and utilized every means to strengthen the uniqueness of the Jewish people and continue the eternal spiritual creative process. They aspired to implant the Torah among all sections of the people, and to make it the eternal source from which the people might draw their spiritual nourishment.

An urgent need, therefore, arose early to create a wall around the Jewish people of prohibitions and barriers, regulations and sanctions. In order that the Torah be maintained as the most basic foundation, as the groundwork valid for all times and all places, it was imperatively urgent to establish a system of explanations, interpretations and methodological research.

To apply the traditional laws of life in their literal and formal sense, without the necessary and proper interpretations, or to regulate Jewish life, which was created by new conditions and needs outside of the traditional regulations, would simply have led away from the historical source, from the original primordial source from which Jewish life originally arose. This would have signified the destruction of the original foundation upon which the Jewish people and Judaism itself have developed.

But not everyone could devote himself to such a difficult and responsible task. A special class of scribes and scholars therefore gradually evolved, studying, interpreting and immeasureably broadening the traditional laws.

The Jewish people regarded these interpreters with great awe and veneration because they were at the same time the elders, the leaders and teachers, and it was therefore considered a sacred duty to observe their instruction with utmost strictness. The scribes and the elders managed the affairs of religious and social life, and their influence was enormous. They not only interpreted, but themselves taught the masses of the people.

Thus, beginning with Ezra the Scribe and throughout the period of the Scribes and the Great Synod, a unique study developed. It was then, so to speak, that the foundations of the Talmud were laid. Ezra and his assistants were practically the first to begin the work of strengthening Judaism, and the Great Synod completed this work and strengthened the foundation for the further development of the Talmud.

Their chief aim at that time was to democratize the traditional laws and to reduce the power of the clergy and the reigning aristocracy. In the first place, it was decided that prayers are as efficacious as sacrifice. And in order to spread and popularize this concept, synagogues and houses of prayer were established in all cities and towns. In order to even further emphasize the equality of the common people with the clergy, it was asserted—naturally on the authority of the Torah—that the laws concerning clean and unclean things are applicable to the layman as well as to the clergyman.

The first regulations were primarily concerned with the sacrificial cult. In order to prevent foreign influences from intruding themselves upon Judaism, especially the false Torah-cult of the Samaritans, Judaism was hedged in by definite prohibitions and sanctions. And since laws were already in existence, it was necessary to explain them in all their details and exactness.

In order to prevent anyone from destroying the validity of any of the traditional laws, the Bible was edited, closed and canonized during the Ezra period. The Talmud compares this achievement to that of Moses. Moses created the Jewish people, and Ezra gave the Jewish people the Torah-culture, and of both created a single essence: Torah and folk, folk and Torah.

The Unwritten Torah, the Talmud, according to tradition, arose from God. Nevertheless, it received its birth and original foundations—its life and existence—from the people themselves. The Jewish people themselves labored over it, bore it and nourished it with its blood and mind. According to the Agada, the human being represents the composition of the Torah. The 248 organs of the human body compare with the 248 positive laws, and the 365 veins compare with the 365 negative laws. The Bible contains 600,000 letters, the number of Jews who were liberated from Egypt in the Exodus.

Even before Ezra and Nehemiah had arrived in Israel, the desire and aspiration existed among the Babylonian exiles to create for themselves a spiritual meaning and essence. The Biblical sources dealing with that period give no details. But it is easy to form a picture of this desire, because in Ezekiel the story is told of three gatherings which the elders of Judah held in his house.

The Jews of the Babylonian Exile took with them into exile all the traditional customs and laws. They also retained the Law of Moses and parts of the Prophets and Psalms. The Torah and the traditions were regarded as certain barriers to national destruction. The relics of their former life became their only support, their only spiritual guide. There is even a conjecture that the institution of the synagogue—the house of learning and the house of prayer—also originated in Babylonia. In their hour of grief and loneliness, the Jews created a spiritual center for themselves, and it was at these gatherings that the Pentateuch and the Prophets were read and studied, that chapters of the Psalms were read and sung collectively, and that they consoled each other with predictions of the return to Zion. These foregatherings in the house of learning and house of study certainly became the beginning of the desire to become better acquainted with the intellectual heritage, to become immersed in it, and to extend its meaning into an actual and realistic body of laws and regulations.

The Babylonian Exile effected the first great transformation in the Jewish people. Before this period, at least in its outward structure, the Jewish people were a nation similar to other nations, having its political ambitions and political intrigues as well as other nations. It is true that Palestine was never a great power and was always threatened by Egypt on the one hand and by Assyria and Babylonia on the other. It always had to be on its guard to defend itself, its freedom and independence. Nevertheless, during the entire period of the First Temple, Palestine remained independent, having its own king and government.

The clergy and the prophets were the chief forces in the religio-political life. But at the same time they were organs of the government, and, speaking very generally, Jewish nationalism expressed itself in political manifestations quite similar to those of other nations. It may sound paradoxical, but it is a fact, nevertheless, that precisely in this epoch of the Temple the clergy, the prophets and Jewish nationalism took virtually secular forms; far more secular, at any rate, than in any later epoch. Needless to say, there was a spiritual aspect to Jewish life even then, but this aspect had a formal rather than an ideological content.

A radical change took place with the first destruction of the Temple, 586 before our present era. The Jewish state was destroyed, the king deposed and exiled, the Jews driven from their land. It is true that this first exile did not last very long. After fifty years the new ruler of Palestine, the Persian king Cyrus, gave the Jews liberty to return to their land, reconstruct the ruined cities, rebuild the Temple and maintain an autonomous regime. Nevertheless, all these concessions could not entirely wipe out the past. The exile became deeply engraved in the soul of the people. After all, if the Jewish state could be destroyed once, it could be destroyed again. Instinctively the people felt that the fall of Judea was the final expulsion of the Jews from the political arena. The Jews somehow felt that the return was not to last and that there would be many more exiles.

But the Jews did not want to be destroyed as a people, neither in their own land nor in exile. Preparations, therefore, began for the struggle for existence. A new mode of living, a new spiritual essence, new habits and folkways had to be invented, which would be binding, have lasting value, and be able to withstand the winds and storms of hostility and persecution. Governmental and political ambitions in the period of the Second Temple virtually ceased to exist. Even the heroic rebellion of the Maccabeans was a result not of political but of religious oppression. The people felt that it was not through political victories that it would achieve eternal existence, but through the establishment of a permanent spiritual life. God and His Torah—this is where Jewish aspirations and hopes should lie.

This radical transformation in the spiritual attitude of the people was brought about by the Scribes.

In the pre-Babylonian period the title "Scribe" was given to the secretary of the court or of the military high command. In Babylonia the scribes devoted themselves primarily to the copying of manuscripts. Among the Babylonians this profession was rather widespread. Among the Jews, it would seem, there were comparatively few scribes in proportion to the Babylonians. They did not know Babylonian and the demand for Hebrew manuscripts was relatively small. But among the scribes in Babylonia one name will always be inscribed in Jewish history in golden letters. This is Ezra the Scribe. This was his title in Babylonia, this was his title when he returned to Palestine, and this title has remained with him throughout history.

Ezra himself apparently did not write much. According to the Talmud he wrote those parts of the Scriptures called Ezra, Daniel and Esther. But his chief merit does not lie in writing. On the contrary, it lies in having ceased to write, in definitively closing what had already been written and in canonizing forever the Written Torah. His ambition was to be the mediator between the past and the present, the continuator of the Torah and its people, the creator of this golden thread which shall continue forever into the future.

On the threshold of a new epoch Ezra came to the people not with a new Torah or with new intellectual modes. On the contrary, he came to pledge the Jewish people to hold fast unto the old, as promulgated by Moses and the Prophets.

He had, to speak metaphorically, again brought the Jews to Mount Sinai and they again called out: "We will do and we will listen."

This conception of his duty and mission—to bring the Torah to the people and the people to the Torah—was soon taken up by his fellow scribes. All of them ceased to be writers and took upon themselves the function of becoming interpreters and translators of the already written Torah.

The first guild of the scribes, the Great Assembly or Supreme Council, is a great enigma for us today. There is no source material concerning it. We do not even know when it was first established and when it ceased to exist, nor how it functioned and what its jurisdiction was. Many monographs have been written about it; Hebrew and non-Hebrew scholars have made many conjectures, and Jewish intellectual history has undoubtedly been enriched by all this study. But in the last analysis we must remember that we are here dealing with a period of *oral* creative activity and that it is therefore entirely bereft of any historical documents. It is therefore far better and more practical to adopt the traditional viewpoint of, and to reconstruct this period in accordance with, the Talmudic sources which were created much after this period. The Talmudic scholars were, of course, far nearer to this period in time, place and spirit than we are, and their historic interpretations are therefore apt to be far more accurate than our own.

According to the Talmud the last prophets, Haggai, Zechariah and Malachi, belonged to this first union, or guild, of scribes, and it was they who transformed this body into the Supreme Council, or Kneseth. After that, the Torah was transmitted directly to the people, from generation to generation. It is perhaps this circumstance which accounts for the fact that in the entire epoch of the scribes, in this entire period of fermentations and crystallization of the Jewish spiritual physiognomy, we hear of no famous names. With the ascendancy of the scribe epoch the ideas of the Torah deeply penetrated into the soul of the people, and since then the Torah no longer belonged to groups or individuals, nor even to God from Whom it stems, but to the entire people. The scribes were sons of the people, their creative force, and they wished to become entirely identified with the people. Jewry and Judaism were thus created by the anonymous will and force of the whole people.

To create and to cultivate a lore of the people which shall serve for all generations and shall derive its strength solely from Mount Sinai was the ultimate aim of the Scribes. The means to achieve this end were proclaimed at the very first gathering. In Nehemiah, chapter VIII, 1-8, we are told: "And all the people gathered themselves together as one man into the broad place that was before the water gate; and they spoke unto Ezra the scribe to bring the book of the Law of Moses, which the Lord had commanded to Israel. And Ezra the priest brought the Law before the congregation, both men and women, and all that could hear with understanding, upon the first day of the seventh month. And he read therein . . . Even the Levites caused the people to understand the Law . . . And they read in the book, in the Law of God, distinctly; and *they gave the sense, and caused them to understand the reading.*"

To read and understand the Torah—this was the new conception. The Torah, as it is written, is a sealed book and one must know how to read and understand it. The Torah is clear and understandable superficially, but inwardly, in its inner essence, it is very elastic and involved: "Turn it (the Torah) and turn it over again, for everything is in it, and contemplate it, and wax grey and old over it, and stir not from it, for thou canst have no better rule than this" (Aboth, chapter V, Mishna 25).

The Torah, that is to say, speaks in a language all its own, in a language which is limited in quantity but unlimited in quality. The scribes are eager to discern this quantitative form of the Torah and they count up all the details. It is interesting to note that in the Talmud there is an opinion that the word "Sopherim"—scribes—means "counters."

The scribes had no difficulty with the quantitative character of the Torah. In the Temple there was the original of the Torah which Ezra had brought with him from Babylonia. Every scribe was able to make a copy of it for himself and arrive at a uniform decision concerning its outward meaning. But with the qualitative essence it was an entirely different matter. This was no task for several scribes or even for generations of scribes, but for all the coming generations of Tanaim, Amoraim, Geonim, Rabbis, and scholars of all sorts. Concerning this task it was said: "It is not thy duty to complete the work" (Aboth, II, 21). On the contrary, the very conception of the tradition is not to complete, but to carry on and continue to cultivate this permanent creative process.

In the tenth chapter of Nehemiah we are told that after the assemblage signed a solemn agreement to observe the

Torah, they specifically obligated themselves to fulfill a number of rules and regulations which the Great Assembly had laid down. Needless to say, these new regulations were not made at once. They were arrived at on the basis of "reading from the Torah and making it understandable." In other words, they were made on the basis of an interpretation of the text of the Torah. We may therefore assume that these regulations in the Book of Nehemiah represent the very first laws, thus starting this tremendous creative process bearing the name of the Halacha. As the first collective bearers of the Oral Torah these men of Ezra's epoch represent the prototype of the Yeshiva, an institution which has remained with us to this day as an organic part of our life.

The first great gathering provided the impulse for a series of smaller gatherings—the synagogues. Although the parallel between these two institutions is only hypothetical, the above assumption seems reasonable enough. At first the Jews would gather in the synagogue primarily to pray collectively. But in time the synagogue became a community institution in which all sorts of matters were taken up. That is why the synagogue is also often called "the house of the people." Ezra's reforms introduced into the synagogue the reading of the Torah on the Sabbath and, as the Talmud states, also every Monday and Thursday, the Torah in the Hebrew text and also translated into Aramaic. Thus the tradition of reading and studying the Torah became a permanent force in the spiritual life of the Jewish people.

The interest in study and interpretation became increasingly greater, and gradually there developed the Beth-Midrash—the House of Study—conjointly with the synagogue; that is to say, a place of study that would attract to itself not casual people for praying, but regular students and teachers to hear lectures in the Halacha and to discuss problems in connection with the interpretation of the Torah. According to calculations of the Talmud, there were at the end of the Second Temple in Jerusalem alone more than 400 synagogues and each one of them had attached to it a school for children and a house of study for students and scholars. In later generations, when the number of scholars and students grew apace, the Beth-Midrash became separated and developed into an independent institution called "yeshiva," or its Aramaic equivalent—Messivtha.

The "Great Yeshiva" in Jerusalem and the small yeshivas throughout the land (although the word "yeshiva" comes in a later period) devoted themselves to serious study, and the voice of the Torah for the first time echoed throughout the mountains of Zion and has not ceased to this day. This was, so to speak, the triumph of the ideology of the Pharisees, long before the Sadducees appeared upon the arena of history. Judaism was formed and became entrenched under the influence of the Pharisees as a continuation of the Torah and the Prophets.

Ezra, as well as the Great Synod, had before him a considerable collection of writings that during the canonization was left out on principle. The Talmud says: "He who takes into his house more than the canonized twenty-four books, brings chaos into his home." The editorial principle apparently was that the Torah must be a uniform work, with one central idea, without confusion and cross-purposes. The Great Synod, therefore, apparently used the maxim of placing prohibitions, of putting a barrier around the Torah, which also remained the principle of the founders of the Talmud.

Later political events, as well as contact with other peoples and cultures, which often introduced radically new trends and divergences, as, for example, Hellenism in practically the entire epoch of the Second Temple, brought new tendencies to the fore in the Jewish creative process. These new tendencies were expressed partly in assimilating those cultural influences that came from the outside world and which, because of their very nature, were able to be absorbed and clothed in a national Jewish form; and partly also in adapting the sacred precepts of the Torah to the economic, political and social conditions.

Thus, from the traditions of the Scribes and from the interpretations and regulations of many generations of scholars to the advent of Rabbi Judah Hanasi arose the Mishna, the chief text of the Talmud.

According to the Rambam, the tradition was developed in the following manner:

In the twelfth year of the wandering in the desert, on the first day of Shebat, Moses convened a gathering of all the Jews and demanded that whoever forgot a law or an interpretation should immediately inform himself of it and study it. From that day until the seventh day of Adar, Moses thus had written up thirteen books of the Torah, one for the Levites and one for each tribe, and then ascended Mount Nebo there to die.

Joshua and the Elders strictly followed the teachings of Moses, and themselves added new interpretations which they inferred from the Torah in accordance with the thirteen qualities of thorough comparison. When differences arose, they were decided by majority vote.

From Joshua the tradition descended directly to Pinchas HaKohen, to Eli HaKohen, to Samuel, David, Elijah, Elisha, Zechariah, Hosea, Amos, Isaiah, Micha, Joel, Nahum, Habakkuk, Zephaniah, Jeremiah, Baruch, Ezra, Simon the Just, Antigonus of Socho, Jose ben Joezer and Jose ben Jochanan, Joshua ben Perachia and Nittai of Arbela, Judah ben Tabai and Simon ben Shetah, Shemaiah and Abtalion, Hillel the Elder, Simeon, Rabban Gamaliel and finally to Rabbi Judah Hanasi, who edited the Mishna.

Many transitions took place in Jewish history, but the act of transition was always systematic, natural and regularly continuous, without any violation to its inner essence.

The Judges, Prophets, scholars of the Talmud, Chassidim and Cabalists, all traveled the same path which reaches back to Mount Sinai, deviating neither right nor left, nor changing anything even by a hair's breadth.

CHAPTER FIVE

THE MISHNA AS A SYSTEMATIZED CODIFICATION OF JEWISH LAW

THE FIRST ATTEMPT AND OPPOSITION. RABBI JUDAH HANASI AND HIS WORK OF EDITING. LANGUAGE AND STYLE. FINAL CODIFICATION.

THE TALMUD CONSISTS OF TWO PARTS: THE MISHNA AND THE Gemara. The Mishna is the main text; the Gemara is the commentary.

The Mishna is the authorized codification of the Unwritten Law, which in the traditional manner passed by word of mouth, basing itself and drawing upon the authority of the Written Torah. These laws consisted primarily of regulations, customs, prohibitions, sanctions, rules and orders, which came down from the Scribes, the Great Synod and the Sanhedrin. The code in the Mishna is also partly the result of the discussions and the decisions of the scholars in the Palestinian Yeshivas.

The first real attempt to systematize the chaotic mass of traditions, customs, laws and sanctions was made by Hillel. Many scholars came to the conclusion that systematized codes of law existed earlier, and began as early as during the period of King Jehoshaphat.

Since the Unwritten Law could not be written down at first, the Talmudic scholars gathered students around themselves and taught them verbally. The study was based on questions and answers which had to be repeated many times until they were firmly impressed in the memory. The word Mishna apparently stems from this period, from the root word "Shonah," meaning to repeat.

The rule was that whatever is transmitted by word of mouth must not be written down. An exception, however, was the writing down of some statement for personal use. Whoever received such a statement or assertion or added something new himself, was permitted to write it down for his own use and even utilize it in teaching his students. But to publish such things publicly was strictly prohibited.

This prohibition lasted for hundreds of years, and during this period innumerable works were undoubtedly lost. Those that have survived were known only to the scholars. It was not until the situation in Babylonia and in Palestine worsened considerably and it was perceived that a danger existed that the Unwritten Torah would be lost entirely, that the prohibition began to be observed less rigidly.

It was then found out that many scholars had written down all that they had learned from their masters and all that they themselves had added. When writing everything down finally became sanctioned, it began to occur to people that this whole mass of material should be systematized and codified.

Rabbi Simon ben Jochai had previously warned against the danger arising from this chaotic condition in the laws and assertions. His authority was a paragraph in Amos (Chapter VIII, 11-12):

[11]Behold, the days come, saith the Lord GOD,
That I will send a famine in the land,
Not a famine of bread, nor a thirst for water,
But of hearing the words of the LORD.
[12]And they shall wander from sea to sea,
And from the north even to the east;
They shall run to and fro to seek the word of
the LORD,
And shall not find it.

The first papers of the Mishna that were found written down were by Akiba ben Joseph (born in 53 of the present era and suffered a martyr's death in the year 132). His student, Rabbi Meir (130 to 160), continued this systematization, although neither was complete. It may be mentioned here that many of the yeshivas had their own individual methods and did not readily recognize the compilations by others. It was not until the end of the second century that Rabbi Judah Hanasi was successful in completing this work.

Rabbi Judah Hanasi was born in 135 of the present era, about 66 years after the destruction of the Second Temple. The wounds were still fresh and unhealed. The persecutions by the Roman government were unbearable and much self-sacrifice was demanded to observe Judaism. There was no longer any central institution to regulate Jewish life. The Sanhedrin still existed, but no longer exerted any influence. It wandered from town to town and could find no permanent meeting place.

The persecution and oppression by the Romans on the one hand, and the internal spiritual disunity and differences among the many independent yeshivas on the other hand, placed the Jews and Judaism in great danger.

In his early years Rabbi Judah, the son of the Patriarch Simon ben Gamaliel II, traveled to the scattered yeshivas and it grieved him to observe this disunity and schism. It would seem that in place of one Torah there were several Torahs, each in contradiction with the others. What was kosher in one yeshiva was not in another; what was clean and permitted in one place was unclean and prohibited in another. It was then that Rabbi Judah conceived the idea of collecting all laws and discussions concerning them and arranging them in one systematic code.

Fate smiled upon his idea, because when he became Patriarch (in 161), the philosopher Marcus Aurelius Antonius was then the Emperor of Rome. The new ruler, a person of high morality and noble ideas, changed the status of the many defeated nations, allowing them some freedom and showing respect and friendship to their leaders.

The Talmud and the Midrash tell many stories about the intimate friendship that sprang up between Antonius and Rabbi Judah. These stories are also related in the writings of the Christian Church Father Hieronymus who lived not long afterwards. Nevertheless, historians are not certain about the truth of these stories. They are not even certain whether Marcus Aurelius lived at the same time as Rabbi Judah. Rabbi Shloime Leib Rapoport in his book "Erech Millin" and Isaac Hirsh Weiss in his "Dor Dor Vedorshov" are perhaps the only ones who adduce definite evidence for these stories.

It may be mentioned that Rabbi Judah was a great scholar and noble character, and that is one reason, undoubtedly, that it was possible for him to persuade the yeshivas to sanction his work. Dissatisfaction arose after Rabbi Judah had completed his codification and had left out a great many laws and statements, which were, years later, carefully collected and added as an addendum to the Mishna.

The collection was at first called after Rabbi Judah, in order to differentiate it from the Mishna of Rabbi Akiba and the Mishna of Rabbi Meir. Later the compilation was accepted as the authorized codification and Rabbi Judah's name was no longer added.

Among scholars there is a great difference of opinion whether Rabbi Judah transmitted the Mishna by word of mouth or in written form. The Rambam says that it was transmitted in written form. So say the modern scholars Geiger, Lebrecht and Isaac Hirsh Weiss.

During the period of the Second Temple the Jews created two different sorts of literature, written in two different styles: (1) Certain parts of the scriptures and almost all the Apocryphal writings, and (2) the greater part of the Mishna.

The Mishna is the greatest literary creation of the Jews in this period. That is why this period is called the Mishna Period, and the language of this period the Mishna Hebrew.

In this Hebrew were written the Mishna writings, the Tosephta, the Mechilta and many other writings, although some of them were written after the Mishna Period came to a close. All the Beraithoth in both Talmuds, the Babylonian and Jerushalmi (Palestinian), are also written in the Mishna style.

Even in later generations, during the days of the Amoraim, when debate and argumentation conducted in the synagogues and study rooms were in the language then in use, that is, in Aramaic, the decisions of Law were nevertheless made in

Hebrew and were thus included in the Gemara. Many of the Agadoth were related and written down in Hebrew. The speeches and sermons before the people, in which the spiritual leaders taught the people the regulations of the holidays, were also made in Hebrew. This even brought about many misunderstandings.

For those who at one time studied the Gemara we will cite just one example.

"Said Rabbi Mattna: When kneading dough a woman must use water that had been prepared a night before" (Pesachim, 42a). Now, the Rabbi used the Hebrew word "Shelonu" to indicate the kind of water necessary for kneading. But "Shelonu" in Hebrew also means "ours." Thus the listeners interpreted the phrase to mean "our water . . . " Had the speaker used Aramaic this misunderstanding could not have been possible.

The language of the Mishna is Hebrew, but already there is a strong Aramaic influence. Old Hebrew grammatical forms have been replaced by Aramaic grammatical forms. Old Hebrew words and expressions are no longer used and are replaced by Aramaic. On the other hand we find many Hebrew words which for certain reasons have not been included in the Scriptures. The Mishna has thus enriched our Hebrew language.

The language of the Mishna was for hundreds of years the spoken language of the Jews in Judea. The Tanaim always used the language of the people.

One marvels at the clarity and breadth of the Mishna language. It is precise, condensed and highly developed. Such a language could have been evolved only by highly intellectual people. Only first-class minds and masters of language could take the tongue of the people and hammer it into a highly skillful and concise prose. When one studies the books of the Mishna one is at a loss what to admire first, the intellectual luminosity of our scholars, their many-sided scientific acumen—as conditioned by the status of science of that time, of course—or their refined and polished style. The genius of the Mishna lies in its style no less than in its contents.

Until this very day we use the rich terminology of the Mishna vocabulary for many scientific disciplines. This rich heritage is far from being utilized to the full. Modern Hebrew will for many years to come derive much from the Mishna source.

The Mishna deals with questions of daily life both of the individual and of the nation. The Law (Halacha) comprises the greater part of the Mishna. Here we find, in addition to religious regulations, various constitutional laws and precepts for the general welfare of the land. The Mishna also contains a complete civil, criminal and family codex. The language of the codex is concise, clear, without any elaborateness.

The second sort of literature of this period, the Scriptures and the Apocrypha, is of an entirely different character. Here are philosophical disquisitions and moral precepts, written in the form of brief aphorisms. Here we also have prayers and songs, stories and historical tales. In such a literature there is also room for poetry and lyrical outpourings. The authors have attempted to imitate the style of the ancient books of the Old Testament, writing in the classical Scriptural Hebrew, although in their days they no longer spoke this language.

Naturally, one also finds the Aramaic influence prevalent

here, in grammar as well as in vocabulary. We also find many Greek and Persian words. But in general, the language is far closer to the classical Hebrew than in the Mishna.

Hebrew was then no longer the living language of the people, and that is apparently the reason that the Mishna does not possess the fertility of expression, the beauty and the picturesqueness of the Hebrew in the Bible. On the other hand, the language in the Mishna is distinguished by its clarity and compactness.

The method of compiling the Mishna was deliberate, and it is easy to understand why a certain subject is found in one place and not in another. Rabbi Judah began with the collection of all subjects concerning liturgy and blessings, and next to them he placed the laws concerning agriculture and the good deeds connected with them. Then he added the good deeds concerning the Sabbath and other holidays, fast days and other historical days. Later he dealt with marriage, divorce and generally everything concerning family life. After that come the laws of vows, money questions, Sanhedrin and laws concerning the relationship among human beings. Finally, he dealt with the laws of sacrifice and cleanliness.

The method and the order are not altogether successful, and the laws seldom have any relationship with one another. Often the relationship is very tenuous and indirect, and subjects follow one another simply because they have the same beginning or the same name.

In the tractate Megilla, for instance, a number of subjects follow one another only because they all begin with "The difference between this and that . . . is only this." Here we find such unrelated subjects as the Sabbath, holidays and Yom

Kippur; the first and the second Adar; food questions, voluntary and involuntary sacrifices, questions of pollution, leprosy questions and many other such questions that should find no place in a tractate of Megilla.

Very often the Mishna deals with various laws in the same place only because they were promulgated by one scholar, one source or one tradition. Thus we find in the tractate Eduyoth four different subjects that have no relation one with another except the fact that Rabbi Chanina, Chief of the Priests, transmitted them all by word of mouth to his students. It is obvious that the collected material was not amenable to classification within prescribed limits and that is why we find laws of faith among laws of sacredness and laws concerning cleanliness among laws of sacrifice.

That is apparently why later scholars changed the Mishna in many subjects and often accepted the interpretation, the purged Mishna, as the original law. There is also reason to believe that even during Rabbi Judah's life important changes were made in the text itself. It is also believed that the reason the Jerusalem Mishna often differs from the Babylonian Mishna is that Rabbi Judah himself in his later years changed the text.

Incidentally, it is interesting to observe that Rabbi Judah himself said: "I learned a great deal from my teachers, more from my colleagues, but most of all I learned from my students."

The rule was not to change anything in the Mishna, not even a letter. The Gemara says (Yebamoth, 9a) that Levi ben Sissi once asked Rabbi Judah to change something in the Mishna and Rabbi Judah became very much angered. But the former did change the text, and many other scholars did likewise.

Among the interpretations in the Gemara it is common to find such expressions as: "Something is missing here, and it is necessary to draw such and such a conclusion." Or: "We interpret thus and so"; "It must be interpreted thus"; "The Mishna should read differently."

That the text was not kept strictly may be seen from the fact that even in our generations corrections have been made, as for example, the corrections of the Gaon of Vilna and of Akiba Eiger.

The Gemara also tells us of interpreters who complained that others are not observing strictly the text of the Mishna and are making too many important changes.

The Gemara, too, followed the above method and included subjects side by side, one with another, simply because they began with the same expression. It is sufficient, for instance, that a subject should begin with the expression "Two which are, indeed, four" to be placed side by side with another subject having no other relation to it. Thus, such unrelated subjects as Shebuoth, laws of uncleanliness and others, are brought together under the same rubric.

The Gemara thus includes in one place laws of damages, laws of work, and laws of uncleanliness.

The order in the Mishna is not very consistent, and there are not seldom in the Mishna itself contradictions between the beginning, the middle and the end. Almost half of the tractate of Kethuboth deals with the laws concerning money. The tractate Kiddushin deals with the laws of slavery. The tractate of Shebiith deals with the laws of robbery and assault.

And so in every volume there is a subject or subjects having no relation with the rest. The reason for this lack of system is that the association of form, style and thought was deliberately adopted as a principle in order to facilitate memorization and transmission of the code by word of mouth.

The one thing that is strongly apparent in the editing of the Mishna is the attitude of veneration to the words of the scholars. Not only did Rabbi Judah transmit the words of the scholars, but with great love he even observed the very style and language of each one. Rabbi Judah observed the unique style of the scholars primarily in the speeches, but he was more economical in the laws and did not even give the name of the scholar responsible for them.

The Mishna is therefore primarily a compilation of the many differences of opinion and discussions lacking the preciseness of a definite conclusion. Many historians, indeed, are of the opinion that Rabbi Judah did not intend to lay down the law for eternity. His intention was merely to save the Unwritten Torah from oblivion, and so far as the determination of the law is concerned, he gave a free hand to future generations themselves to determine the law in accordance with the necessity of the times.

The Mishna is arranged under six general classes, called "Sedarim" or "Orders." Each Seder is being divided into a number of tractates or treatises called "Masechtoth," and these are again subdivided into "Perakim," chapters, and each chapter again into "Mishnayoth," sections. The whole is called "Shas," the initial letters of Shishah Sedarim, six orders or series of these orders. The initials of the six names yield the mnemonic term Zeman Nakat, which means "a time accepted."

The first Seder relates to the productions of the earth as forming the staple sustenance of human life.

The second Seder relates to times and seasons, involving the religious observance of years and days, feasts and festivals.

The third Seder deals with the institution of marriage, which lies at the basis of the system of human society.

The fourth Seder relates to civil controversies, and treats of the rights of persons and things.

The fifth Seder comprises laws and regulations regarding the service and worship of God upon the provisions of the Levitical ritual, or things consecrated.

The sixth Seder exhibits the prescriptions requisite to the maintenance or recovery of personal purity according to the Levitical ideas.

The following is an analysis of the contents of each tractate of the six orders.

I. SEDER ZERAIM (Seeds). The Seder contains the following eleven tractates:

1. *Berachoth,* "Benedictions." Regulations dealing with the liturgy. Contains nine chapters, and there is Gemara to that Masechta in either of the two Talmud compilations: the Palestinian and the Babylonian.
2. *Peah,* "Corner." Questions arising out of the law concerning the "corners of the field" (Leviticus XIX:9). Contains eight chapters, and Gemara only in the Palestinian Talmud.
3. *Demmai,* "Doubtful." Treatment of corn bought from persons suspected of not having given thereof

the tithes. Contains seven chapters. Gemara in the Palestinian Talmud.

4. *Kilayim,* "Mixtures." Treatment of the prohibited mixtures in plants, animals and garments (Leviticus XIX:19). Contains nine chapters. Gemara in the Palestinian Talmud.
5. *Shebiith,* "The Sabbatical Year." (Exodus XXIII:11; Leviticus XXV:2-7; Deuteronomy XV:1-11.) Contains ten chapters. Gemara in the Palestinian Talmud.
6. *Terumoth,* "Heave-offerings." (Numbers XVIII:12.) Contains 11 chapters. Gemara in the Palestinian Talmud.
7. *Maasroth,* "Tithes." Law of the tithe to be given to the Levites (Leviticus XXVII:30-33; Numbers XXVIII:21-24). Contains five chapters. Gemara in the Palestinian Talmud.
8. *Maaser Sheni,* "The Second Tithe." Regulations based on Deuteronomy XIV:22-26. Contains five chapters. Gemara in the Palestinian Talmud.
9. *Challah,* "Dough." The portion of dough to be given to the priests according to Numbers XV:21. Contains four chapters. Gemara in the Palestinian Talmud.
10. *Orlah,* "Uncircumcision." Treatment of the fruits of a tree during the first four years of planting (Leviticus XIX:23-25). Contains three chapters. Gemara in the Palestinian Talmud.
11. *Biccurim,* "First Fruits." Treats of the first fruits to be brought to the Temple (Deuteronomy XXVI:

1-11). Contains three chapters. Gemara in the Palestinian Talmud.

II. SEDER MOED (Season). The Seder contains the following 12 tractates:

1. *Sabbath.* Prohibited labor during the Sabbath. Contains 24 chapters. Gemara in the Palestinian and Babylonian Talmud.
2. *Erubin,* "Amalgamations." Treats of a technical point which arises out of a Sabbatical law, *viz.,* the boundary which may not be overstepped on the Sabbath and how it may be extended. Contains ten chapters. Gemara in the Palestinian and Babylonian Talmud.
3. *Pesachim,* "Passovers." Observance of the Passover festival. Contains ten chapters. Gemara in the Palestinian and Babylonian Talmud.
4. *Shekalim,* "Shekels." The annual tax to the Temple (Exodus XXX:12-16). Contains eight chapters. Gemara in the Palestinian Talmud.
5. *Yoma,* "The Day." The ritual of the Day of Atonement (Leviticus XVI:3-34). Contains eight chapters. Gemara in the Palestinian and Babylonian Talmud.
6. *Succah,* "Booth." Observance of the feast of Tabernacles. Contains five chapters. Gemara in the Palestinian and Babylonian Talmud.
7. *Betzah,* "Egg." Also called *Yom Tov,* "Festival." The name Betzah is taken from the first word in that Masechta. Treatment of the kinds of work which, according to Exodus XII:16, were prohibited

or permitted on the festivals. Contains five chapters. Gemara in the Palestinian and Babylonian Talmud.

8. *Rosh Hashanah,* "New Year." Observance of the feast which marks the New Year. Contains four chapters. Gemara in the Palestinian and Babylonian Talmud.
9. *Taanith,* "Fast." On the public fasts. Contains four chapters. Gemara in the Palestinian and Babylonian Talmud.
10. *Megillah,* "Scroll." Concerning the public recital of the Book of Esther on the feast of Purim. Contains four chapters. Gemara in the Palestinian and Babylonian Talmud.
11. *Moed Katan,* "Minor Feast." Concerning the intermediate days of Passover and Tabernacles. Contains three chapters. Gemara in the Palestinian and Babylonian Talmud.
12. *Chagigah,* "Festival Offering." On the private offerings on the three Pilgrimage-Festivals. Contains three chapters. Gemara in the Palestinian and Babylonian Talmud.

III. SEDER NASHIM (Women). The Seder contains seven tractates.

1. *Yebamoth,* "Levirate Marriage." Deals with the law of marriage with a childless sister-in-law and forbidden degrees of relationship in connection with marriage (Leviticus XVIII). Contains 16 chapters. Gemara in the Palestinian and Babylonian Talmud.

2. *Kethuboth,* "Marriage Documents." Treats of the dowry and marriage-settlement. Contains 13 chapters. Gemara in the Palestinian and Babylonian Talmud.
3. *Nedarim,* "Vows." Treats of vows and their annulment, particularly with regard to women (Numbers XXX:3ff.). Contains 11 chapters. Gemara in the Palestinian and Babylonian Talmud.
4. *Nazir,* "The Nazarite." Treats of the laws concerning the vow of the Nazarite (Numbers VI). Contains nine chapters. Gemara in the Palestinian and Babylonian Talmud.
5. *Sotah,* "Suspected Adulteress." On the woman suspected of adultery, according to Numbers V:12-31. Contains nine chapters. Gemara in the Palestinian and Babylonian Talmud.
6. *Gittin,* "Divorces." Laws relating to the annulment of marriage (Deuteronomy XXIV:1 ff.). Contains nine chapters. Gemara in the Palestinian and Babylonian Talmud.
7. *Kiddushin,* "Sanctification." On the marriage status. Contains four chapters. Gemara in the Palestinian and Babylonian Talmud.

IV. SEDER NEZIKIN (Torts). The Seder contains ten tractates.

1. *Baba Kamma,* "The First Gate." Treats of damages and injuries and their remedies, with reference to Exodus XXI:28-37; XXII:1-5. Contains ten chapters. Gemara in the Palestinian and Babylonian Talmud.

2. *Baba Metzia,* "Middle Gate." Treats of laws concerning found property (Deuteronomy XXII:1-4), concerning trust (Exodus XXII:6-14), concerning buying and selling (Leviticus XXV:35-37), concerning lending (Exodus XXII:24-26; Leviticus XXV:35-37) and concerning hiring and renting. Contains ten chapters. Gemara in the Palestinian and Babylonian Talmud.
3. *Baba Bathra,* "Last Gate." Treats of laws concerning real estate and commerce, mostly based on traditional law; and also of the laws concerning hereditary succession, based on Numbers XXVII:7-11. Contains ten chapters. Gemara in the Palestinian and Babylonian Talmud.
4. *Sanhedrin,* "Courts." Deals with courts of law and their procedure and capital crimes. Contains 11 chapters. Gemara in the Palestinian and Babylonian Talmud.
5. *Maccoth,* "Stripes." Treats of false witnesses and their punishment (Deuteronomy XIX:16-19); of the cities of refuge (Numbers XXXV:10-32), and of crimes punished by stripes (Deuteronomy XXV:1-3). Contains three chapters. Gemara in the Palestinian and Babylonian Talmud.
6. *Shebuoth,* "Oaths." Treats of the different kinds of oaths, those made in private life as well as those administered in court (Leviticus V:4-5, 21-22; Exodus XXII:6-10). Contains eight chapters. Gemara in the Palestinian and Babylonian Talmud.

7. *Eduyoth,* "Testimonies." A collection of traditional laws and decisions gathered from the testimonies of distinguished Rabbis. Contains eight chapters. No Gemara.

8. *Abodah Zarah,* "Idolatry." Laws concerning idols and the relation to the worshippers thereof. Contains five chapters. Gemara in the Palestinian and Babylonian Talmud.

9. *Aboth,* "Fathers." An ethical treatise collecting the favorite maxims of the Mishna teachers. Contains five chapters. There is also an appendix called "the chapter of R. Meir on the Acquisition of the Torah." No Gemara.

10. *Horayoth,* "Decisions." Treats of the consequences of acting according to erroneous decisions rendered by religious authority, with reference to Leviticus IV; V. Contains three chapters. Gemara in the Palestinian and Babylonian Talmud.

V. SEDER KODASHIM (Sanctities). The Seder contains 11 tractates.

1. *Zebachim,* "Sacrifices." Treats of the animal sacrifices and the mode of their offering (Leviticus IV; V). Contains 14 chapters. Gemara in the Babylonian Talmud.

2. *Menachoth,* "Offerings." Deals with the meal and drink offerings (Leviticus II). Contains 13 chapters. Gemara in the Babylonian Talmud.

3. *Chullin,* "Profane Things." Deals with the traditional manner of slaughtering animals, and dietary

laws. Contains 12 chapters. Gemara in the Babylonian Talmud.

4. *Bechoroth,* "First-borns." Deals with the laws concerning the first-born of man and animals (Exodus VIII:12-13; Numbers XVIII:15-17). Contains nine chapters. Gemara in the Babylonian Talmud.
5. *Arachin,* "Estimations." Treats of the mode in which persons or things dedicated to the Lord by a vow are legally appraised in order to be redeemed for ordinary use (Leviticus XXVII:2-27). Contains nine chapters. Gemara in the Babylonian Talmud.
6. *Themurah,* "Substitution." Treats of the laws concerning sanctified things having been exchanged (Leviticus XXVII:10-27). Contains seven chapters. Gemara in the Babylonian Talmud.
7. *Kerithoth,* "Excisions." Treats of the sins subject to the punishment of excision, and their expiation by sacrifices. Contains six chapters. Gemara in the Babylonian Talmud.
8. *Meilah,* "Trespass." Treats of the sins of violating or profaning sacred things (Leviticus V:15-16). Contains six chapters. Gemara in the Babylonian Talmud.
9. *Tamid,* "Continual Offering." Describes the daily morning and evening offering in the Temple (Exodus XXIX:38-41; Numbers XXVIII:2-8). Contains seven chapters. Gemara in the Babylonian Talmud.
10. *Middoth,* "Dimensions." Contains the measurements and description of the Temple, its courts,

gates and halls; also description of the service of the priestly guards in the Temple. Contains five chapters. Gemara in the Babylonian Talmud.

11. *Kinnim,* "Birds' Nests." On the offerings of birds (Leviticus I:14; V:7; XII:8). Contains three chapters. Gemara in the Babylonian Talmud.

VI. SEDER TEHAROTH (Purities). The Seder contains 12 tractates.

1. *Kelim,* "Vessels." Deals with the ritualistic defilement of utensils, garments, etc. (Leviticus XI:33-35). Contains 30 chapters. No Gemara.
2. *Ohaloth,* "Tents." Treats of tents and houses conveying the ritual uncleanness of a dead body (Numbers XIX:14-15). Contains 18 chapters. No Gemara.
3. *Negaim,* "Plagues." Laws relating to leprosy (Leviticus XIII; XIV). Contains 14 chapters. No Gemara.
4. *Parah,* "Cow." Regulations concerning the Red Heifer and the use of its ashes for the purification of the unclean (Numbers XIX). Contains 12 chapters. No Gemara.
5. *Teharoth,* "Purities." A euphemism for the defilements which last until sunset (Leviticus XI:24-28). Contains ten chapters. No Gemara.
6. *Mikvaoth,* "Baths." On the requirements of cisterns to be used for ritualistic purification (Leviticus XV:2). Contains ten chapters. No Gemara.
7. *Niddah,* "Uncleanness of Menstruation." Treats of the legal uncleanness arising from certain conditions

in women (Leviticus XV:19-31). Contains ten chapters. Gemara in the Palestinian and Babylonian Talmud.

8. *Machshirin,* "Preparations." On liquids as a conductor of defilement (Leviticus XI:34-38). Contains six chapters. No Gemara.
9. *Zabim,* "Persons Suffering from a Running Issue." Treats of uncleanness caused by physical issues (Leviticus XV:2-18). Contains five chapters. No Gemara.
10. *Tebul Yom,* "Immersed During a Day." On the status of a person who has undergone immersion, but his purification is not complete until sunset. Contains four chapters. No Gemara.
11. *Yadayim,* "Hands." On the defilement of the hands and their purification. Contains four chapters. No Gemara.
12. *Uktzin,* "Stalks." Treats of stalks and shells of fruit in regard to conveying ritual uncleanness. Contains three chapters. No Gemara.

In addition to the 63 Masechtoth which compose the Mishna and Gemara, there are certain minor ones which are connected with the Talmud as a kind of Apocrypha or appendix, under the title of Masechtoth K'tanoth or smaller treatises. These are:

1. *Aboth d'Rabbi Nathan,* divided into 41 chapters and a kind of Tosephta to the Mishnaic treatise "Pirke Aboth," the ethical sentences of which are here considerably enlarged and illustrated by numerous narratives. In its present shape, it

belongs to the post-Talmudic period, though some elements of a Beraitha of R. Nathan (who was a Tana belonging to the fourth generation) may have been embodied therein.

2. *Sopherim* (scribes), divided into 21 chapters. This treatise is important for the Masorah as it contains the rules for the writing of the Sefer Torah and the liturgical laws for the service on the Sabbath, Holidays and Fast days. A separate edition with notes, was published by J. Muller (Leipzig, 1878).

3. *Ebel Rabbathi* (the large treatise on Mourning), euphemistically called Semachoth (Joys), is divided into 14 chapters. This treatise deals with the laws and customs concerning burial and mourning. References to a treatise by that name is made in the Talmud (Moed Katon, 24a, 26a; Kethuboth, 28a).

4. *Callah* (bride), contains only one single chapter. This minor Masechta concerns itself with the duties of chastity in marriage. References to a treatise with that name are made in the Talmud (Sabbath, 114a; Taanith, 10b; Kiddushin, 49b; Jerusalem Talmud Berachoth, chapter II, Halacha 5).

5. *Derech Eretz* (the conduct of life), divided into 11 chapters. The first chapter treats of prohibited marriages, and the remaining chapters, of ethical, social and religious teachings. References to a treatise by that name are made in the Talmud (Berachoth, 22a; Jerusalem Sabbath, chapter VI, Halacha 2).

6. Derech Eretz Zuta (a minor treatise on the conduct of life), divided into ten chapters. This treatise is replete with rules for the learned and maxims of wisdom.

7. *Perek Ha-Shalom* (chapter on peace), contains only one single chapter. As already indicated by the title, it treats of the importance of peacefulness.

The *Masechtoth K'tanoth* (smaller treatises) are as follows:

(a) *Sefer Torah,* concerning the writing of the Torah. Contains five chapters.

(b) *Mezuzah,* concerning the writing on the door-post. Contains two chapters.

(c) *Tephillin,* concerning phylacteries. Contains one chapter.

(d) *Tzizith,* concerning fringes. Contains one chapter.

(e) *Abadim,* concerning servitude. Contains three chapters.

(f) *Kuthim,* concerning Samaritans. Contains two chapters.

(g) *Gerim,* concerning proselytes. Contains four chapters.

CHAPTER SIX

THE ACHIEVEMENTS AND SIGNIFICANCE OF THE GEMARA

THE DRIVE TOWARDS CONTENTS. THE TENDENCIES AMONG THE BABYLONIAN JEWS. THE RELATIONS BETWEEN PALESTINE AND THE YESHIVAS IN OTHER COUNTRIES. ABBA ARECA AND RAV ASHI. THE BABYLONIAN TALMUD AND THE JERUSALEM TALMUD.

THE CREATIVE PROCESS WAS IN NO WAY LESSENED WITH THE close of the Mishna. The evolutionary development of the legislative code and the religio-cultural sphere extended beyond the limits of the Mishna. They continued to evolve at the same rate and with the same richness, and furthered the deepening of religious life and the refinement of the individual and the social morality.

Indeed, the development could not cease, because many of the motives which called into life the Unwritten Torah did not lose their potency when the Mishna was closed. The national creativeness had shown the creators of the Mishna how to make possible the continued existence of the Jewish people when Rome sought to destroy the political unity of Judea. And this same national creativeness also dictated to the

Talmudic scholars the continuance of this work so that the Unwritten Torah might become the chief driving force of the perpetuation of Jewish life within the broad religio-spiritual norms.

The purpose of this continued development was to conserve the Jewish traditions and impregnate them with the new values which life itself creates in its eternal process of renewal.

The forces which impelled the further development of the Talmud must not, however, be looked for only in the persecutions of the Romans and must certainly not be considered an unconscious psychological reaction. They must be sought in Judaism itself, in the very inner essence of Jewish spiritual life.

The entire Jewish history constitutes in essence one single epoch and one single purpose: to maintain the Jewish people as a nation; and throughout our entire history it was the Torah, later broadened through the Talmud, which prevented our extinction.

For what purpose?

Thus history demanded and commanded.

From their earliest arrival in Babylonia the Jews concentrated upon the rebuilding of traditional Judaism and upon the maintenance and strengthening of the link with Palestine. However, not everything from their native land could be transplanted to the Diaspora. The sacredness of the Temple, the religious services of the Priests, the feeling of security which one's own home and country give, were lacking. Babylonia gave the Jews truly great opportunities. It allowed them to live according to their beliefs and social customs, gave them the broadest cultural autonomy and full civil equality. Nevertheless, Babylonia was a foreign country, a place of exile, and the spiritual sustenance of the Jewish people had to be drawn from Palestine.

When the first Babylonian exiles returned to Palestine in the days of Ezra and began again to build a spiritual center, the Jews remaining in Babylonia exhibited great devotion and love to the Holy Land. They sent annually munificent gifts, were tremendously interested in the fate of the Jews in Palestine, and themselves sought to return many times.

This link with Palestine greatly helped to establish their own spiritual center. The reigning powers in Babylonia as well as the local population there considered the Jews citizens of their religion which, in fact, meant a recognition of Jewish nationality and political unity. Despite the fact that the Jews were an exiled and defeated people, they were, nevertheless, accounted a religio-political entity, not merely as a theoretical concept, but as a reality.

As soon as they arrived in Babylonia, the Jews therefore began to build their life upon the ancient Jewish foundations. The majority of the exiles soon established themselves and built up purely Jewish cities and towns under a well-organized Jewish community. They had only one goal and one purpose before them: to make Jewish life in the Diaspora stronger, more spiritual and more unique.

Their economic conditions greatly helped in this task. The Jews led a normal economic existence in Babylonia as if they had been natives there. They engaged in agriculture, brewing, fruit cultivation, export, clothing, canal building, furniture, and other trades.

Babylonia, generally speaking, was a rich and beautiful country, containing many hills and valleys, forests and fields, minerals and other natural resources. The earth was rich and well cultivated, and no one suffered poverty.

During the few hundred years between the First and the Second Destruction of the Temple, the Jews in Babylonia developed their own independent, unique life. The rich Persian culture and the various religious cults exerted considerable influence, but they were casually set off from the main stream of Jewish life.

The Jews also had their own head of the community, the Resh Galuta, representative to the government, who reigned in truly royal fashion. He was elected by the Jewish people and the government ostensibly sanctioned the election. The Resh Galuta possessed princely powers and was supposed to derive from David's dynasty. He ranked fourth behind the king and was therefore very close to the court, and he also wore royal clothes. The Jews saw in all this a reflection of the old independent state, and it also evoked the respect on the part of other countries.

In the course of many decades, a system of synagogues and schools in which serious studies were conducted, was established in Babylonia. The Jews in Palestine had an ancient tradition which held them in the Jewish way of life and it was therefore unnecessary for them to become immersed in study in order to maintain Judaism. The Jews in Babylonia, however, had no such tradition, and in addition were faced with problems and questions concerning which the Palestinian Jews had not the slightest inkling. Intensive studies and profound scholars, able to analyze and interpret thoroughly, therefore arose.

The Palestinian Jews at first looked with great contempt upon the yeshivas and the learning of the Jews in Babylonia. Perhaps this feeling was slightly motivated by jealousy, and perhaps they felt that their hegemony was threatened.

At the end of the period, however, in the days of the last Mishna scholars, a movement began in Palestine itself to transplant the Torah to Babylonia. Young men from Babylonia in great numbers were then studying in the Palestine yeshivas in order to return home and sow the seeds of their learning.

The Jews in Babylonia even boasted that whenever the Torah is forgotten in Palestine, they, the exiles, bring it back to its former glory. Thus it happened in the days of Ezra the Scribe, thus it happened in the days of Hillel, and thus it happened later when Babylonia boasted its famous yeshivas in Sura and Pumbaditha. Nevertheless, it took hundreds of years until the yeshivas in Babylonia achieved their full splendor and glory.

The reason for this is the fact that the great scholars seldom returned from Palestine to Babylonia. Only the lesser scholars returned to the Babylonian yeshivas and they could not accomplish a great deal. They simply lacked the great strength required for the responsible work of establishing yeshivas capable of achieving the stature of the Palestinian schools.

Furthermore, the Babylonian Jews were dependent upon the Nasi, head of the Jews in Palestine, who was the only authority empowered to ordain rabbis and give decisions in case of dispute. The Nasi of the Palestine Jews was never in a hurry to ordain Babylonian scholars. Not to be unduly critical of this practice, we must assume that the intent was a purely national one: the Nasi wished to continue the close link between the two great Jewish communities, and this was possible only through the maintenance of Palestine as the only authoritative and concentrated spiritual center.

But the opposite effect was achieved. The relationship between the two great centers became very strained and, in the best of circumstancs, very unequal. The Babylonian Jews were proud of the fact they were always on guard and maintained the Jewish religion and traditions; while the Palestinian Jews looked slightingly upon them and regarded them as fools who "eat bread with bread."

The Palestinian Jews considered themselves the superiors of their Babylonian brothers and complained that "because of the travelers from Babylonia the insects in Palestine are multiplying."

It goes without saying that such a situation could not exist for very long, and a revolt soon occurred. The Babylonian Jews considered themselves justified and well prepared. They had their yeshivas, their great leaders and scholars, their Resh Galuta who was practically a king, they were devoted believers and with great zeal maintained the Jewish tradition, and above all, they, the Babylonian Jews, preserved the purity of the Jewish race, did not have mixed marriages and did not suffer from mass rapine as did the Palestinian Jews on whose soil foreign wars were always being fought.

As soon as the edited and canonized Mishna was brought to Babylonia, a new epoch began. The prestige of Palestine gradually declined and Babylonia increasingly began to emerge in the foreground.

One of the most talented students of Rabbi Judah, Abba Areca, intended to return to Babylonia to take over the leadership of the local yeshivas. Before he left, he wanted to be ordained by the Nasi of the Palestinian Jews, as was the custom and law. He did not himself dare to visit the Nasi and he therefore sent his uncle, Rabbi Chiya, who was, incidentally, Rabbi Judah's favorite pupil. When Rabbi Chiya told the Nasi about his mission and asked him whether Abba Areca might have the power to give judgment, Rabbi Judah answered in the affirmative. When Rabbi Chiya pursued him and asked whether Abba Areca might have the power to decide marriage problems, Rabbi Judah again answered in the affirmative. But when Rabbi Judah was asked whether Abba Areca might have the power to absolve the first-born from certain laws, he answered in the negative.

Abba Areca was greatly chagrined at this restricted ordination. But his determination to become the leader of the yeshivas in Babylonia was nevertheless greatly strengthened. Upon his arrival in Babylonia, he quickly became the head of the Sura yeshiva and soon won the respect and love of everyone. From all over the country students flocked to his yeshiva, and in a short period it had about 1,200 students. The period was also favorable for this development, for at this time the Persian king who was very friendly to the Jews reigned in Babylonia. Abba Areca, who received the title of Rav, became closely acquainted with the king and received from him many privileges and favors.

Abba Areca came from a very distinguished family and was also a distant relative of the Resh Galuta of the Babylonian Jews. To be a relation of the Resh Galuta was considered a great privilege because he derived his lineage from King David through his father's side, while the Nasi of the Palestinian

Jews derived his lineage from David through his mother. Nevertheless, Abba Areca did not put on any airs and he and his family led a modest existence and befriended members of the lower classes. Of course, the people loved this and he soon became the most popular leader among the Babylonian Jews.

When Abba Areca returned from Palestine in 219 C.E., he found the academy already established under R. Shila, who bore the title of "Resh Sidra." Abba Areca was elected to head the academy, but, instead, handed over the office to Mar Samuel, while he founded another academy on similar lines at Sura. The two academies flourished side by side, each attracting numerous scholars.

The Babylonian Talmud must be considered principally as the work of the academy at Sura, though Pumbaditha, and for a little while also Nehardea, became recognized as principal seats of learning whose decisions were accepted wherever Jewish communal life existed.

In connection with his yeshiva in Sura, Abba Areca also established a semi-annual conference at which the achievements of the scholars and students were discussed. The conference lasted a month and attracted more than 10,000 students.

Thus Abba Areca transplanted the study of the Torah to Babylonia, where it was further broadened and developed. This process of creation and development continued for centuries until Rav Ashi, a scholar of the fourth generation, decided to undertake the task of collecting and editing everything which had been created until his time.

Under his own leadership and under the leadership of Rabina, Rav Ashi gathered a number of scholars and together they collected all the traditional laws, differences of opinion, interpretations, sanctions, doubts and judgments.

Rabina was actually older than Rav Ashi and was in reality the very last editor and compiler of the Gemara. Nevertheless, he is considered a student of Rav Ashi. Rabina's relation to Rav Ashi was that of a student to his teacher.

From the time of Abba Areca's establishment of the yeshiva in Sura until the time of Rabina and Rav Ashi (219 to 427), the interpretations, discussions and statements around the Mishna increased to such an extent that even the greatest scholars and savants could not possibly memorize them all. Rav Ashi thus complained: "Whereas the heart of the previous generations was as broad as the gate of a palace, our heart is as small and insignificant as the ear of a needle" (Erubin, 59a).

Rav Ashi was then the head of the yeshiva in Matha Mahesia and possessed a magnetic personality. All great scholars eagerly listened to his every word. It was said about him: Since the days of Rabbi Judah there was no one who united as successfully as he did learning and wealth.

Rav Ashi apparently also possessed the great energy required to undertake such important and responsible work. He was also aided by scholars from Palestine, and thus the customs of the Palestinian Jews were also included in his works (Sabbath, 150b).

It must be remarked that at this time the Palestinian Jews had already compiled their Talmud—the Jerusalem Talmud—and this fact undoubtedly stimulated the speedy compilation of the Babylonian Talmud.

Rav Ashi, however, never concluded his work. After Rav Ashi and Rabina there were two generations of Talmudic scholars, but they added nothing to the already compiled code.

The Gemara part added to the Mishna a wealth of new laws and assertions, the essence of which it is not easy to cull. The Gemara often resolved the contradictions in the Mishna, but on the whole it merely complicated matters. In place of the more or less codified Mishna, we now have the great labyrinthine structure consisting of the Mishna, the Gemara, and the various commentaries. Even the Agada is often intermingled with the pure legal code and it is difficult to determine what is law and what is Agada.

The Rambam tells the following story about himself:

"Once a judge came to me with a copy of my 'Mishna Torah,' and pointing to a law he asked me where this law might be found in the Gemara. I told him that most probably the law will be found in its proper place in the tractate of Sanhedrin. He then answered that he had searched for the law in the Jerusalem and Babylonian Talmud, in the commentaries and could not find it. I was astounded and told him that most likely he would find the law in the tractate of Gittin. We both searched for it and could not find it. It was only after he had left that I recalled that the law in question is found in the tractate of Yebamoth, in connection with another law."

Many important questions are treated in the Talmud cursorily, and other questions that could easily be condensed are drawn out at interminable length in elaborate discussions. It is not surprising that the Talmud itself says concerning many of its arguments that they are "mountains that hang upon a hair."

Even the spirit of the Mishna, this free, liberal encompassing spirit which was dominant until the rise of the Talmudic scholars, was completely negated by the Gemara. Very often it overlooked explicit law in the Mishna and made its effect considerably more severe.

After the close of the Gemara, many scholars, some more and others less, strongly criticized these changes and pointed out that there are no errors in the Mishna.

Both the Babylonian and the Jerusalem Talmud maintain a like attitude towards the Mishna. Both often and consciously overlooked the law as stated in the Mishna, although the Jerusalem Talmud by no means had the same influence as the Babylonian. Both indeed had the same aim, but did not share the same fate. Even the greatest scholars as a rule study only the Babylonian Talmud and seldom look into the Jerusalem Talmud.

The language of the Jerusalem Talmud is Talmudic Hebrew with a strong infusion of Western Aramaic, then common in Palestine. Maimonides in his introduction to his Mishna commentary ascribes the authorship of the Jerusalem Talmud to R. Jochanan who flourished in the third century. In its present form, the Jerusalem Talmud is supposed to belong to the fourth or fifth century.

The Jerusalem Talmud was first published by D. Bomberg at Venice, without date; then with brief glosses at Cracow in 1609, and Krotoschin, 1866, folio. An edition in four volumes was published at Zitomir, 1860-1867.

The first commentary on the Jerusalem Talmud was composed in the 17th century by R. Joshua Benveniste, and was only on 18 Masechtoth. In 1710 Eliyahu Fulda wrote a commentary on the order of Zeraim and partly on the order of Nezikin. A complete commentary was written in the 18th century by Moshe Margolies. His commentary is embodied in the Zhitomir edition (1860).

Regarding some other commentaries on single parts of the Jerusalem Talmud see Z. Frankel, Mebo Ha-Jerushalmi, 134a-136a.

The commentaries on the Babylonian Talmud may be divided into (a) Perushim, (b) Tosaphoth, (c) Chiddushim and (d) Hagahoth. The Perushim are running commentaries accompanying the text. The Tosaphoth (additions, supplements) are glosses on Rashi's commentaries. The Chiddushim (novellae) are explicit comments on certain passages of the Talmud text. The Hagahoth are marginal glosses.

It must also be stated that the Babylonian Talmud is much larger than the Jerusalem Talmud which has a Gemara of only four sections: Zeraim, Moed, Nashim and Nezikin. The tractate of Nidda has a discussion of only the first three chapters. And the Gemara of the tractate of Shabbas (Sabbath) begins the discussion at the twenty-first chapter. Why that is so no one knows. It is said that once there was a Gemara for five whole sections, but it got lost in the stormy days after the close of the Talmud in Palestine.

That is why apparently the Jerusalem Talmud could not become the great popular work of the people. Too much was lost and what was preserved is actually only in fragments and incomplete. That is also why whenever there is a difference in laws between the Babylonian and the Jerusalem Talmud, the Babylonian Talmud is the authority. All the early and later interpreters also base themselves upon the Babylonian Talmud.

The Jerusalem Talmud which developed in Palestine and under quite exceptional circumstances has been canonized, but has at the same time been relegated to the background. Since the close of the Talmud the interpreters, savants and scholars, as well as the entire Rabbinical world, have always watched over the Babylonian Talmud and have with great zeal sought to cleanse it of the many errors and imperfections which have crept into it through the negligence or malice of the copyists. The great majority of interpretations and comments that have been written deal with the Babylonian Talmud. Only a small portion, almost an insignificant portion, deals with the Jerusalem Talmud.

Even the holy deed of studying the Torah, of studying the Gemara and its commentaries, seems to be applicable only to the Babylonian Talmud. It was universally agreed that no virtue accrued to the study of the Bible by man unversed in the Talmud.

CHAPTER SEVEN

THE HALACHA AND ITS RELATION TO JEWISH LIFE

SOCIAL AND ECONOMIC INTERESTS. THE ESSENCE AND CONTENTS OF TALMUDIC LAW. ITS SYSTEM AND METHOD. THE TENDENCIES TOWARDS LENIENCY AND SEVERITY IN THE LAW. THE RULES FOR EXPOUNDING THE SCRIPTURES.

THE HALACHA IS OFTEN COMPARED WITH A STORMY SEA which engulfs everything around it with its billowing waves. The Halacha is also often compared with a dense forest, the intertwining branches of its trees completely blotting out the sky. Others have compared it to a labyrinth containing blind alleys in which only the very experienced and trained can find their way.

There is no question that Talmudic Law is subject to analysis only by minds of utmost profundity and keenness, and that is no doubt the reason why it has always been the special subject of our intellectual giants. The Halacha demanded of its students a trained logical mind and the ability to analyze hair-splitting arguments. In the course of many years the Halacha became so extended that it was difficult to find one's way in it.

In extenuation, it must be said that the dry and logical Law helped greatly to maintain Jewish life. It kept the Jews away from the primitive Christian hypotheses and held them bound to a purified monotheistic concept.

The word "halacha" is Aramaic and its meaning in that language is "a way of life." In the Talmudic language it has a meaning similar to "Mishpat," an accepted custom or law based upon a custom or event (Ha'Aruch).

By the word "halacha" the Talmud signifies a custom which has received general assent and recognition. "If it is a law we must accept it; if it is only an opinion questions may still be asked" (Yebamoth, 76b; Kerithoth, 15b). When the Talmud cites many opinions concerning a given matter and wishes to indicate the final, authorized opinion, it expresses it in the following manner: "The Law is such and such." Or, "the Law is as stated by such and such a Tana."

The word "halacha" is also often used to designate definite and established rules and regulations, which bear no relation to laws. Thus the rules concerning etiquette and decency are called "laws of established custom" (Berachoth, 22a). Medical regulations are called "laws of physicians" (Yerushalmi Yebamoth, chapter 5, halacha 2). Thus the Talmud also speaks of the laws of creation (Sanhedrin, 67b), laws of witchcraft, etc. Within the rubric of Laws were included also such laws as are specifically mentioned in the Torah. They are called in the Talmud "Gufei Halachoth"—matters of law (Yerushalmi, Sabbath, chapter 2, halacha 7).

At first the debates and discussions concerning the laws were conducted purely on a theoretical level, and they very often remained on that level because the concrete historio-political conditions did not allow of carrying them out in practice. Nevertheless, for the Jews such laws were always sacred, and with the rise of the Sanhedrin in the last century before the destruction of the Temple, the scholars received a mandate from the people to formulate them. Even in those years when the Sanhedrin was not officially recognized by the reigning powers, the decisions of the scholars were nevertheless law, and the new regulations, if they were arrived at unanimously, were readily accepted by almost all the people. Incidentally, at this time it was already believed that Abraham had observed all the 613 precepts in all their details and nuances (Yoma, 28b).

Among the many chapters of the Torah recited daily in the Temple was the chapter on the Ten Commandments (Tamid, 32a). This custom was sought to be likewise introduced in the synagogues, but the Tanaim Rabbi Judah, Rabbi Samuel and Rabbi Nathan did not allow this because of the objections of the pagans (Berachoth, 10b). Rashi explains: "So that the pagans may not be able to declare that the rest of the Torah is untrue, since only the chapter on the Ten Commandments, handed down by God Himself and heard from his own mouth on Mt. Sinai, is recited in the synagogues." The Gemara (Yerushalmi, Yebamoth, 1,5) also states: "So that they should not be able to say that only the Ten Commandments were given to Moses on Mt. Sinai."

In the course of years simple interpretation became transformed into the Law. The purpose of the first investigations was to establish the ordinary meaning of the Torah. But with time these interpretations grew enormously in number and inevitably contradictions arose. Then a new method had to be used of making comparisons and deducing one law from another. Such methods lost their previous character entirely and had little to do with the original text. They were at first studied in a theoretical manner and upon the basis of purely logical considerations and comparisons.

At first, as stated previously, these discussions and debates were purely on the theoretical level and often remained on that level. The longer the Torah was studied and the greater frequency with which customs and virtues were defined by the aid of purely logical arguments drawing from them untold consequences, the greater became the number of sayings which finally, in the language of the scholars, received the term Halacha—Law.

The Halacha which was transmitted by tradition was called "The Law given to Moses on Mt. Sinai"; i.e. established at the very birth of the Jewish faith and nation. In the Talmud there is a great debate concerning these laws. Many scholars apparently doubted whether the tradition upon which these laws were based was authentic. Whenever it was not known whence a given Halacha stemmed or for what reason it was established, it was attributed to this ancient epoch.

The "Rosh" and the "Beth Joseph" state that not always are these laws, that are asserted to stem from this period, really so, but they are merely as sacred as if they had really stemmed from this period, since they are ancient and were transmitted by tradition from generation to generation.

In his treatise upon "The Rambam's Commentary on the Mishna," S. Z. Setzer wishes to establish that the Rambam also did not believe that all laws attributed to the ancient period are really from that period. He even asserts that the

Rambam, in his interpretation of this term, was far more radical than the "Rosh" and "Beth Joseph." However, the ultra-orthodox rabbis will hardly agree with him, since, after all, the Rambam never stated this specifically and it is merely a hypothesis or Talmudic Pilpul.

The fact is that the roots of Judaism were even in primitive days deeply sunk in the life of the people. Even then the Jew stood on a higher pinnacle of civilization than other nations and had his definitive and traditional moral and ethical precepts and regulations. The Divine Vision at Mount Sinai is only the affirmation of an already existing social order based upon the existing foundations of the Torah, and this remains to this day the basis of the entire Judaic historical view.

The Talmudic scholars merely sought to establish these traditional ways of life upon a more solid footing, and they therefore sought to cultivate and extend these traditions. The first task, therefore, was to confirm these customs theoretically. General rules had to be worked out, as well as the details. This work could not be done without general assent and recognition, and the scholars therefore had to discuss these problems jointly.

Although the Halacha is perhaps to some extent dry and scholastic, it embodies perfectly the pure Jewish spirit—a spirit which expresses our entire centuries-old spiritual creative process. Halacha means progress and development (from the Hebrew verb "holach"—to go); Halacha means continued and expanded development of the unique Jewish way of life and its view of life and man.

The seeds of Jewish spirituality had been deeply sown in the life of the people even in primitive times. Even in ancient times the Jewish ethic towered above that of the other peoples, and even then they were already in possession of definite traditional moral and ethical laws and customs. Receiving the Torah at Mt. Sinai was only the affirmation of already existing governmental and social order. Jews had been living under a definite code of morals and ethics long before receiving the Torah. The Torah was the written document and holy testament of an established social order, and it is upon this foundation that Jewish history and the Jewish future were to be built. The Talmudic scholars strove to implant these traditional precepts deeper in the lives of the people. In order to achieve this they were forced to broaden and refine these precepts so as to eliminate all possible contradictions.

Their first duty was therefore to expand and to give a philosophical basis to these customs and habits. It was necessary to establish broad principles and at the same time to work out all the details.

An instance of this is the observance by the Jews of rites involving "Tefillin" (the phylacteries tied on the arm and head), "citrus" (one of the four plants used on the Feast of Tabernacles), "fringes" (the show-fringes worn in the four corners of the Talith), etc. The text in the Torah concerning these is not clear. The Torah says: " . . . and it shall be for a sign upon thy hand and for frontlets between thy eyes." But how do we know that it means phylacteries? Again, the Torah says: "Thou shalt make thyself fringes upon the four corners of thy vesture." But how do we know that it means Tzitzith? In this connection other difficult questions arose: Should phylacteries be worn on Saturday? Is a female obligated to put on phylacteries?

The Torah speaks sparsely about these questions and is not clear concerning any of the duties that have to be performed, and yet each one of them demands a concrete explanation and interpretation based upon logical principles. This necessity existed immediately after the first destruction of the Temple and continued to exist in every period and in every country that the Jews emigrated to.

Not only did the Halacha itself have a direct link with Jewish life, but even the method of interpreting it was likewise influenced by socio-political and economic conditions. When a Talmudic scholar resorted to the method of "rigid interpretation" of the Law, it was precisely because Jewish life demanded such an approach.

Generally speaking, the Halacha grew out of a number of political, economic and social causes. To the many Talmudic prohibitions (the term Halacha also includes the various laws that we call prohibitions, sanctions, restrictions and vows) also belong, for example, the following statements: One, that Jews residing outside of the Holy Land are unclean. Another, that glassware is just as susceptible of becoming unclean as copper and earthen vessels.

It has always been thought that these two statements are of the kind that the Talmud calls abstract discussion, without any relation to real life, or something that concerns a distant period, without any logical purpose. Now, however, we know more.

In the dark days of Antiochus the tyrant, many Jews fled from Palestine and emigrated to other countries where persecution could not reach them. The Talmudic scholars perceived in this a danger to the continuance of the Jewish people. There was grave danger that the majority of Jews might flee Palestine and leave the country in the hands of the enemy. They therefore issued a decree that all territory outside of Palestine is unclean and Jews residing there are also unclean. The reasoning was that no Jew would wish to be unclean all his life and would therefore remain in Palestine.

This restriction, which superficially seems to have no sense, was thus, as we see, evoked by a purely political and national condition. The restriction concerning glassware also stems from the necessities of life itself, although in this case the factor motivating it was a purely economic one.

Even in the period of the first Temple there was a great shortage of glass in Palestine. The glass-makers were Canaanites from Tyre and Sidon, who gradually undermined the important Jewish industry of earthenware manufacturing. Jews ceased to buy the home-manufactured earthenware that was susceptible of becoming unclean and bought instead the imported or Palestine-manufactured glassware made by the Canaanites. The scholars therefore issued a law that glass dishes were also subject to becoming unclean and thus put an end to foreign competition with an important Jewish industry.

Class interests often played a role in the determination of a given law and gradually two powerful and representative groups of scholars were evolved, each representing a different class and group in the society of the time.

The House of Shamai and the House of Hillel both represented such different classes and groups. Hillel and his yeshiva represented the poor, although Hillel himself derived his lineage from the House of David. The yeshiva of Shamai arose among the so-called bourgeoisie and aristocracy—to use modern terms—although Shamai himself was not a rich man, nor an exploiter of labor.

There is a discussion in the Talmud whether a certain type of coarse bread may be baked on a holiday. Beth Shamai asserts that it may not, whereas Beth Hillel asserts the contrary. Without knowing the class differentiation of the two schools it would be difficult to understand why Beth Shamai should impose a prohibition on baking this coarse loaf when it is usually permitted to bake and cook on holidays for eating purposes. However, when we study the class interests which these two schools represented and defended we may learn the motive for this prohibition.

Beth Shamai declares that this coarse bread may not be baked, because in the rich and aristocratic society which this school represented, this coarse loaf was not considered a food. On holidays, and perhaps even on ordinary days, the rich undoubtedly ate fine white bread, cakes, cookies, etc. Beth Hillel gave permission to bake this bread because for the poor it was a vital food, and even at a holiday feast it was considered a necessary food.

This class differentiation existed not only in the Hillel and Shamai yeshivas, but practically during the entire period of the development of the Talmud. Even as early as during the rise of the Pharisees, in the days of the Hasmoneans, the institution of "pairs" in the leadership of the Sanhedrin arose. One was the head, the other a sort of vice president. These two represented the two wings in the camp of the Pharisees.

One was the conservative wing; the other, the progressive wing. This division in leadership lasted about 150 years, and Beth Hillel and Beth Shamai were the very last to represent these different groups and classes.

At first, the majority in the Sanhedrin consisted of conservatives, and the head of the Sanhedrin therefore always represented the conservative wing. In later generations the progressive element became increasingly dominant and so the head of the Sanhedrin represented that wing.

The House of Shamai was the last to represent the conservative school. Its chief point of departure was that although times and conditions may change, the law must remain unchanged. Beth Shamai therefore stubbornly fought for the retention of the old and did not allow any changes to be brought about. Beth Hillel, on the other hand, held that the Jew was not created for the Torah, but the Torah for the Jew, and the law must therefore accommodate itself to changing conditions of life.

The general tendency in the creation and development of the Halacha was on the whole liberal and humanistic. The Talmudic scholars were, generally speaking, more liberal concerning those laws that did not bear a strictly religious character. In later generations the law became lenient even in those matters that concerned the relations between God and man. Thus, the Gemara (Erubin, 32b) states that he who would conduct himself only according to the strict interpretations of Beth Shamai and Beth Hillel would be regarded as a fool who walks in the dark.

The Talmud also argues sharply against the fanatics who seek to be more pious than is necessary. The Jerusalem Talmud asserts (Sabbath, chapter I, section 2) that one who takes upon himself a duty that is not required according to law is an ignoramus.

The general rule was that it is better to permit than to prohibit. A voice from Heaven was supposed to have declared that in the controversy between Beth Shamai and Beth Hillel, the lenient interpretation shall prevail. Also in the controversy between Rabbi Acha and Rabina, the law is likewise loosely interpreted in accordance with Rabina.

It is, incidentally, no accident that the Talmudic scholars showed considerable zeal to interpret the laws liberally. It is generally a good principle to strengthen and maintain the law by adapting it to human needs and human psychology. "The Torah was not given to angels in heaven" and is not for use in an ethereal and Utopian atmosphere.

The Law thus became the key to everything that was creative in Jewish life. The entire Jewish past, the old way of life, the ancient attitude to the world and to man may be interpreted through the Halacha.

The main essence of the Halacha is, on the whole, the law which bears a direct relationship to Judaism. First come the laws concerning worship in the Temple and the manner of sacrifice. Then come the laws concerning the holidays, such as the Sabbath, Passover, Rosh Hashana, Yom Kippur, Succoth, and the others. Still later come the laws concerning Heave-offering, Tithe, First-born, First fruit, Annual Temple Tax, Vows, and finally, the laws concerning cleanliness and uncleanliness.

In addition to these purely religious laws, the Halacha also deals with all those matters that concern relations between man and man. There are the civil laws, criminal laws (particularly in the tractates, Baba Kamma, Baba Metzia, Baba Bathra, Sanhedrin, and Succah), and laws which are in essence practical advice about life and bear a strictly ethical and moral character. These latter laws are scattered without any order throughout the Talmud.

There are also laws which express such altruistic motives as cannot be found in the juridical code of any other nation. There are laws which answer the eternal question whether the Jews constitute a nation, a religious group, or both. There are also laws whose principles seem to be based upon psychology, others that seem to be based upon morality. Jewish history as a whole may best be understood through the Halacha.

Many historians were misled in their researches because they have failed to probe the depths of the Halacha. Without this understanding it was difficult for them to get to the essence of Jewish ideals and ideas, to the uniqueness of Jewish character, molded by the Talmud and most clearly expressed in the Halacha.

The Talmud gives practically a stenographic description of the history and development of every law. It gives a detailed report of the entire process of the making of the Halacha, its germination from a sentence in the Torah, often from a single word. Such a story is very often not less dramatic than a complex court trial. Several scholars give their opinions and each one supports his opinion by many arguments and facts. Mountains are built and as quickly torn down. Brilliant images flash every now and then. Here someone has fallen into a trap and desperately tries to extricate himself, giving a number of new logical arguments and thus emerges the victor. It is a legal chess game which intrigues and stimulates, sharpens the intellect, and teaches one to think critically and analytically.

The first beginnings of this system of assertion and argument in the establishment of a law arose as a consequence of the fact that the intent and significance of many old laws and customs had been forgotten. Gradually assertion and argument became established as a system and method. Rabbi Akiba adduced an overwhelming number of laws concerning every dotting of an "i" or crossing of a "t." Although many of his laws were accepted in his day, they were altogether superseded in later generations through new arguments.

According to the Agada God showed Moses a method of interpreting the Written Torah in several different ways. He showed him 49 arguments in favor of one set of hypotheses, and 49 other arguments in favor of an opposite set of hypotheses. And when Moses pleaded with God to tell him what the law really was, God answered him: "The Law is what a majority of the judges shall decide."

In order for a given law to become valid the assent of at least a majority was necessary. If a majority of the judges assented, the law was established and had to be strictly observed, because in those days every prohibition or permission was deemed to be under divine guidance.

But the Talmud itself does not always reach unanimous agreement. Often there are conflicting opinions, and the law is not determined. This made Judaism elastic and flexible and left it to existing authority to choose the most feasible opinion. In his great thesis "Yad hachazaka," Maimonides attempted to do away with this elasticity and once and for all establish the definiteness of every law, but his attempt evoked strong opposition.

Every law which was established by a majority of the judges was deemed valid even though there was no direct evidence for it in the Torah. However, it was strongly desired to always find such evidence in the Torah itself.

In order to establish a law the Talmudic scholars made use of modern methods of jurisprudence, logic and philosophy. At first, only the ordinary meaning of the Written Torah was followed, what is called in Hebrew "peshat," or meaning. Later, they sought not merely the ordinary meaning, but also the more hidden significance and intent, or what is called "derash" in Hebrew, meaning study and search.

The pursuit of *derash* became an absolute necessity. At first, the tradition of the people were quite sufficient. The accepted laws had been an essential part of the Jewish way of life long before they had been written down and the Talmudic scholars therefore had no need of scientific methods and logical propositions in order to base the laws upon the Torah. The simple fact that a law had been handed down from generation to generation was sufficient to make it binding forever.

Thus a mass of religious and national laws and customs had been accumulated, accepted by the people in the course of many centuries, and transmitted from father to son in every generation. These customs and laws were as a rule established as laws through interpretations made by the Sopherim and later by the Sanhedrin.

Thus it continued until the Sadducees began to question the legality of the Oral Torah, rejecting every law and custom which was not indubitably based upon the Written Torah. It may be remarked, incidentally, that this period coincided with troubled and uncertain times in Palestine, times in which the authority for many laws and customs is easily forgotten. The Talmudic scholars were therefore forced to fence every tradition with the complete and unquestioned authority of the Torah.

Thus, in order to extend and widen the sphere of the Written Torah so that it could become the fundamental basis for the explanations and interpretations of the Laws which are not explicitly outlined in the Torah, scientific and logical methods had to be adopted.

The *derash* method thus adopted never became an exclusive method. Although it was widely utilized, the ordinary meaning of the word was never discarded altogether. The general principle followed in the Gemara was that one may search and study, but never depart too far from the plain meaning of the word.

Hillel is the first to be credited with establishing rules and principles in the hermeneutic study of the Halacha. Many of these rules and regulations were undoubtedly known before him, but Hillel was the first to systematize them and establish them as standards for all students.

Hillel's rules are seven in number:

1. *Kal Vechomer,* meaning light and heavy, minor and major. According to this method we learn the easier from the more difficult. First, the premise of the easier proposition is established, then the premise of the more difficult one, and

the conclusion flows from the two. If the easier thing is prohibited, the more difficult one is most certainly prohibited. This rule is also reversible. If the more difficult thing is allowed, the easier is most certainly permitted.

An application of the above rule is the following: From whatever is said about ordinary holidays we may learn by inference about the Sabbath. Since a holiday is not such a sacred day as the Sabbath, therefore if a given task is prohibited upon holidays, by inference this task is most certainly prohibited upon the Sabbath.

This rule can be applied in converse fashion. The Sabbath is a most holy and sacred day. If a given task can therefore be performed on the Sabbath, it may certainly be performed on holidays.

To this principle of *Kal Vechomer* three important limitations were later added:

a. A law derived from another law should be equivalent to the law from which it is drawn. The inference based upon the principle of *Kal Vechomer* must not be any more severe and exacting than the original law upon which it is based.

b. The inference from minor to major is not to be applied in the penal law. A law may be derived based on the principle of the *Kal Vechomer,* but no harsher punishment can be inferred based upon this principle. Punishment for transgressing the inferred law must be the same as for transgressing the original law.

c. A new law cannot be established by inference from a traditional law. The method of *Kal Vechomer* does not permit the establishment of a new law by inference from an already established law.

2. *Gezera Shava* ("Similar Decree"): This means establishing a new law by analogy in the contents or the meaning of a word in two different passages.

This method, too, was severely limited in the following manner:

a. In order to make a fruitful analogy, one or both of the analogical expressions must be completely superfluous.

b. No one can draw an analogy on his own authority. The analogy must be accepted in tradition by previous generations or by the highest legislative bodies.

3. *Generalization from one passage:* It is permitted to derive a general rule from one passage in the Torah. A given law may be erected into a generalization and other cases may be grounded upon this law, if they are sufficiently similar.

4. *Generalization from two passages*: A generalization may be drawn from two passages in the Torah. If two different passages possess similar qualities, the law can be applied to both.

5. *General and particular:* The determination of the general by the particular and the particular by the general. If a given passage begins with a general statement and ends with a specific statement, the particular does not exceed the general and the law remains as outlined in the particular. If the passage, on the other hand, begins with a particular statement and ends with a general statement, the law is as asserted in the general, not in the particular.

6. *Two contradicting passages*: When two texts contradict each other, the meaning can be determined only when a third text bearing on this matter is found which harmonises them.

7. *A passage explained by its own subject matter*: If a passage is insufficiently clear, the subject matter of the passage may be used to clarify the matter.

In addition to the above seven rules, there is still another principle called the *Heckesh,* or comparison. This is not an analogy in a word or expression, but refers to the similarity between two themes in the same passage.

A peculiar sort of analogy, which bears a certain similarity to the *Heckesh,* is the *Semuchin* or principle of contiguity between two different passages. For example, one passage in the Torah states that a bastard may not enter the congregation of God. A contiguous passage states that a man may not marry the wife of his father. The Gemara therefore interprets the former passage to mean that the Torah prohibits such bastards only who have been born out of relations between a man and woman whom the Torah prohibits from marrying. For example, father and daughter, brother and sister, aunt and nephew, and other incestuous cases.

In addition to the above kinds of analogies, there are several others.

On the basis of the above seven principles, Rabbi Ishmael later elaborated 13, differing from the original seven only in minor details.

Rabbi Eliezer, in turn, increased these 13 principles to 32. But these apply only for *Derash* and the *Agada.*

Rabbi Akiba formulated his own method, based upon the words "only," "also," and "with," and other such peculiar expressions. His method, however, is not obligatory for students of the Law and his interpretations based upon this method have been little accepted.

Another of the Talmudic methods was to permutate the symbols underneath the letters of a given word. Often they used the similarities of sound and syllable. These methods, however, were not used to derive any laws, but merely to explicate a thought.

The Talmudic scholars were apparently well versed in the Hellenic systems of logic, although they did not completely follow them. The unique characteristic of the entire Talmudic creative process is that it proceeds under the assumptions that the Torah does not follow any chronological order, that a given passage must first be disarranged before it is interpreted and that there is no consistent pattern in the Mishna. Such assumptions are in direct contradiction to Greek principles. The underlying reason for this is that the Talmudic scholars laid very little emphasis upon pure form. The essential thing was contents and purpose, the inner essence of the thought and its moral and ideological value.

The Halacha is therefore formulated in moderate style and tone, in folksy and simple language, through open and free argument, democratic and tolerant discussions. The Halacha has therefore exerted a most powerful influence in Jewish life.

The Agada, on the other hand, possesses great literary value. It possesses truly poetic qualities, is rich in imagery, and contains many historical traditions. At the same time, however, it is most dangerous to rely upon the Agada. True enough, it expresses the Jewish national soul, is undoubtedly profoundly bound up with the life of the Jewish people, and has most certainly exerted a great influence upon Jewish thought. Nevertheless, it does not possess the great reserve power of the Halacha. The Agada floats in fantastic worlds, whereas the

Halacha is built upon solid foundations. The Agada exerted great influence upon the heart and feelings of the Jews, but the Halacha molded and formed the Jewish character and the Jewish way of life.

The Halacha is a uniquely Jewish product, called forth directly by life itself and all its constituent elements.

CHAPTER EIGHT

THE AGADA AS AN EXPRESSION OF THE JEWISH SPIRIT

THE AGADA (FOLK TALES) AS A COMPLEMENT TO THE LAW. FOLK TALES AMONG THE JEWS AND OTHER PEOPLES. THE CREATORS OF THE AGADA AND OF THE LAW. FOREIGN TALES IN A JEWISH DRESS. THE FOLK TALES, THEIR STYLE AND PURPOSE.

TALMUDIC SCHOLARS INTENDED PRIMARILY TO STRENGTHEN the religio-national and socio-ethical life of the Jewish people. In order to achieve this purpose, they utilized two methods which seem on the surface to be contradictory; the Halacha and the Agada. While they developed and refined the Halacha portion of the Talmud, their poetic instincts also prompted them to create the Agada with its splendid homespun style.

In essence, the Halacha, the Law, was the more important element in holding the Jews together as a united people. Nevertheless, this did not diminish the sacredness of the Agada. On the contrary, the Jews drew inspiration from these phantasies in which were reflected their own dreams and aspirations.

The Halacha was the guide and the Jews eagerly observed all the laws, customs, restrictions and sanctions. But by means of the Agada, the Jews were able to imbue the observance of the law with the breath of life, to divest it of its dryness and clothe it with poetic beauty. The Agada is therefore a complement of the Halacha, because it explains the spiritual value of the observance of the Law; because it is concerned with justice; and because it partakes of the divine character of the Law.

In the Agada the Jews found their consolation, their salvation and their victory. The Agada is the poetry of the Jewish people, and the Talmud and the Midrash have reared the Jews upon the soil of this poetic creation. The Bible is the chief source of Jewish poetry, but with the Agada this source became deeper, cleaner and more refreshing.

The Agada is the most sensitive expression of the Jewish spirit. The Agada is tender, warm-hearted, and looks upon the human being as a mother does upon her helpless child. The individual is always honest, good, sacred, and does not even know the meaning of sin. The same drive which impels man to sin, impels him also to build and create.

The Agada practically dissolves human sin, and every human weakness is purified and explained. The Agada sees only the spiritual and raises it to the highest degree.

The Agada may be compared with a blooming garden riotous with color, and its fruits are rich with the Jewish spirit and Jewish genius. Through the Agada we are able to perceive clearly and sharply the unique character of the Jewish people, their attitude to God and man, those they hated and those they idolized. Not dry facts there, but something far more important: the poetry of the time.

What is called history is either completely false or else written by partisan, sometimes even corrupt, writers. Even in the best of circumstances history is molded and trimmed according to the opinions and prejudices of the historian. History is true only insofar as it deals with the intrigues of individuals, who played with the people as with figures on a chess board. Seldom do we see in the history of the older nations the free action of the people themselves. The folk tales, legends and stories, however, were born out of the very depth of the masses of the people. It is the Agada which is the proper source material for the historian, because it is in the Agada that the heart, the soul, the deeds and dreams, the ideals and aspirations of the entire people are reflected.

History tells us what happened. The Agada tells us what the people wanted and hoped should happen. History is in essence false even when it is true; the Agada is true even when—or perhaps because—it is fiction.

The political and economic conditions of the Jews were for the most part deplorable in exile, and this insecurity exerted a profound influence upon the Jewish spirit. The Jews therefore sought something which would excite their imagination, stimulate their inspiration, and console them with hopes of the future, of a world beyond this earth, of a heaven in which the brotherhood of all mankind shall exist.

The Agada provided this hope and this consolation to the oft-discouraged Jews. The tone, the language, the style of the Agada were warm and intimate throughout, and clothed the form of duty and law with a veil of tenderness and poetry.

The Jewish Agada is a most brilliant gem from which the most beautiful and sublime thoughts on ethics, morality, divinity, and man radiate. It was created by a fertile and artistic imagination, and the fictional heroes are for us a source of inspiration and love.

What else could the Jewish people do for its great spirits except to spin around them stories plucked from its very heart?

Through the Agada we see, as through a brilliant mirror, the entire culture of the times. Every branch is represented in it: magnificent allegory, profound legend, tender humor, biting satire, the idyllic novel, romantic and historic story, fable, epigram, aphorism, proverb.

Through this compact literature we become thoroughly acquainted with the life of the people in that period, with the greatness of its heroes, the philosophy of its teachers, its struggles and martyrdom, its sorrows and anger, hopes and joys. We see before us a living people in all its manifestations.

Other nations also created legends around their leaders and heroes. But how different these were! The Romans and Persians flooded the world with a sea of blood. Every adult person was busy destroying other countries and robbing other peoples. The greater the number of slaves one had, the greater his prestige. The greater the number of people he had killed, the greater his heroism. Even their gods were always warring, fighting each other or intriguing against each other, because of a woman or lust for power. The maxim was: the strong is the victor and to him belong the spoils. The Greeks also sought to conquer peoples and countries, if not always by force then by their erotic culture, by lust and adultery.

Murder and adultery, war and power, robbery and brute strength—these were the ideals and idols of those nations. They, too, idolized their leaders; they, too, spun a web of legends and stories around their heroes; they, too, found inspiration and hope in legend and story; they, too, sang about their historic events. But how different these were!

Their creations reflected their actual lives. They were warriors, murderers and robbers, and so they created their heroes in their own image—heroes who gloried in blood, who murdered entire peoples in order to satisfy their passion and lust.

And the Jews? They, the persecuted and tortured, the driven and pained, raised their eyes to heaven and dreamed of the millennium. The Jews did not idealize war and lust unless they strayed from the path and assimilated the customs of the surrounding peoples. And even then, they regretted it afterwards and did penance. The ideal of the Jews was a symbol and example of all virtues and spirituality.

The Talmudic scholars set the tone for the idealization of our heroes and leaders. Beginning with the very first generations they devoted themselves day and night to the study of the Torah. Shem and Eber had a yeshiva, Samuel the Prophet had his yeshiva, Boaz had his yeshiva. Jewish heroes were those only who were models of conduct, who were saintly and god-fearing.

A story in the Agada relates:

Pappus ben Judah criticized Rabbi Akiba for endangering his life and continuing to teach his students despite the prohibition of the government.

I will answer you by a parable, Rabbi Akiba told him, so that you may understand better. One day a fox saw some fish swimming at the edge of a river. He spoke to the fish in this wise:

Come upon the shore, so that we may live together in opulence and in joy, like our forefathers were wont to do.

The fish thereupon answered the fox:

We are surprised that you, Mr. Fox, whom everyone considers the wisest of all animals, should speak such nonsense. If here, in the water, our very life and food, we are always in danger of being swallowed up, how much more would we be endangered if we were to be on dry land!

In the Talmud many stories are expressed through a parable, containing some profound thought or example of a virtue. The authors of the Agada were in essence not story writers or writers of parables, but ordinary preachers and interpreters. They, as well as the Halacha authors, based everything upon some text in the Torah, but since they mingled with the people they combined all sorts of stories and legends with their speeches.

The majority of the authors of the Agada paid little or no attention to the Law. For them, the Law was presumably too dry to make use of among the broad masses of the people. They therefore utilized the great riches of the people's imagination and drew their moral from them.

This habit of drawing a moral from some story was, truth to tell, not the exclusive property of the Jewish people. The Christian preachers also utilized this method. They, too, created stories based upon some text of the Bible. In the writings of the Christian Fathers we find extensive use made of the Midrash. Their stories are in essence copied from the Jewish Agada, but are cloaked by Christian interpretation. The Christian Fathers simply took them from us and put a Christian stamp upon them.

That is why, apparently, we find in the Talmud and in the Midrash selections that may be interpreted as criticism of the early Christians. The Talmudic scholars carried on a bitter struggle against the early Christians, who were of course Jews, and who adopted the Talmudic system and method of interpretation based upon the Torah, and therefore in the heat of the struggle made many rather pointed remarks. Sometimes this was done quite openly and freely, and sometimes the criticism was veiled in a story or aphorism. Here and there we also find stories containing a double meaning or completely not understandable. However, in such a case it is not certain whether the text is authentic. Often the Jews themselves made changes because of fear of the Christian Church, and at other times our enemies deliberately made damaging changes in order to be able to incite the populace against us.

Incidentally, it must be remarked that not all stories were written down. Many were lost, and others were not included by the editors. The editors were very strict, and those stories that had no direct relationship to the Jews or contained foreign elements which could not be assimilated were rejected. In those stories that were retained, the editors utilized only the main plot, leaving the significance and meaning to the imagination of the reader and the student.

The Written and the Unwritten Torah became, so to speak, The Jewish Book, the only book, and it was from this book that the people sought not only the word of God, not only the law and the custom, but also the story for the child, the exciting romance for the wife, and the wonder stories about the heroes.

The Jews were not always able to free themselves from the foreign and pagan elements. Very often they also allowed exaggeration to creep in and gave their imagination free play. Such stories were, apparently, firmly implanted among the people. When the editors were faced with this colossal number of stories and legends so deeply rooted in Jewish life, they first of all sought to cleanse them of the foreign, pagan elements. To reject them entirely was practically impossible. It would have exerted a harmful effect and would have allowed the foreign story, stemming from the old mythology and the new Christianity, to break the barrier erected around the Torah.

To the extent possible the Talmud therefore rejected the dross, and clothed the story with Jewish contents. The foreign story was planted upon Jewish soil, received a Jewish imprint, although often it lacked the Jewish spirituality and high Jewish ethic. Many of these foreign stories were later rejected, but not entirely discarded. The stories themselves continued to live among the people for generations. That is why, perhaps, there are so many Jewish stories scattered in foreign literatures and in ancient archives. In the early Christian Church books there are numerous such stories which were rejected by the Talmudic scholars as foreign and harmful.

In addition to the Talmud and the Midrash, the Jewish stories are scattered in the Greek, Latin, Arab, Ethiopian, Aramaic and Syrian literatures. Recently, these stories were even found in Armenian literature. How they got there has not been investigated as yet. One thing, however, is certain: the editors of the Agada were well acquainted with these stories, but declined to include them in the collections of the Agada because they contained elements of mythology and paganism. Furthermore, these stories and legends were not based upon any given text in the Torah, although in the Talmud and Midrash there is a numerous body which is likewise not based upon any such text.

Because of the uncertain intention and significance of the Agada, it has sometimes been considered as something unimportant. The Halacha, on the other hand, was emphasized and stressed quite as much as the Written Torah. Only the common people, the man in the street, held fast to the study of the Agada. In the little Russian or Polish town, the lower classes read the Midrash or some other text, while the elite, the student-husband living with his in-laws, studied the elaborate discussions of the Halacha.

Jewish scholars, particularly those of the Spanish period, looked down upon the study of the Agada. Because of their rationalized philosophy, which incidentally was influenced by Greek and Arab philosophy, they introduced to the study of the Talmud the scholastic arguments, philosophical theses and syllogisms, thus diminishing the value of the Agada.

"There is nothing to learn from the Agada except what can be rationally understood," said Rabbi Samuel Hanagid in his "Introduction to the Talmud."

"The Agada is only a story which one tells another," states the "Rambam" in his "Milchamoth Chovah" ("Urgent War").

Rabbi Samuel Hanagid and the Rambam were not the only ones who looked down upon the study of the Agada. All other scholars of that period devoted themselves only to the Law, philosophy and poetry. On the other hand, the Ashkenazi scholars were devoted to the Agada and carefully collected and edited it. Thus we have the Yalkut Shimoni, the Lekach Tov, and many others, which are truly gems of literature.

In the Talmud itself we find innumerable selections sharply criticizing the authors of the Agada and the Agada itself. The Christian scholars, particularly those who were hostile to the Jewish religion, very often utilized this criticism as a weapon against the Jews. The truth, however, is that the Agada remains as important as the Law, and is perhaps of even greater importance. The Gemara itself says: "The Law may be compared to bread, while the Agada to water." An interpreter asserts this to mean that just as a man must drink before he eats, so the Agada must be studied even more than the Law.

In our own times some small-town half-baked intellectuals and free-thinkers looked down upon the Talmudic Agada as upon a collection of grandmother tales. Even religious and often profound scholars looked down upon the Midrash and silently regretted that many of the stories had not been discarded.

These religious critics of the Agada based themselves most often upon the many assertions in the Talmud, and, although their scholarship seldom extended to the Talmud of Jerusalem, they were all able to cite from memory the statement of Rabbi Chiya.

In the Jerusalem Talmud (Tractate Sabbath, chapter XVI, Halacha I) it is told that Rabbi Chiya once saw a book containing the Agada and cried out: "Even if there are some good things in this book, the hand of its author should be severed."

It is no wonder that Rabbi Chiya was so bitter against the Agada. In another part of the Jerusalem Talmud it is told that once Rabbi Chiya had to deliver a lecture in the same city as Rabbi Abbahu of Caesarea, who was speaking on the Agada. The latter drew a tremendous crowd, while Rabbi Chiya, who was speaking on the Halacha, hardly had an audience.

The Agada was criticized practically at all times and in all places. This attitude, however, has now virtually disappeared. It is precisely because of the fact that the Agada is like a shut palace to which the key has been lost that the Agada excites so much attention, attracts and appeals. If we sometimes encounter a story which is greatly exaggerated and irrational, it is not the fault of the Agada, but of our feeble mind. Many stories were at first deliberately told in an exaggerated and concealed form, "in a wise manner," as the Gemara says, because they contained sharp and mordant criticism against the existing regime.

Various scholars have attempted to decipher the terminology and explain the secrets hidden in the Agada. But all their attempts and all their knowledge have proved in vain except in a very few cases. Only a few doors of the palace have been unlocked. To find the key to all doors is at the present time impossible. Every Talmudic and Biblical scholar had his own style, his own artistic temperament, his own rich terminology. One, for instance, built his story upon the foundations of the Cabala and mysticism. Another built his upon philosophy and logic. A third upon the language of riddles, which was an accepted study and literary style in those days.

The main criticism is, of course, directed against those Agadoth that tell supernatural and impossible tales; tales about devils, evil spirits and dreams. Nevertheless, these exaggerated and impossible tales are among the most beautiful pearls, the pride of our folklore. The best evidence for this is that the people found in them a path to their own souls and have cherished them for many generations.

The stories were not intended to be believed literally. The Talmud states very clearly that the scholars spoke in exaggerated language, in a language which makes the event bigger, more wonderful and more amazing than it actually is. To write in an exaggerated manner was the fashionable style not only among the Jews, but among other peoples as well at that time.

The Agada also has great value inasmuch as it records all historical events, legends, aphorisms, fables, parables, stories, criticism, and free translations from the Bible. In most cases it is a part of the Halacha and so serves as a diversion from the difficult mental gymnastics. Sometimes, on the other hand, it stands by itself in a mass that may outweigh the Halacha.

The Agada is divided into six parts, according to its contents and character:

1. The exegetic Agada, which gives plain or homiletic and allegorical explanations of Biblical texts.

2. The dogmatic part, which explains God's attributes and His direction in the creation of the world and Man, the Revelation of God, reward and punishment, the future, and the coming of the Messiah.

3. Ethical—containing aphorisms, maxims, proverbs, fables,

and speeches, which teach and illustrate man's moral and ethical duties.

4. Historical—Traditions and legends concerning the lives of Biblical and post-Biblical figures in national and universal history.

5. Mystical—Cabala, demonology, astrology, magic, dreams and their significance, panaceas and medicines.

6. Miscellaneous—anecdotes, observations, practical advice and miscellaneous information concerning old philosophy and science.

That which is found in the Agada is beautiful, and has the charm of eternal youth. The long centuries have not tarnished it, nor diminished its value, but have made it even more beautiful.

CHAPTER NINE

THE IDEOLOGY AND TENDENCIES OF THE PHARISEES, SADDUCEES AND ESSENES

SACREDNESS AND LAW OF LIFE. THE ESSENCE OF THE PHARISEES AND THEIR DIFFERENCES FROM THE SADDUCEES. JEWISH CONTENTS AND JEWISH FORM. FAITH AND NATIONALISM.

THE PHARISEES WERE ORIGINALLY CHILDREN OF THE PEOPLE, and although they devoted themselves to the study, research and interpretation of the Torah and thus went above the common man, they nevertheless dedicated themselves to serve him and him alone. The Pharisees were the common people in practice as well as in theory. To them is accredited the saying that the Sabbath was made for the people and not the people for the Sabbath.

The Pharisees recognized the written Torah as the basic foundation of the Jewish faith. Nevertheless, they considered the Torah to be merely a means to life. The Sadducees, on the other hand, held that the Torah is something sacred and must be sanctified; a sort of commemoration of a distant past. To the Pharisees the Torah was the lore of life for all generations.

The Pharisees did not permit reality to come into conflict

with the demands of religion. They insisted that life must be carried on in strict accordance with religious law, but that religious law must be so interpreted as not to hinder the functions of life. Indeed, it must be added that the Torah itself was based in part upon custom and folkways which for centuries had been a part of the Jewish way of life.

The Pharisees maintained the long view and did not desire the Jewish faith to suffer from rigidity. Their view of the Torah was as of something which is organically linked to the people. In the Torah they saw the obvious, essential, indissoluble link with Jewish life.

Their horizon was vast and they looked into the distant future, not just into one epoch or one place, but into all eternity and all lands. The Pharisees looked into broad vistas and linked the past with the present and the future.

The Pharisees had no faith in the power of the mortal and they were unconcerned with the apparent fact that a virtuous man may suffer while an evil man may thrive. They believed in a Divine Providence that superintends everybody and everything. Naturally, they believed in the immortality of the soul and in a life after death in which everyone is either rewarded or punished.

Every letter, every dot in the Torah had deep significance for them. And that is why they based every law upon some text in the Torah. Whenever it was impossible to find a relevant support in the Torah they leaned upon tradition and upon the words and interpretations of previous scholars and writers.

The Pharisees were truly religious and devoted themselves zealously to the study of the Torah. They led a life apart from the people and conducted themselves in strict morality. Anyone could join their ranks provided he led a life comporting with morals and ethics. He also had to be sternly religious and guard against coming in contact with infidels.

Because of their natural isolation and extreme scrupulosity in the law concerning cleanliness and uncleanliness, the Pharisees gradually also became estranged from the common or ignorant people. There is a controversy in the Gemara (Sota 22a; Berachoth, 16b) concerning who may be called an ignorant or common person. Rabbi Eliezer says: "He who does not read 'Shema' three times daily, etc." Rabbi Joshua says: "He who does not wear phylacteries." Ben Azai says: "He who does not wear 'fringes' " (Tzitzith). Rabbi Nathan says: "He who does not educate his children in the ways of the Torah." It is apparent that the concept of the common or ignorant man then was quite different from that of today and that this schism between the Pharisees and the common people came about because of the suspicion that the common man was not altogether particular in the observance of the laws concerning tithes and the offerings due to the priesthood.

The Pharisees were on their guard not to fall under evil influence, and if anyone of them violated a law or transgressed a restriction or barrier he was considered a sinner. Nevertheless, in the matter of punishment for such sinners they were patient and careful because they adhered strictly to the principle that one must be cautious in meting out justice.

When the Pharisees became a well established force in political and religious life, certain elements, not altogether sincere, infiltrated into their ranks—as is always the case. In the Talmud such people were called hypocrites and the populace was warned against them. It was because of these hypocrites and their despicable deeds that a hatred finally developed against all Pharisees and the very word "Pharisee" practically became an insulting term. The early Christian sect easily utilized this hatred and helped to fan it. In the Christian Testament the word "Pharisee" is always mentioned with scorn, hatred and contempt. It is on the basis of these writings that the word "Pharisee" has been defined in practically all dictionaries as a hypocrite.

It is characteristic that the Talmud itself did not spare these hypocrites and the Gemara (Sota, 22b) lists a number of Pharisees who were bent on following their selfish interests.

Nevertheless, it would be incorrect to accuse all Pharisees of falseness and hypocrisy. The majority consisted of sincere people who, with the utmost zeal and honesty, practiced whatever they preached and studied. They were also essentially democrats and always fought for the principles of equality and social justice. They maintained that there should be one law for everyone—for the poor as well as for the High Priest and Prince.

It is told that when a slave of King Jannai killed someone, Simon ben Shetah demanded that the king stand trial before the Sanhedrin. When the king arrived at the trial and sat down, Simon ben Shetah cried out: "Jannai, arise and listen to what the witnesses against you have to say." Jannai felt that he was insulted in being treated as a commoner and replied: "If all the other judges will so command I will do it." Jannai turned to the right and the judges remained silent; he turned to the left and the judges likewise maintained silence. Simon ben Shetah then cursed all the members of the Sanhedrin for their cowardice (Sanhedrin, 19a).

The first Hasmoneans were all Pharisees, because they were merely priests and princes and not kings. The Pharisees at first did not allow the Hasmonean victors to become kings. The Pharisees, and before them the Great Synod and the Chassidim, were staunch opponents of a Jewish monarchy. They looked with disfavor upon the creation of a privileged caste, under law. The Pharisees maintained in this connection a consistent principle: the unabridged rule of the Torah. The people saw in this principle the maintenance of their own interests and eagerly supported the Pharisees.

The Pharisees essentially were not an ideological grouping and it is therefore incorrect to designate them as a party. The tendencies and the direction of the Pharisees did not exhibit any characteristics to mark them off from what came before them. The word "Pharisee," etymologically speaking, means separation, but this is to be regarded only in the sense of maintaining their unique conduct and in the strict observance of all laws and customs.

The Pharisees arose as a separate group during the period of the Hasmonean revolt. At first they were known as the party of the Chassidim, and it was not until the time of Johanan Hyrkanas that they adopted the name of Pharisees.

During the revolt (165-168 B.C.E.) they were active participants and helped greatly in achieving victory. Their chief aim then was to free the Jews from religious persecution, but they were totally disinterested in any political aspirations, if there were such. So long as the struggle against the enemy bore a religious character, the Chassidim took part in it. But as soon as the revolt of the Hasmonean assumed a secular character the Chassidim appear as the Pharisees and become the avowed opponents of the ruling Hasmonean dynasty. Their principles did not harmonize with secular politics, involving as it did power and rule, and under no circumstances allowed of compromises.

The Pharisees regarded government policies from the viewpoint of religion and they therefore made no distinction between Jewish or foreign rule. Whenever government policies interfered in any manner with the development and extension of the Unwritten Torah they fought resolutely against them. Their zeal and energy in fighting the Jewish kings Johanan Hyrkanas and Alexander Jannai were as great as against the Greek tyrant Antiochus Epiphanes.

Very often the Pharisees bore the yoke of foreign rulers with greater equanimity than that of their own rulers. Sincerely believing in divine guidance and in reward and punishment, they looked upon foreign rule as upon divine punishment for the sins of the people of Israel.

In the great revolt against Rome the most outstanding Pharisees adopted the viewpoint that the yoke must be borne patiently. Later, this viewpoint was rejected by the majority of the Pharisees. But this trend came about as a result of the revolutionary tendencies of the masses, which, incidentally, gave rise to the party of the Zealots.

In every event the Pharisees saw the finger of God and Divine Providence. It is true that they believed in free will, in man's ability to choose good and evil. Nevertheless, in the deeds of the individual as well as of the people, they saw the will of God. Everything is previsioned, and yet man has the freedom to choose. In these two opposite viewpoints the Pharisees detected not the slightest contradiction.

The concept of reward and punishment obviously developed out of the above-mentioned concept of "prevision" and "freedom to choose." Since man has freedom to choose the good, he is therefore responsible for his evil deeds, and liable to an accounting. And if we nevertheless see that in this world the good man suffers while the evil man prospers, it is an indication that reward and punishment come after death.

The nature of the Pharisees is clear and their philosophy and achievements can be readily understood. But it is altogether different with the Sadducees. It is difficult to achieve a full understanding concerning the essence of their philosophy. They lack the uniform characteristics which are so clearly defined with the Pharisees.

However, one thing is clear. Although many of the modern scholars and students attempt to paint the Sadducees in a rosy light and ascribe to them the pioneer struggle for progress and secularism, all our historical sources show the exact opposite.

The Sadducees were the aristocrats of the day and maintained a snobbish attitude towards the common people. Only the rich joined their system; the masses, on the other hand, were always hostile to them.

The leaders of the Sadducees were mostly the priesthood who formed the aristocracy of the Jews in this period. True, not all priests were Sadducees, but they all considered themselves privileged in one way or another and aristocrats. The more outstanding of the priests in that epoch—those who were also high government officials—quite readily abandoned the strict demands made by the Pharisees and very often came out against the Unwritten Torah.

It is not especially clear how the name Sadducees originated. There are many differences of opinion and conjectures, all of them leading to the same conclusion: the Sadducees from the very beginning drew their nourishment from the priesthood.

The most probable theory is that the name Sadducees stems from the family of Bnai Zadok, who were all priests and had maintained this station since the days of Solomon. After the Babylonian exile the priests of other families also received the right to perform services in the Temple, but the family of Bnai Zadok maintained their privileged position.

It is also told that one of the great-grandfathers, the High Priest Zadok, was a student of the scholar and chief of the Sanhedrin, Antigonus of Socho, and when the latter preached that man must not serve God as a slave does his master in order to receive his reward, Zadok interpreted this to mean that there is no reward in heaven for man. It is then, according to the story, that Zadok established the party of the Sadducees.

Other historians hold that the first Sadducees were indeed the children of Zadok, and that they established the party during the period of the Hasmoneans, because their prerogatives in the office of the High Priest were taken away from them.

However, these are all conjectures and it is more feasible to believe that the Sadducees consisted of the aristocracy of the priesthood and government officials, whose personal interests came into strong conflict with the severe demands of the Pharisees.

The Sadducees avowedly believed in the sacredness of the Written Torah and held that every word must be interpreted literally. They even rejected the traditional customs which had in the course of many centuries become an integral part of the Jewish way of life.

The Sadducees did not believe in reward and punishment. They argued that the pleasure that a man derives from doing a good deed is sufficient reward. They also did not believe in divine guidance over the individual and asserted that if man has a free will and may choose good or evil, then God cannot exert any tutelage over him. Man alone, they reasoned, is the cause of his fortune or misfortune and no one has any influence over him.

The Sadducees, the aristocrats, were more interested in life in this world rather than in reward and punishment in the next, and it is only natural that they could not accept the concept of divine interference in man's private affairs and punishment or reward according to deeds. Because their interests lay mainly in political affairs, their entire ideology was in conformity with these interests and principles. The stronger these interests became, the more did they push them to the foreground and reject everything else which interfered with them.

Since their political interests were often linked to the culture of foreign nations it was natural that they should adopt foreign cults and tendencies and thus gradually become estranged from the Jewish way of life and thought.

The Sadducees intermarried with the Kutheans and Samaritans, who in the course of many years had transformed the

Jewish religion which they had adopted into a mixture of paganism and Jewish lore (Chullin, 81a).

The Sadducees accepted the Torah as a foundation, but failed to erect a structure upon it. They preserved only the religious ritual, but rejected all other obligations and practical precepts. The Sadducees became a party of egoistic and self-seeking magnates who utilized the cult of sacrifices to rob the poor people. Sometimes the Sadducees would stimulate and incite nationalist feelings and at other times sell themselves to the enemies and oppressors of the Jewish people. They considered all means justified if it served their end to grasp power and rule over the people with an iron hand.

Perhaps the Sadducees intended to maintain a Jewish essence, in a national or religious sense, but they sought to clothe this essence in a foreign dress, in a Hellenic garb. They thought that essence without form can be durable and is fundamentally national. But the truth is that essence is fundamentally a-national. In its first stages, perhaps, contents may be national, but it gradually becomes universal. That is why other faiths undoubtedly broke through every national barrier and became rooted among many nations—nations often with hostile and quite different cultures. Faith and morality are essentially anti-national tendencies, and throughout world history they have united nations that did not in the least possess any common characteristics.

A foreign essence could easily be assimilated by the Jewish people endowing it with a Jewish stamp and form, but a foreign form could never become a part of Jewish life.

The Jewish-Greek philosopher, Philo, based his theory upon the principle that essence is the sole factor in the maintenance of a people. His works and theories, however, have had a lasting influence and found a permanent place only outside of Jewry. Another example is the Jewish-Arabian literature which influenced Jewry only to the extent that it was translated into Hebrew and thus was incorporated in a Jewish form.

It is also believed that the German dialect would never have become metamorphosed into Yiddish if it had not adopted the external Jewish form—the Hebrew alphabet. A national criterion can be built only upon a national form, because it is only form that bars the road to assimilation.

This principle was undoubtedly the foundation upon which the Talmudic scholars sought to base Jewry and Judaism as a religio-national entity. The Sadducees, who sought to base Judaism upon the sacredness of the Torah and yet would have allowed the Jewish people to assimilate foreign cultures, became involved in internal contradictions and as a result were forced to make ever new compromises and accommodations.

Their religious conservatism demanded a strict observance of the laws of the Torah, but their social conservatism demanded a way of life in direct contradiction to the spirit of the Torah. What then should be done? They simply declared a good deal of the Torah invalid and moribund.

Whenever the Sadducees captured leadership they abolished all the regulations and laws in the Torah which were a hindrance to them. They also created their own lawbook, which superficially seemed to be an interpretation of the Torah in the style and in the manner of the Pharisees, but which in reality did not contain any of the principles of social justice and fair play embodied in the Talmudic socio-juridical and economic writings.

Many of the Sadducees, those who were more consistent and logical, gave up Judaism altogether. To them belong the Herodians, the family of King Herod the Idumean, and the free-thinkers who are mentioned in the Talmud as well as in the New Testament.

Very little is known about the origin of the Essenes and the many conjectures that exist are not at all based upon facts. Little is spoken about them in the Talmud, and when they are mentioned it is with contempt or ridicule.

Professor Graetz believes that the Essenes arose out of the Chassidim. This hypothesis is not improbable since the Chassidim were extremely religious and it is quite possible that in later times a number of them, the more religious ones who did not wish to accept the many licenses granted by the Hasmonean rules, separated themselves from the rest. For instance, the Chassidim believed that one may not violate the Sabbath even when one's life is endangered, a thing which the Pharisees sanctioned.

Because of their fanaticism and isolation the Essenes gradually became complete ascetics and carried their strict observance of the laws to extremes. The Sabbath became so holy that even going out of the house or carrying an object from one room into another was not permitted.

This severity made it impossible for them to remain living in the cities and in every-day society. They therefore sought out isolated and abandoned places and there lived like hermits. They formed a community by themselves under strict regulations and were completely uninterested in events outside their own little world.

The Essenes did not devote themselves to the study of the Torah and did not engage in arguments as to the meaning of a word or sentence. Their chief aim was solitude and contemplation. They prayed a good deal, individually and in groups, and principally sang and recited chapters of the Psalms. It goes without saying that they observed all the laws and precepts, but this was not sufficient for them. They were always searching for inner significance and that is why they were always preoccupied with thought of God. They sought in religion not the externals, the practical guidance, but the higher fulfillment and integration of the spirit. The Essenes conceived the Jewish religion only in its purely spiritual essence and it is through this spirituality that they sought to reach the Heavenly Kingdom.

While the Sadducees devoted themselves to the sacrifice cult and the Pharisees to setting up barriers around the Torah, the Essenes went to the wilderness and into the mountains and there ordered their life upon communal foundations. There, in the isolated communities, they lived apart from the world and occupied themselves with spiritual work. They knew nothing of worldly pleasures, but sent their thoughts heavenward.

In the archive studies of Professor Solomon Schechter he tells us that in that period there were many other groups and sects who left behind them many written records. These fragments did not become canonized and were forgotten in history. From what has been ascertained we have found out that among these sects there was one that later on played a significant role in Jewish life. But what sect it was and whether it was the Essenes we do not know.

Professor Levi Ginsberg of the Hebrew University in Jerusalem studied these fragments and came to the conclusion that this influential sect arose in the time of King Jannai. Since this king was a tyrant and shed much Jewish blood, evoking bitter anger and struggle on the part of the Pharisees, he befriended the Sadducees and gave them complete power. A group of about 8,000 Pharisees remained adamant and militant and fought so long that they had to flee Palestine.

They then formed a religious group of a high moral standard and finally became far more exacting than the Pharisees.

The Essenes, who were the largest group among these exiles, slowly separated themselves entirely from life around them and began their own extreme existence. They discarded every vestige of material pleasure and lived in a world of their own.

However, the Essenes were not always so ascetic. In the course of many years they softened and many of them even married. The majority, however, continued their old way and led an isolated life.

At first the Essenes even refused to work, but when they began to suffer hunger and privation they decided to work on a cooperative basis, that is to say, rejecting private property. All earnings went into a communal treasury and no one received more than the next fellow or could have greater privileges than the other. Everyone had to work and could not have any servants.

It was not easy to become a member of the Essenes. Every candidate had to undergo a trial period of three years and to achieve many degrees, like the Freemasons today, before he could become a full-fledged member of the group. It is interesting to note that while the Essenes considered swearing a great sin, every new member had to take an oath.

In this oath he vowed never to swear, to love God and serve Him even at the risk of life, to love every human being and animal, to help everyone, never to lie or cheat, and, what is most important, never to divulge the secrets of the group.

The chief teachings of the Essenes were:

1. Not to participate in war, even in a just war.
2. To keep the body clean by bathing in cold water three times daily.
3. To lead a communal life, live collectively, work collectively, eat collectively, and not to profit more than anyone else.
4. Not to have sexual intercourse and not to marry.
5. To prepare oneself for the next world and seek to achieve the Heavenly Kingdom.

The Essenes believed that through their mode of life they could achieve the status of the prophets and possess the Holy Spirit. Many of them considered themselves prophets and, as it is told in Josephus, two of them predicted the future. One of them, Menachem, told Herod that he would become king and the latter rewarded him for his prediction by making him Chief Justice of the Sanhedrin under the patriarchate of Hillel. Another, Judah, was said to have predicted the death of the Jewish king Aristobolus.

Their mode of life is also described in detail by Josephus:

They arise long before dawn and bathe themselves in cold water. Then they say their morning prayers and begin their daily work collectively. About 11 in the morning they bathe themselves again in cold water, don white linen clothes and sit down at the table. No one utters a word and no one touches any food until the elder says Grace. After the meal they say their prayers collectively, change their white clothes for work-clothes and work until sunset. Then they bathe themselves again, don the white clothes, say their evening prayers together, and eat their supper. From their evening bath until after supper they do not speak to one another.

Each member possesses only his own linen clothes, a towel, and a shovel. He can not own anything else, neither in the group nor anywhere else. The towel is for use after bathing and the shovel is for covering the earth after fulfillment of physical needs.

This severely disciplined life made the Essenes strong and healthy. They all lived to an advanced age and many of them reached 100 years and more. When a member became sick he was healed with medicinal herbs and prayers.

The Roman rulers maintained a friendly attitude to the Essenes, because they knew that they would never participate in a Jewish revolt.

The national ideal which, with the Pharisees and also partly with the Sadducees, was an end in itself, was slowly forgotten among the Essenes and they had practically no relations with the rest of the Jewish people. That is apparently the reason why they left no traces of themselves.

CHAPTER TEN

THE MIDRASHIC LITERATURE

MIDRASH AND AGADA. THEIR BEAUTY AND SIGNIFICANCE. THE SCHOOL OF AKIBA AND THE SCHOOL OF ISHMAEL. MIDRASH RABBA, MECHILTA, TANCHUMA AND PESIKTA.

THE ENTIRE MIDRASHIC LITERATURE IS ESSENTIALLY A PART of the Agada and was created by the desire to gather together into one place the entire Hebrew folklore of all times.

In the Midrashim we find a wealth of parables, fables, stories and aphorisms, interwoven with bits of folk wisdom and divine inspiration. In a unique manner they combine profound faith and oppressive pessimism, passionate hope for the millennium and black despair over the present.

The origin of the Midrashim lies most probably in the sermons which religious leaders used to deliver in the synagogues in conjunction with the reading of the Torah. The purpose, of course, was to influence the audience to live in the spirit of the Torah and to implant in them principles of virtue based upon the highest conception of morals and ethics.

In order to exert the proper influence upon their auditors, the preachers, among whom could often be found the most prominent Tanaim and Amoraim who, as a rule, were dry legalists and strict adherents of the Halacha, found it necessary to speak in artistic images and poetic similes. These were often noted for their psychological insight and understanding of human beings. Through these artistic images the preachers were able to penetrate into the innermost essence of human phenomena. As Jewish patriots they lamented every Jewish sorrow and exulted over every Jewish hope for better and happier days.

The word "Midrash" stems from the verb "Darash," meaning to search and to seek. It is the reverse of the word "peshat," which signifies meaning. The first to distinguish between these two words was Rabba Kahana (Sabbath, 63a) and Rav (Yebamoth, 24a). Although the Midrash never deviates too far from the ordinary meaning of the word, it seeks to penetrate into its more profound significance.

The word "Midrash" also assumed the connotation of delivering a speech, because it had always been the custom of beginning a sermon with a passage from the Torah.

The Midrashim were, as a rule, written and compiled in such a way as to make them readily accessible to every individual without much education. The Midrashim are generally divided into two parts: Tanaic and Amoraic. The Tanaic Midrashim are commentaries and interpretations of those portions of the Pentateuch which contain rules and regulations. They are, therefore, called the Midrash of the Halacha. They are free expositions of these passages of the Torah and they aim at establishing new laws based upon the authority of ancient tradition. These Tanaic Midrashim are among the very oldest, and although it is not certain when they were first composed, we do know that they go back at least as far as the second century.

Those Tanaic Midrashim which were later compiled by the Amoraim contain two parallel opposing tendencies: One, the School of Akiba or Be Rav; the other, the school of his opponent, Rabbi Ishmael.

The following are the Midrashim of the Akiba School:

A. *Siphra,* or "The Book." It is also known under the name of Torath Kohanim. This Midrash is an interpretation of Leviticus, apparently because in the ancient schools study began with Leviticus instead of with Genesis. The Gemara (Sanhedrin, 86a) calls it merely The Book of Rabbi Judah, but the truth is that he was not its sole author. The first collection may have been his, but the others are undoubtedly of a later period.

B. *Siphre,* or "Books." These are exegetical writings upon the strictly legal parts of Deuteronomy.

C. *Mechilta* of Rabbi Simon ben Jochai. This is an interpretation of Exodus. The larger portion of this Midrash is contained in other Midrashim and there is controversy among scholars whether Rabbi Simon was really the author.

D. *Siphre Zuta* is an interpretation of Numbers. It is not certain who is the author of this Midrash. Many scholars, however, believe that it stems from the School of Eliezer ben Jacob.

The Midrashim of the School of Rabbi Ishmael are:

A. *Mechilta* upon Exodus. Mechilta is an Aramaic term meaning measure and form, "Midah" in Hebrew meaning the same. This Midrash seeks to give an exposition of the laws and observances found in Exodus. However, only the beginning and the end of this Midrash deal with the Halacha, the bulk of it containing stories of the Agada.

B. *Siphre* on Numbers. These are also known as "Midrash Wishallehu." Here too we find a good portion containing stories of the Agada.

C. *Siphre* on Deuteronomy. These contain portions of unconnected chapters from the fifth book of the Pentateuch, with a good deal of Agada material intermixed.

D. *Mechilta* of Rabbi Ishmael upon Leviticus. This Mechilta is mentioned in the Gemara, but no copy of it has ever been found.

The most important Midrashim are subdivided into exegetical and homiletical literature. The exegetical writings are: *Bereshith Rabba, Eichan Rabbathi, Shir Ha'Shirim Rabba, Midrash Ruth, Midrash Koheleth, Esther Rabba, Midrash Samuel, Midrash Jonah, Midrash Tehillim, Midrash Mishle and Midrash Job.*

The Midrashim are called "Rabba" or "Rabbathi" (large) in order to differentiate them from an older, but smaller Midrash which is ascribed to Rabbi Oshaya, who was a Palestinian Amora of the first generation.

Bereshith Rabba (Genesis) explains in simple manner words and sentences often having only slight relation with each other. These explanations are made through the use of short, and sometimes long, Agadaic expositions, interwoven with wise sayings, aphorisms, and parables. Sometimes one finds words and terms of foreign languages nowhere else to be found in the entire Hebrew literature. It must also be added that the language is Neo-Hebrew throughout, mixed with Aramaic, particularly in the longer stories.

The entire Midrash is divided into *parshioth,* or chapters, but different manuscripts contain a different number of chapters.

The Midrash *Eichah Rabbathi* (Lamentations), is one of the oldest Palestinian Midrashim and contains a large number of sermons. This is undoubtedly due to the fact that it was customary in those days to deliver a sermon in the morning and evening of Tishah B'Ab.

The exposition here is virtually the same as in *Bereshith Rabba* and follows the passages of *Eichah* with Agadaic interpretations. There is considerable controversy among scholars as to the age of this Midrash.

The Midrash *Shir Hashirim* ("Song of Songs") is full of repetitions and lengthy sermons without any order or proportion. In this Midrash we find many excerpts from the Jerusalem Talmud, Bereshith Rabba, Wayyikra (Leviticus) Rabba, and Pesiktha.

The Midrash *Ruth* contains expositions and compilations of the Agada divided into eight sections. Every section begins with an introduction. In the first introduction we are told that wherever we find in the Torah the words "Wayehi Bimei" ("And it came to pass"), it is an indication of trouble and evil.

The Midrash *Koheleth* (Ecclesiastes), with but minor exceptions, follows the text of the original word for word. The author has also included many of the older Midrashim and excerpts from the Babylonian as well as the Jerusalem Talmud. That this Midrash came much later than the others is indicated by the fact that it specifically mentions the *Pirke Aboth* and the tractates *Gerim, Abadim, Zizith, Tephilim,* and *Mezuza.*

It is distinguished by its rather successful blend of allegorical exposition and simple interpretation.

The Midrash *Esther* contains material of considerable age, but its exposition is not particularly felicitous. On the other hand, it contains many beautiful stories about Esther's appearance before King Ahasueres.

The Midrash *Samuel* or *Agadoth Samuel,* as it is sometimes called, is an Agadaic exposition of the book Samuel in the Scriptures and is composed of considerable ancient writings. Since this Midrash mentions only the names of Palestinian Amoraim, one may assume that it was compiled in that country.

The Midrash *Jonah* consists of two parts. The first part is virtually a repetition of the Yalkut, while the second part also seems to have had its origin in the latter work. Here we also find borrowed passages from *Pirke Eliezer,* the Jerusalem and Babylonian Talmud, and even the Zohar.

The Midrash *Tehillim* (Psalms) consists of two unequal parts, which is conclusive evidence that it was not compiled at one time or by one person. There is a conjecture that this Midrash was composed in the last generations of the Gaonim period, although the language and method used lead one to believe that it must have been composed in Palestine. In this Midrash the numerical values of a word or letter are used as a basis of interpretation.

The Midrash *Mishle* (Proverbs) bears more the nature of a commentary than of a homily. The sources for this Midrash are the Babylonian Talmud and older Midrashim. It is therefore believed that it was compiled in Babylonia.

The Midrash *Job* has been completely preserved, and all its citations and excerpts from other writings are thus gathered together in one place.

The Amoraic Midrashim are wholly collections of the Agada and aim primarily at expounding new views of life and concepts of ethics and morality. The entire character of the Midrashim, generally speaking, is far more universal and appealing than the Talmudic Halacha. They speak more to the heart and their influence was far greater.

As works of literature they are often of a very high order and can compare favorably with the greatest works in world literature.

The homiletical Midrashim are:

A. *Pesikta* of Rabbi Kahana, or as it is called for short, *Pesikta.* It consists of 32 sermons on Hanukah, the Sabbath before Passover, the 12 Haftaroth for all other holidays. This Midrash is the oldest collection of all *Pesiktas* and was probably compiled in the seventh century.

B. *Wayyikra Rabba* (Leviticus) consists of 37 sermons and is also considered one of the oldest of the Midrashim. Both the *Pesikta* of Rabbi Kahana and the *Wayyikra Rabba* are distinguished by their original form and structure.

C. The *Midrash Tanchuma* or *Yelamdenu* consists of sermons about the entire Pentateuch. The arrangement of these sermons is very interesting. They always begin with the Halacha, then go on to several introductions, then to an exposition of the first few sentences in the chapter, and at the end there is promise of the coming of the Messiah.

The name "Tanchuma" was given to it probably because many of the sermons begin with a sentence "Began Rabbi Tanchuma bar Abba." There is also a theory that Rabbi Tanchuma laid the basis for this collection. The name "Yelamdenu" was given it because the Halachas in this Midrash begin with the words meaning "let the rabbi teach us."

D. *Pesikta Rabbathi* also consists of homiletical discourses upon the entire Pentateuch, all the special Sabbaths, and Haftoroth. This great *Pesikta* was compiled in the middle of the ninth century and is almost entirely a repetition of other Midrashim.

E. *Shemoth Rabba* (Exodus), *Bamidbar Rabba* (Numbers), and *Debarim Rabba* (Deuteronomy). *Shemoth Rabba* has 52 sections, the first 14 constructed in one fashion, the rest in another. The most interesting are the latter, although they lack freshness of style and originality of thought. According to the available evidence this Midrash belongs to the eleventh or twelfth century.

Bamidbar Rabba contains 23 sections divided into two parts. The first part, occupying virtually three-fourths, is chiefly an Agadaic composition. Several of the sermons, expounded at tedious length, are obviously a repetition of the *Midrash Tanchuma.* This Midrash, too, belongs to the twelfth century.

Debarim Rabba consists of 27 discourses, two of them merely fragments. Every sermon has an introduction expounding the Law and a conclusion containing happy prophecies. At the end of the Midrash there are supplements containing vivid descriptions of the death of Moses. It is believed that this Midrash was composed towards the end of the ninth century.

In addition to the above-mentioned Midrashim there are several other major ones, such as *Yalkut Shimeoni, Yalkut Hamakiri, Midrash Hagodol, Yalkut Reuvenu, Yalkut Ha'Chodosh, Lekech Tov,* as well as a good deal of smaller Midrashim.

Actually, these are not really Midrashim, but collective works passing under the name of Midrashim.

The *Yalkut Shimeoni,* or *Yalkut* for short, is primarily a dictionary compiled from about 50 other volumes, most of them lost beyond redemption. It is a commentary upon the entire Scripture and is divided into two parts: one part deals with the Pentateuch in 963 paragraphs, while the other deals with the rest of the Scripture in 1085 paragraphs. The order in this volume follows that in the Scripture, except that the Book of Esther precedes Daniel and Ezekiel precedes Isaiah. The name of the author is Simon Darshan. It was apparently composed in the first half of the thirteenth century.

The *Midrash Hamakiri* is a compilation of older Midrashim and other writings and deals with all the Prophets and three of the larger books of the third part of the Scripture (Hagiographa). The author is Makir ben Abba, who lived in Spain in the second half of the fifteenth century.

The *Midrash Hagadol* is a commentary upon the Pentateuch and was composed in Yemen. Since this Midrash gives frequent citations from the Rambam's work Yad Hachazaka (Strong Hand), it is surmised that the author must have lived long after the Rambam's death.

The *Yalkut Reuvenu* is a collection of Kabbalistic commentaries upon the Pentateuch collected by Reuben ben Joshua Hakohen, who died in Prague in 1673.

The *Yalkut Hachadash* is also a Kabbalistic collection, but bears no name of any author or compiler. It was first printed in Lublin in 1648.

Bereshith Rabba, it is believed, was compiled by Rabbi

Moses Hadarshan of Narbonne in the first half of the eleventh century and is mentioned in Rashi and in Rabbenu Tam.

The Midrash *Lekah Tov* contains a good deal of Agada material and commentaries upon the Pentateuch and the Scrolls. The author is Tevie ben Eliezer, who was born in Bulgaria in the eleventh century.

The Midrash *Sechel Tov* was largely taken from the Midrash *Yelamdenu* and is very far from being a real Midrash.

There are many collections of the Agada which possess narrative value. Among them especially worthy of mention are the *Pirke* of Rabbi Eliezer and of Tanei Debei Elijah.

The *Pirke* of Rabbi Eliezer or *Beraitha* of Rabbi Eliezer aim at inculcating the Jews with principles of pure ethics. In order to achieve this aim they give a detailed description of divine deeds and wonders in the creation of the world. In addition to these moral precepts there are many scientific treatises on astronomy, the world calendar, as well as many exotic legends and stories. The entire book reads like a novel of morals and contains a wealth of wonderful Biblical characters and episodes.

This book was credited to the pen of Rabbi Eliezer ben Hyrkanus, the pupil of Rabbi Jochanan ben Zakkai, but it really stems from a much later period, with most indications pointing to the eighth century. It mentions, for instance, the Mohammed's family and Arab rule over Palestine.

The book is divided into 54 chapters. The first two chapters are an introduction, relating the life of Rabbi Eliezer. Nine chapters are devoted to the creation of the world, including a treatise on astronomy and a calendar. Ten chapters tell the history of Adam and Eve and their sons. Then we have chapters on Noah and the flood, Abraham, Isaac, Jacob, Joseph, Moses, the giving of the Torah on Mount Sinai, and the war with Amalek. It breaks abruptly with the story of Miriam and her punishment. This sudden end indicates that the book was never completed.

The author of the work, whoever he may be, had a great fondness for numbers and the various subjects he deals with are discussed in groups of seven and ten. It is written in Hebrew and often rises to great heights of beauty, especially in the portions dealing with the coming of the Messiah.

The second book, *Tanei Debei Elijah,* is a true pearl in religio-ethical literature. The name it bears, "The teachings of Elijah" or "The Agadaic Order of Elijah" *(Seder Elijah),* made many believe that the author was the Prophet Elijah. Truth to tell, the book is of such high quality that it would be no discredit to Elijah, the lover of Israel, the Herald of good tidings, and the savior in time of need. Nevertheless, the holy prophet must be deprived of the honor of being the author of this excellent work.

The book was written by a mortal man whose age is known to us. He tells us himself who he is and that 900 years have passed since the destruction of the Temple. There are varying opinions concerning the place where he lived. Many say that he lived in Babylonia, while others say that he lived in northern Italy. Recent researches have uncovered that the author was Abba Eliyahu of Palestine, who wandered a great deal throughout the Orient and also often visited Babylonia.

The book is divided into two parts, a larger and a smaller part: *Eliyahu Rabba* and *Eliyahu Zuta.* The larger portion contains 41 chapters, the smaller 25. This work is distinguished from all others by not being a commentary upon the books of the Scriptures. It is merely a series of ethical sermons upon the necessity and value of observing certain virtues. The main subject matter is the Torah, love of Israel, and good deeds. All virtues, the author asserts, merely provide the flicker of a feeble light, but the Torah radiates sufficient light to illuminate the entire world from one end to another. People have many faults, but the greatest fault of all is not to know the Torah, because those who do not know the Torah are indeed blind, deaf and crippled.

His love for Israel is unbounded. "Many say," he writes, "that the Torah is to be preferred above all else, but I say that love of Israel is above the Torah." He condemns those Jews who are not honest in their dealings with non-Jews. Every injustice, he says, is a desecration of God, and it does not matter a whit whether it has been perpetrated against a Jew or non-Jew.

It may be said that *Tanei Debei Eliyahu* is the most beautiful book in the Agada literature. It is full of poetic imagery and contains an immense number of literary fables, parables and stories.

CHAPTER ELEVEN

THE INSTITUTION OF "PAIRS"

NASI AND AB BETH DIN. THEIR ROLE IN THE DEVELOPMENT OF TALMUDIC LAW. THEIR MORAL AND ETHICAL SAYINGS.

FIVE PROMINENT FIGURES IN JEWISH HISTORY HAVE COME down to us linked in pairs. Jose ben Joeser and Jose ben Jochanan are the first of these pairs. Jose ben Joeser was the president (Nasi) of the Sanhedrin, while Jose ben Yochanan was its vice-president (Ab Beth Din). This system of dual authority continued for five generations. It was not entirely novel, however. Already during the rein of Jehosaphat, king of Judah, power had lain in the hands of another pair: the priest Amariah and Zebadiah ben Ishmael (II Chronicles, XIX, 11). When the Jews returned from their Babylonian exile the pairs were Zerubbabel and Jeshua ben Jehozadak; also Ezra and Nehemiah.

In the period of Jose ben Joeser and Jose ben Jochanan, about 230 years before the destruction of the Second Temple, Hebrew culture had become virtually entirely Hellenized. The High Priest himself, the traitorous Alcimus, worked hand in glove with the Greeks to destroy Judaism and Jewish life. Only a few remained loyal to Hebrew traditions and energetically fought against the evil deeds of the High Priest. Jose ben Joeser and Jose ben Jochanan were the leaders of this tiny minority among the Jews.

Together with 60 other pious Jews Jose ben Joeser lost his life in this unequal struggle against Hellenistic culture. As they were being led to their execution the treacherous High Priest visited Jose and attempted to convert him.

According to the Midrash the following conversation took place between them:

"Well, you can see for yourself how well off I am for obeying our Greek rulers," the High Priest argued, "and just see the fate that visits you for not obeying."

"If those who anger God lead such a good life," Jose answered him calmly, "imagine how well those who do God's will will fare."

"Perhaps you can point to anyone who was more loyal to God than you have been?" the High Priest asked.

"If that is the case," Jose replied, "if those who do God's will have such a bitter end, what must be the fate of those who have angered Him?"

Josephus and the Apocryphal Writings relate that after this conversation the High Priest was seized with apoplexy and died. The Midrash, however, tells us that he committed suicide.

Whether Jose ben Jochanan shared the fate of his colleague is not known. Generally speaking, there is very little information that we have concerning his life. The conjecture is, therefore, not improbable that he also died a martyr's death.

Be that as it may, the role that both of these great men played in the development of the religious literature is very great indeed. Their few statements that have come down to us in the *Pirke Aboth* are imbued with unlimited faith in the Oral Law as the only force capable of sustaining a Jewish national life. From these statements we also derive their view of life of man's moral consciousness as the fundamental impulse of human fellowship.

Jose ben Joeser said: "Let thy house be a meeting place for the wise, dust thyself with the dust of their feet, and eagerly drink in their words" (Aboth 1).

This piece of advice has a purely moral and practical value. Whenever one is in the company of scholars and savants one naturally falls under their influence, one gains a positive attitude to learning and good manners, and one thereby becomes spiritually uplifted and developed.

Jose ben Jochanan said: "Let thy house be wide open, and let the poor be members of thy household. Do not multiply speech with a woman. If this applies to one's own wife, how much more to that of another man's wife? Wherefore the wise men said: Every time a man talks overmuch with women he brings evil upon himself, and he escapes from the words of the Torah, and his end is he inherits Gehenna."

The beginning of this statement continues the thought of Jose ben Joeser. One's home should be open not only to scholars, but to poor people as well. Learning and piety without liberality are insufficient. One must lead to the other. The Torah must bring one to brotherhood and compassion. There is an opinion that this particular statement was directed against the Hellenizing influences of the period. Greek philosophy and culture took no note of the weak in relation to the strong.

The second half of the statement, advising against idle conversation with a woman, was also directed against Greek culture. In Greek civilization the woman held a high position, and lust and adultery were considered quite honorable. The Jews at this time had already become strongly influenced by Greek culture and men and women engaged in sports and gymnastics in complete nudity. In time, Jewish youth became ashamed of their circumcision and allowed operations to be made on their genital organs to hide the fact that they were Jewish.

Joshua ben Perachiah said: "Get thee a teacher; and get possession of a companion; and judge every man favourably."

Nittai the Arbelite said: "Keep thy distance from an evil neighbour; and associate not with a wicked man; and despair not of retribution."

The slogans of this second duo of Hebrew scholars to a certain extent reflect the philosophy of the Pharisees, which later became the philosophy of the Talmudic scholars: unlimited devotion to the study of the Talmud, lofty standards of moral conduct, and love for one's fellow beings.

Judah ben Tabai said: "Be not as those who seek to influence the judges; and when the litigants are standing before thee regard them as guilty; but when they have been dismissed from thy presence regard them as innocent, since they have received their sentence."

Simon ben Shetah said: "Examine the witnesses thoroughly; and be cautious with thy words lest from them they learn to bear false witness."

Simon ben Shetah was the brother of King Alexander Jannai's wife, Salome Alexandra. Alexander Jannai was at first a bitter opponent of the Pharisees and at his command all the Pharisee members of the Sanhedrin were killed. Only Simon ben Shetah was spared from death. Later he even succeeded in ousting the Sadducees from the Sanhedrin and in reinstating the Pharisees. His task was made considerably lighter after Jannai died and his wife ascended the throne.

Simon ben Shetah introduced two important reforms. One concerned the marriage contract. Since ancient times the unwritten terms of the marriage contract obligated the husband to pay a certain sum to his wife in case of divorce, or to set aside a certain sum for her and her heirs in case of his death. This obligation was, however, in fact a mere moral obligation and was dependent upon the husband's will or upon that of his heirs. In accordance with the new regulations introduced by the reform, this obligation was written into the contract and put the husband's property under lien. In case of divorce or death the wife was legally able to demand her portion from the property of her husband or from his property which had been inherited by others. This reform of Simon ben Shetah has remained to this day a part of the marriage contract.

The other reform was the introduction of compulsory education for Jewish children. Every Jewish community became obligated to establish and maintain a school for children, where the Torah, prayers, and other subjects were taught. By this reform, the first of its kind in the history of Judaism, Simon ben Shetah gained for himself a prominent place among the pioneer builders of education among the Jewish people.

Shemaiah said: "Love labour; and hate domineering; and make not thyself known to those in authority."

Abtalion said: "Ye wise men, be cautious in your words, lest ye be guilty of the sin (which will bring about) exile, and ye be exiled to a place of evil waters, and the disciples that come after you drink and die, and it be found that the name of Heaven has been profaned."

Both warned that we must zealously guard the traditional interpretation of the Torah.

Special prominence has always surrounded the fifth and last of our pair: Shamai and Hillel. In distinction to the other eight personages, whose role in the literature of the Law is strictly circumscribed, their work has left an indelible mark throughout the breadth and depth of the Talmudic ocean. They are the main pillars upon which the entire structure of the Law has been erected, and the entire world of Talmudic scholars draws its nourishment from them. Without them we can hardly envisage what character the Mishna and the Gemara might have taken.

Through his fine character, limitless modesty, endless patience, and wonderful tenderness for all human beings, Hillel soon became a legendary character. All sorts of stories and legends have sprung up around his personality and quickly spread from generation to generation.

Hillel became famous, as the Talmud tells us, in the following way. Once the Benei Bethirah, about whom we know practically nothing, asked Hillel whether it is necessary to make the Passover sacrifice if Passover eve falls on Saturday. Hillel answered in the affirmative and based his opinion upon accepted texts. The scholars, however, were not convinced, and argued that they cannot trust anyone who comes from Babylonia. Hillel then said: "I heard this opinion from my teachers Shemaiah and Abtalion." This finally convinced the other scholars. Hillel's decision was accepted and he was appointed president of the Sanhedrin.

This story shows how strong the power of tradition was rooted even in those days: whatever our ancestors did is sufficient argument for us to do the same thing.

Hillel said: "Be of the disciples of Aaron, loving peace and following after peace, loving men and bringing them nigh unto the Law."

He used to say: "He that exalts his name destroys his name; he who increases not decreases; and he who learns not deserves death; and he who makes gain out of the Crown shall perish."

He used to say: "If I am not for myself, who is for me? And if I am for myself, what am I? And if not now, when?"

Shamai said: "Make thy (study of the) Torah a fixed habit; say little and do much; and receive every man with a pleasant face."

CHAPTER TWELVE

BETH SHAMAI AND BETH HILLEL

THE CHIEF TRAITS OF THEIR CHARACTERS.
THE CONTRADICTORY SYSTEMS OF THOUGHT.
SHAMAI'S COURAGE AND DETERMINATION.
THE VALUE OF BOTH SCHOOLS.

MOST OF US FLEE FROM STUDY AND CONTEMPLATION. THE intellectual fashion today is to believe in direct action. We lack vigor and therefore longingly wait for the day when a strong personality will arise and put the will of the people into effect.

Perhaps it is therefore not out of place to take a glance at our past and study the great personalities of the area who can serve us as guide posts in our present troubled times.

From this standpoint it is hardly possible to look with indifference upon such a giant as Hillel. Our sick world can learn a great deal from him. Hillel is one of those figures in world history which has to be put down upon paper.

Hillel of Babylonia is one of the most brilliant Talmudic lights, and personifies most perfectly the great ideal of uncompromising love for mankind. How much worldly wisdom is embodied in his wonderful stroke of genius to transform the positive but utopian dictum, "Love thy neighbor as you would thyself," into the negative but realizable, "Do not unto others what you would not have others do unto you!"

Hillel possessed almost superhuman patience and faith. Nevertheless, they did not blind him to the concrete needs of daily life, just as his unlimited respect for the laws of the Torah did not prevent him from modifying them to bring them more into consonance with changing needs. How much wisdom there is in his creation of the fictional "Prosbul," which nominally does not abolish the impractical law of "Shemittah" (the law that a loan was wiped out after seven years), but circumvents it entirely.

In a broader sense Hillel is a most consistent humanitarian who believes that man is responsible for his own fate ("If I am not for myself, then who will be?"). But the individual cannot fulfill himself when he remains alone, but he must be part of the community ("And if I am for myself only, what am I?").

As a rule we see in Shamai only the severe fanatic, who rigorously observes the letter of the Torah, interprets everything literally, and who sets up all sorts of barriers against the violation of the precepts. But all this severe exaggeration really aimed at the preservation of the Jewish nation. It is no accident that most students of the School of Shamai perished in active struggle against the Roman aggressors.

It is amazing to observe, however, that despite this rigid code there is evident in the School of Shamai an inner dichotomy and psychological ambivalence, to use modern terms. One could even make out a good case for Shamai's pessimism.

There is a story in the Gemara that for two and one-half years a debate raged between the School of Shamai and the School of Hillel concerning the value of man's life. The scholars of Shamai's School held that it would have been far better for man not to have been created at all. The scholars of Hillel's School, on the other hand, maintained that the creation of man must be considered as a grace from God. The debate was decided in favor of the Shamai School. Pessimism won out. But the qualification was added that now that man has been created it is necessary that he be careful in his deeds.

The result of all this was that the Jew, created, so to speak, against his better interests, could hardly take a step in the immoral world at large unless he leaned entirely upon the Torah and its precepts.

Hillel was born in Babylonia in the year 75 before our present era. His brother, Shebna, was a wealthy merchant and wanted Hillel to become a partner in his business. Hillel declined the offer, however, and chose instead the career of a scholar (Sota, 21a).

The study of the Torah in this period was apparently not pursued very diligently, and the yeshivas in Babylonia—if such existed at all—were not held in great esteem. Judaism, as a religious creed, on the other hand, was maintained on a high spiritual level. The Sabbath was strictly observed, and the annual Temple Tax, as well as gifts and sacrifices, was regularly sent to Jerusalem. But the study of the Torah was perfunctory, since the Babylonian Jews were in this respect dependent upon Palestine.

Yet even in Palestine the study of the Torah was much neglected. Herod's tyrannical reign was greatly responsible for this, and with the death of Shemaiah and Abtalion the light of the Torah was virtually extinguished. The rise of Hillel, the continuator of the Torah in his generation, was therefore almost a miracle (Succah, 20a).

Hillel left his homeland, Babylonia, and came to Palestine to study at the feet of Shemaiah and Abtalion. In order to exist, Hillel became a laborer. During the first half of the day he worked hard in order to eke out a miserable existence, and the rest of the day he spent in study. Once it happened that he could not pay the house guard and therefore could not enter the yeshiva. But since he did not wish to miss the wise words of these two famous Tanaim, he climbed up upon the roof of the yeshiva, although it was cold and snowing outside, and listened in to the class through the skylight. The snow covered him up completely, and thus he lay frozen throughout the night. The next morning, when the students gathered, they noticed that no light came from the skylight. It was then that Hillel was discovered upon the roof and taken down. He was thoroughly washed, rubbed with ointment, and placed near a fire to warm himself. This happened on a Sabbath, but the elders of the yeshiva decreed that in honor of such a man it was permissible to violate the strict regulations of the Sabbath (Yoma, 35b).

Even while in Babylonia Hillel had achieved high standing, but he and the other scholars could never feel certain that their interpretation was in consonance with the decisions of the Tanaim in Israel. Hillel undoubtedly had many such doubts, but the Talmud tells us about three causes for which Hillel undertook the dangerous voyage to Palestine at a time when that country was in a state of unrest and one's life was not safe.

One case concerns the cleanliness and uncleanliness of a leper (The Siphra, chapter 9). The second deals with the question whether it is permissible to eat matzoth made of newly threshed wheat. The third case concerns sacrifices during festivals (Yerushalmi: Pesachim, chapter 6, Halacha 1).

The Babylonian scholars very often were at sea as regards their interpretation. As a result of this they were in a difficult position. They were never sure whether or not their decision would be adhered to, as on many occasions the Halacha in Palestine was at variance with that in Babylonia. To be sure, Hillel's interpretation did invariably square with the Babylonian one. But to avoid uncertainties he left for Palestine to acquaint himself with the Palestinian decisions on the spot.

Hillel did not spend much time in Palestine on his first visit. He soon returned to Babylonia, but later, when the tyrannous rule of Herod slackened somewhat, he again returned to Palestine.

The Talmud and the Midrash tell many stories illustrating Hillel's amazing learning. Thus, it is told that he knew all the 70 languages of the world, and the language of all the beasts, trees and plants, hills and valleys.

The chief traits in Hillel's character were his kindness and modesty, and the Talmud tells many charming stories on this score. His modest character grew out of his profound moral conscience and deep understanding. The main idea running through all his work is human fellowship, and religion is for him merely a means to achieve this end.

This is indicated in his very first saying: "Be of the disciples of Aaron, loving peace and pursuing peace, loving thy fellow-creatures, and bringing them nigh to the Torah" (Aboth, chapter I, Mishna 12).

In the Aboth of Rabbi Nathan (chapter XII) it is told that Aaron was an excellent psychologist and possessed an acute understanding of human nature. Whenever he found out what someone was contemplating doing or was actually perpetrating some evil, he befriended that person and thus brought him back to the ways of the Torah. Such a person would soon feel deeply humiliated and mortified that Aaron considers him, who is such a sinful person, quite a decent fellow.

Hillel was the first of the Tanaim to make love for one's fellow man the mainspring of the Jewish religion. Once, when a gentile came to him and asked him to teach him the entire Torah in one sentence, Hillel told him: "What you do not wish to be done unto you, that you should not do unto others. This is the entire Torah and the rest is merely an elaboration of this virtue. As you will study the Torah you will find that out for yourself" (Sabbath, 31a).

Hillel's prestige was immense, and as it was said about Ezra the Scribe that he renewed the Torah with his additions and improvements, so it was said about Hillel that he renewed the Torah by his great erudition and noble character. Eighty of the most eminent men of his generation were his students. Thirty of them merited the Divine Presence resting upon them, just as it rested upon Moses. Thirty others merited that the sun should stop in its path, just as it stopped for Joshua, the son of Nun. The other 20 students were of lesser caliber, and, nevertheless, among these was Jonathan, the son of Uzziel, whose zeal for the Torah was so great that when a bird fluttered by him while he was immersed in study, it was consumed by the flames of his inspiration (Succah, 25a).

The populace loved Hillel, and his home was always open to anyone who wished to ask him anything. Once, the Agada tells us, several serious minded men came to him and asked him:

"Tell us, dear teacher, what is the best way to find favor in God's and in man's eyes?"

"Three things will merit it," Hillel replied. "Work, modesty, and a life of sorrow and suffering which is so anchored in faith that it is never weakened."

And Hillel illustrated this with a story:

A linen cloth freshly washed and ironed lay on the table and boasted about its beauty. I will soon, so the cloth dreamed aloud, be raised in stature. A new garment will be made of me to be worn by a person to whom great respect will be paid.

At the very instant that the piece of cloth was spinning its dreams an old and dirty overcoat came into view, dusty and sullied, having been trampled underfoot and thrown from one place to another. The linen cloth took one look at this filthy overcoat and laughed uproariously:

"Woe to you, you old rag."

Some time passed and as the cloth foresaw, it was made into a new jacket. Its owner put it on and over it a beautiful overcoat. The jacket immediately recognized the old overcoat and could not refrain from expressing its amazement:

"Tell me, my good friend," the jacket asked, "you were already an old rag. How is it that you merited to be placed over me?"

With modesty and wisdom the overcoat began to recount its sorrowful past:

"At first they took me to a washerwoman, where I was beaten with long sticks until all the dust and dirt were gotten rid of. Then sharp needles and coarse brushes pricked my hide until I was hardly to be recognized. Finally, I thought, an end came to my trials and tribulations. But soon I was thrown into a cauldron of boiling water, where I was burned and scalded, then I was again pricked and beaten until a new overcoat was made of me."

"Thus," Hillel concluded his parable, "it is with the Jew. It is impossible to exalt him to higher spheres before he has patiently borne all persecutions and oppressions."

Hillel stemmed from the dynasty of King David and is one of the few intellectual giants in all history. His thirst for knowledge was immense, but this zeal did not prevent him from also having an interest in secular learning. He studied foreign languages and literatures, all for the sake of learning itself (Tractate Sopherim, chapter 16). He implanted this same zeal in his students and they too did not forsake foreign sciences (Succah, 28a; Baba Bathra, 134a).

Hillel became the symbol of modesty. Be humble like Hillel, it was said. But modesty was not his only characteristic. He was also a great moralist whose precepts are still used as values in the life of society.

Once, someone wagered that he would be able to evoke Hillel's anger and impatience. He went to Hillel's home just before the Sabbath evening, when Hillel was taking a bath, and called him out for a reply to some foolish question.

Hillel presently came out covered by a cloth, and he was asked:

"Why are the eyes of the Tarmudites red?"

Hillel patiently answered him: "Because they live in a very sandy place."

Several minutes later the person returned and again called Hillel out to answer another foolish question. This was repeated several times, but each time Hillel answered the questions patiently and seriously (Sabbath, 31a).

Hillel's faith was very deep. He would always say, blessed be God today and every day. He never worried about tomorrow, as long as he had enough for today. For tomorrow, he said, let God worry! (Betza, 16a).

The reverse of the soft-hearted and kind Hillel was the aged Shamai. The Mishna tells the following story about his severity in upholding the law:

Once, when his daughter-in-law bore a son just before Succoth, Shamai ordered the roof over the mother's room to be torn down and covered with greens, so that the newly born infant might observe the rules and regulations concerning Succoth.

The Torah commands fasting on Yom Kippur, and Shamai interpreted this to require fasting on the part of everyone, even children and pregnant women.

Shamai is particularly well known for his saying in Pirke Aboth: "Fix a period for thy study of the Torah; say little and do much; and receive all men with a pleasant countenance" (chapter I; Mishna 15).

Shamai, who had the reputation of an irascible person, always maintained that the Law must move mountains and must never be adopted to changing situations. The Torah is fixed once and for all and cannot be interpreted to suit the times. What has once been written remains sacred for all time. Reason must bow to tradition and can never make any changes or allow for exceptions.

Shamai was not completely blind to the fact that time evolves new necessities and calls for reinterpretations which could not previously be foreseen. But such interpretations must be made in the light of tradition and must be based upon the Law. He had little regard for original opinions. Nevertheless, he too made his own interpretations and gave new arguments, but always based strictly on what was already set down.

Many students gathered around Shamai, as around Hillel. And thus two separate and contradictory systems of thought in the Law developed: The school of Shamai and the school of Hillel. As the teachers differed, so differed the students. Both schools played a tremendous role in the development of the Law, although in the Mishna they are mentioned barely a dozen times.

Hillel's school, in essence, interpreted most laws with a view to making their observance easier. The Shamai school, on the other hand, was the strict constructionist school.

In reality, of course, there was no difference between the schools on grounds of principle. Both were unanimous in the stress they laid on the necessity of observing the Unwritten Torah. The Hillel school did not intend to carry out any reforms in the Law. The difference lay in methodology, and eventually the Hillel school gained dominance.

In the Law it was the school of Hillel that can claim most credit, but in history it is the Shamai school that proved of greater utility. Those conservatives who did not bend to the needs of the times and did not deviate from the Law as written also did not bow before kings and oppressors. For them the Law applied equally to everyone and in order to maintain it they showed great courage and determination. History will never forget the speech which Shamai, the founder of conservatism, held at an open session of the Sanhedrin. His speech exhibited greater courage than any other since the Prophet Elijah. His words had a deep impact upon many generations and his long vision proved right in many respects.

After being conquered by all the empires, such as Assyria, Babylonia, Persia, Egyptian-Greece and Syrian-Greece, Palestine finally fell under the rule of the greatest world empire the world had ever seen, Rome. At first, Rome ostensibly afforded Israel its protection, but it soon became a despotic and tyrannical ruler.

During this period Judah still had its own king, but Rome was already sending there its consuls, generals and procurators, who were in fact the real rulers of the country. One of these governors was the Idumean Antipater, who utilized cunning and wiles to bring his son Herod on the Jewish throne.

Herod's first important post was as commander of the military forces, and even as early as this period he exhibited the cruel traits of the tyrant, traits which made him infamous in Jewish history, when he became king of the Jews for 40 years. The soil of Palestine was made to flow with Jewish blood, thousands perished without trial, and every Jewish home was in mourning.

The Sanhedrin, under the leadership of Shamai and Hillel, forced the then reigning Jewish king, Hyrkanas, to charge Herod with murder. Herod appeared before the Sanhedrin, but came dressed in his military uniform, armed from head to toe, and accompanied by Roman guards. His demeanor was arrogant and fear fell upon the judges. All remained quiet and bowed their heads to the ground. Only the old Shamai stood up against this attempt at terrorization and he spoke to his colleagues proudly and courageously:

"Comrades, judges, and king! Most certainly you and I never saw an accused coming into court in this manner. Every accused is wont to come in here frightened and uneasy, attempting to evoke our pity. He would come here not brushed and combed, but dressed in black. But Herod, who is accused of murdering untold numbers, this great criminal comes dressed in purple, his hair curled as if this were a holiday, and in the company of the military. I do not condemn Herod, who is more concerned about his own safety than about the safety of the court. You alone, and the king with you, have allowed him thus to conduct himself. But you must know that God is greater than all of us, and the day will come when this man whom you all fear to judge will one day punish you as well as our king."

Nobody supported Shamai's daring outburst and Herod was not condemned. But Shamai's words came true. Herod destroyed the king and the entire Hasmonean dynasty, suppressed the Sanhedrin and its judicial functions, killed many of them, and only by a miracle were Hillel and Shamai spared.

Later on, when the Jews rebelled against Roman oppression, the students of the Shamai school were the foremost fighters in the war for liberation, while the students of the Hillel school remained most passive. Thus, from methodological differences arose political differences, which often led to deep hatreds and even to physical quarrels.

But the Jewish people grasped the value of both yeshivas and both schools. In both, the School of Shamai and the School of Hillel, the principle of the Torah was prevalent and adequately made a part of Jewish life. Both schools have considerably helped in the development of the Halacha, the traditional Jewish law, and no wonder that on the day the quarrels between the two Schools broke out the Jewish people sorrowed and considered it as the day of the Golden Calf.

The contribution of the two Schools to the development of the Halacha is that the Oral Law at once became the means of absorbing the currents of social behavior into the purposefulness of the spirit. The quarrels of the two Schools gave to Torah-Judaism the elasticity and plasticity that prevented the Halacha from becoming dogmatic along the catechisms of the other religions. In a very definite sense it may be said that the quarrels between the two Schools have democratized and humanized the Oral Law.

CHAPTER THIRTEEN

THE ROLE OF THE SANHEDRIN IN JEWISH LIFE

THE HISTORICAL ASPECTS. ITS EXISTENCE AND AUTHORITY. THE POLITICAL AND JURIDICAL CHAMBERS. THE FUNDAMENTAL MOTIVE IN CRIMINAL CASES. PROCEDURE AND DECISIONS.

AT THE BEGINNING, DURING THE TIME OF EZRA AND NEHEMIAH, a Supreme Court of Justice (Beth Din Hagadol), regulating the life of the Jewish people, was gradually being established. At first it was called the Great Assembly (Kneseth Hagdolah) but later it became known as the Sanhedrin.

The transformation of the Kneseth Hagdolah, the Great Assembly, took place gradually and was actuated by momentary expediency. The "Small Assembly" established throughout the length and breadth of the country, was undoubtedly a blessing to the Jews since it helped to strengthen and maintain Judaism. Nevertheless, at the same time it helped to weaken the central authority of the Great Assembly, and a danger arose that different and contradictory interpretations of the Halacha might be given. The original character of the Great Assembly as the highest legislative body had gradually been forgotten, and it was most natural that its very prestige and existence should be placed in jeopardy. In order, therefore, to insure the necessary consistency and uniformity of the Oral Torah a new institution arose: this was the Sanhedrin.

Sanhedrin is a Greek word and signifies a gathering of high military men. In Hebrew it was called Beth Din Hagadol, the Great Court House. The Sanhedrin differed from the Great Assembly inasmuch as it was not an academic institution for the study of the Torah, but an official governmental institution whose main purpose it was to centralize and maintain the unity of the multicolored cultural and spiritual life of the Jew throughout the world.

All the problems and doubts that would arise in the synagogues and courts all over the country would thus be resolved by the Sanhedrin, and no one ever dared to oppose any of its decisions. If any of the scholars throughout the land had the temerity to make a law or interpret a law against the accepted judgment, he was declared to be a traitor who deserved the death sentence in accordance with the Torah.

Thus was the colossal accumulation of laws and regulations, which in the course of generations had been gathered by the scribes of various systems and yeshivas, cemented and made uniform. The danger of chaos and confusion concerning the interpretation of the Torah was thus avoided.

In the previous epoch, the epoch of Ezra the Scribe and the Great Assembly (Kneseth Hagdolah), the historical task was to awaken the latent forces of Jewry, to evoke the desire to study, and to imbue the entire people with the spirit of the Torah. But now, when this aim had been achieved, it was necessary to curb and discipline the newly awakened drive to independent study and interpretation of the law.

A central institution like the Sanhedrin, whose task it was to gather and preserve all the authentic elements in the creation of the people, could not remain an anonymous body. Its existence and authority were therefore symbolized and represented by recognized personalities. The writers and scholars of the previous epoch despite their participation in the creation of the Talmud, could remain unknown, but the supreme governmental power of the Sanhedrin, representing as it did the organic unity of the entire people, could not otherwise be expressed than through prominent individuals possessing great personal authority and influential renown.

According to the Agada, the Sanhedrin was a direct continuation of the Assembly of the Elders in the time of Moses. There is a controversy in the Talmud (Sanhedrin, Mishna I) concerning the number of members that should comprise the Sanhedrin. One opinion is that there should be 71 members since the Assembly of the Elders consisted of 70 members exclusive of Moses, who was the chairman. Another opinion, however, holds that 70 members are sufficient.

It is difficult to determine precisely how the Sanhedrin was established and how it functioned. The source materials for this phase, as for all matters concerning the period of the Second Temple, are very meager, and what does exist is riddled by internal contradictions. According to Greek sources, the New Testament and Josephus Flavius, it would seem that the chairman of the Sanhedrin was the High Priest, the representative of the Sadducees, who denied the authority of the Oral Law. But according to the Mishna it would seem that at the head of the Sanhedrin were two prominent authorities of the Oral Law.

Much has been written concerning this controversy by Jewish as well as non-Jewish scholars. A composite view proposed here is that the Sanhedrin was divided into two chambers, one political and one juridical. The political chamber was in the hands of the Sadducees, and their representative was usually the High Priest. The Pharisees, on the other hand, were interested primarily in the religious and cultural aspects of the Sanhedrin's work, and were headed by those two leaders, the Zugoth (the Pairs), of whom the Mishna speaks.

The Talmud (Sanhedrin, 52b) specifically speaks of the Court of the Sadducees, although it tells us very little about its functions. On the other hand, it deals in detail with the religious and legislative chamber of the Sanhedrin, which was controlled by the Pharisees.

The Sanhedrin consisted of 71 members and 23 members constituted a quorum. If one of the members had to leave the chamber, he first had to make certain that 23 members remained sitting. If in his absence only 22 remained he could not leave. The Sanhedrin sat in the Chamber of Hewn Stones daily from early morning, when the morning offering was made, until evening, when the evening offering was made. On the Sabbath and holidays the Sanhedrin sat in the synagogue and only matters concerning the Halacha could then be brought up.

The Sanhedrin played the chief role in Jewish life. Its authority was supreme in all civil, political, social, governmental, religious, and criminal matters. Even the king could be judged by the Sanhedrin.

The Sanhedrin was truly an institution of the people, and its spirit was homespun and simple. The majority of its members consisted of the Pharisees, whereas the Sadducees, the aristocracy, seldom exerted any influence in its councils. The dynasty of the Hasmoneans was generally favorably disposed to the people and therefore always supported the Pharisees who had the complete confidence of the people.

Even King Jannai, who became an enemy of the Pharisees because they did not tolerate his ambitions for absolute rule, finally was forced to give in to the will of the people and reinstate the Pharisees in the leadership of the Sanhedrin. This is likewise true of King Herod, one of the most wicked kings in Jewish history. He, too, was finally forced to succumb to the will of the people. His greatest ambition was to do away with the institution of the Sanhedrin and destroy it forever. Indeed, he began his reign by murdering practically all the members of the Sanhedrin. Nevertheless, he did not dare to abolish it, but appointed such members as he thought would not interfere in his affairs of the state and whom he could completely dominate. In the end, however, the Sanhedrin defeated him also and returned to its former unlimited power and jurisdiction.

The Sanhedrin was divided into two parts: political and juridical. The juridical part was the most important and its decisions and rulings had a significance for Jewry everywhere and at all times. In the juridical part were handled purely religious questions and every one of its interpretations was canonized as the law of the Torah. In the juridical part were also determined such things as the dates of the new moon, the calendar, the holidays, and generally all religious matters.

In addition to the Great Sanhedrin, consisting of 70 or 71 members, there were also Minor Sanhedrins which functioned in the provinces and which consisted of only 23 members. In Jerusalem itself and in many Jewish communities outside of Palestine there were Minor Sanhedrins, each one having at its head a chairman bearing the title Mufla, or "Outstanding Personality."

The minor Sanhedrins in Jerusalem were one at the entrance of the Temple Mount and one at the entrance of the Temple Court. Whenever the minor Sanhedrins outside of Jerusalem could not reach any decision, their wisest and greatest judge together with the litigants took the case to the minor Sanhedrin of the Temple Mount. From there the case was transferred to the minor Sanhedrin of the Temple Court. In both of the latter courts the judge of the local Sanhedrin expounded the opinions of every member of his court. Finally, the case reached the Great Sanhedrin in the Chamber of Hewn Stones. Here the matter would be ultimately decided by majority decision.

Financial matters were decided by three judges.

Court procedure was as follows: The judges sat while the litigants stood. The plaintiff was the first to present his case. The witnesses were inducted into a separate chamber and warned to tell nothing but the truth. Then all but one were led out of the chamber. The latter would be asked what evidence he has that the defendant owes money. If the witness stated that the defendant had told him that, or that someone else had told him, his testimony was not accepted. The first witness is then led out of the chamber and another witness cross examined. If their testimony agrees, the case is then taken up. Every judge is free to express his opinion. If two judges believe the defendant to be innocent while the other judge believes him to be guilty, the defendant is freed. If two judges declare him to be guilty and the third believes he is innocent, the defendant is sentenced. If one judge believes he is guilty, the second believes him to be innocent, while the third is undecided, other judges are called in. Once the decision is rendered the litigants are called in and told of the judgment. No judge may tell the defendant that he had rendered a decision in his behalf, but that the other judges were in a majority and overruled him. This would be considered slander against the other judges and revealing secrets out of court.

Criminal cases were decided by a Sanhedrin of twenty-three members.

The witnesses were led in first and warned that if their testimony is based on conjecture or upon hearsay, even from a trustworthy person, they will have to be thoroughly cross examined. Because criminal laws are unlike civil laws. In civil law cases a person may offer money to wipe out his offense. But in criminal cases the responsibility for the life of an innocent person rests squarely upon the witnesses. And this means not merely one life, but the life of whole generations. As our wise man said: Whoever destroys one life destroys a whole world of people. And whoever saves a life saves a world. And if the witnesses should say, why should we give testimony if we are likely to get into trouble ourselves, this too is wrong. If they know the truth, that the defendant is a wicked man, then it is their duty to eradicate the wickedness, the evil and the murder in the world.

The cross examination of the witnesses was done in a most thorough manner. What year, month, week, day, hour, and place? Do you know the defendant? Did you warn him, etc.?

If the testimony of the witnesses agreed, extenuating circumstances in behalf of the defendant were sought. If there were sufficient mitigating circumstances, he was freed immediately. If not, the trial was postponed to the next day. In the meantime, the judges discussed the case informally among themselves. The judges ate very little, drank no wine during the day, and sought to establish the truth. On the next day they got to the court early in the morning and immediately took up the case. A judge deeming the defendant innocent could not change his mind. On the other hand, judges holding the defendant to be culpable may. Then a vote was taken. To find a defendant guilty a majority of at least two was necessary. To free him, a majority of one vote was sufficient.

Important political trials, such as the case of a city corrupted by nascent Christianity or some form of idolatry, or a High Priest who leaned towards the Sadducees or who did not strictly observe the traditional regulations at the Service in the Temple, were always conducted by the Great Sanhedrin. Also without the sanction of the Great Sanhedrin it was prohibited to carry on a war or enlarge the territory of Jerusalem.

The Minor Sanhedrin was a purely juridical institution, having the power to judge in criminal cases. Its decisions were final and absolutely binding. Only when there was a difference of opinion among the judges could the decision be appealed to the Great Sanhedrin in Jerusalem.

The existing Sanhedrin, whenever it was necessary, always added new members to its ranks, although often the influence of the king or of his court played a role in the selection of new members. But even in such cases the new member had to be highly qualified and suited for his position. Every new member had to undergo a severe mental and physical examination. For example, he had to be healthy and strong physically, not too old, and not ugly. He could not be a poor man, so as not to be exposed to the temptation of bribery and corruption. But the most important qualification was erudition in Jewish lore and general knowledge. Aside from his knowledge of the Law, he also had to possess knowledge of medicine, astronomy, biology, mathematics, and languages.

Litigants at trials could conduct their arguments in whatever language they knew best and the Sanhedrin had to understand this language without the aid of an interpreter (Menachoth, 65a; Sanhedrin, 16b).

Every judge of the Sanhedrin had to be an ordained rabbi. The ceremony of ordination consisted of laying hands upon the head of the one to be ordained. This stemmed traditionally from Moses, who thus ordained Joshua, and Joshua who in his turn ordained his followers. This ceremony was later abolished and in its place was substituted the ordination ceremony of bestowing the title "Rabbi" upon the younger colleagues by the older scholars. Proselytes could not become members of the Sanhedrin.

At first any ordained rabbi could himself ordain someone else. However, Hillel abolished this custom and ruled that only the Nasi, the president of the Great Sanhedrin, could ordain rabbis.

The Nasi, who was also considered a viceroy, was the chairman of the Sanhedrin and every new member had to receive his sanction. The Vice-chairman was Chief Justice and could not participate in any affairs outside of the Sanhedrin. There was also another assistant to the Nasi called the Chacham, Wise Man. His function was to listen to the arguments of the litigants, examine the evidence, and prepare the trial for the Sanhedrin.

The Talmud records the names of 23 Nesiim, Patriarchs, who held office consecutively. From this record it is evident that the era of the Nesiim lasted about 600 years. However, there is still doubt whether all the chairmen of the Sanhedrin bore the title Nasi. As evidence for the negative view we may cite the fact that the chairmen in the first quarter of this era were not called Nasi in the Talmud. The first one to be thus called is Hillel.

Because Hillel derived his lineage from the House of David, the office of the Nasi became after him a sort of dynasty and was transmitted in his family from generation to generation. Thus, with the exception of a small interruption, the position of Nasi remained for 13 generations the heritage of the Hillel progeny.

It is interesting to note that the Jewish king could not be a member of the Sanhedrin, although the High Priest could at the same time be the Nasi. The law in those days severely prohibited the violation of the kingly dignity, thus making it impossible for the members of the Sanhedrin to differ in their opinions from the king. No one would go against the decision of the king, and innocent people, opponents of the government, would thus be sentenced to death (Sanhedrin, 18b).

The sessions of the Sanhedrin were always public and anyone had a right to enter and express his opinion. The sessions were held in the Temple and years later a special room in the Temple, the Lishkat Hagazith, the Chamber of Hewn Stones, was richly furnished and care was taken that it should be kept up with the greatest dignity and reverence.

During the session the members of the Sanhedrin sat in a semi-circle, similar to an amphitheater. In the center sat the

Nasi, next to him on the right the Ab Beth Din, Chief Justice, and on his left the Chacham. At the two ends of the semi-circle were two secretaries. One took down the arguments in favor of the accused, the other the arguments against him. There were also other secretaries of the court, attendants, guards, and police.

The principle in criminal jurisdiction was justice and righteousness. The court was impartial and had no leaning to the rich or well-born. Everyone was treated the same way, with no special severity towards one or sympathy towards the other.

A judge, says the Gemara (Sanhedrin, 7a), who judges rightly even for one hour sustains the world and causes God to come among the people.

The text (Pirke Aboth, chapter I, Mishna 2): "The world is based upon three things: upon the Torah, upon Service, and upon deeds of loving kindness," is interpreted thus: The world is based upon justice, upon fear of God, and upon pity.

Justice is the fundamental motive in Jewish life. The Mishna (Sanhedrin, chapter VI, 7) says: What does God say when a man feels himself to be aggrieved? I suffer everywhere, in my arms, in my head. And if God himself grieves so as a consequence of the death of a wicked person, how much more does He grieve for the blood of an innocent person!

The universe is based upon three elements: truth, justice, and peace. And all three elements mutually depend upon each other. Wherever there are justice and order, there we can also find truth and peace (Aboth, I, 18).

A judge who issues a just verdict thereby becomes a partner of the Creator and the act of Creation. Contrariwise, if he renders an unjust verdict he causes the Divinity to depart from Israel (Sanhedrin, 7a).

Whenever we observe a generation suffering trials and tribulations we should investigate its courts and its judges, because all its troubles stem therefrom (Sabbath, 139a).

A judge who takes from one and gives to another without justice and right is deprived of his soul by God Himself.

A judge sitting in court and administering justice must imagine that a sword is hanging over his head and the jaws of hell are gaping underneath him (Sanhedrin, 7a).

We can learn wisdom from the ants. When an ant drops a speck of food, no other ant will pick it up. And the ants are neither "civilized," nor do they possess leaders and judges.

A judge must be wise, humble, understanding, God-fearing, possess a good record, and be a prominent and beloved person (Tosephta Sanhedrin).

It happened once that a judge was appointed who was not sufficiently qualified. Jehuda bar Nachmani, the interpreter of Resh Lakish, was then asked to be the judge's interpreter. But when Jehuda discovered that the new judge was not much of a scholar he quoted the following saying from the Bible: "Wo unto him that saith to the wood, Awake! and to the dumb stone, Rouse up!" Can this teach us anything? It is bedecked with gold and silver and no breath whatever is in it." (Habbakuk, II, 19) God will judge those who have appointed such a judge.

The judges themselves can sometimes debase and lower the prestige of the law among the people. For instance, when a judge condemns a man for usury, theft, robbery or some other crime and is himself a usurer, a robber, and a thief.

Where there is no justice, there the sword rules. There is no justice nor judges and everything is in a state of chaos.

A judge should be like a king who depends upon no one. Only then can he administer justice fairly and squarely. But if he is like the priest who goes about the farm holdings to collect his tithes he is capable of destroying the world.

Bribes should never be taken, not even in order to clear an innocent person (Kethuboth, 105a).

A judge should never accept a fee for meting out justice, except remuneration for his time.

One who accepts a bribe becomes one with the man who gives it and is bound to judge in his favor no matter how clear the case may be the other way. Those who accept bribes are so blinded that they cannot see the truth. When a person has poor eyesight he goes to an eye doctor and asks to be helped. But the judge accepts a farthing and deliberately closes his eyes. A judge who accepts bribes and slants his decisions sooner or later becomes dependent upon other people.

Not only is the taking of money bribes prohibited, but bribery by words is equally prohibited (Kethuboth, 105b).

Rabbi Papa says: A judge should not render decision involving his friend or his enemy. His friend, because he could not condemn him; his enemy, because he could not exonerate him (Sanhedrin, chapter III, Mishna 4).

Resh Lakish interprets the Biblical verse: "Fear no man," in the following manner: When two people come to court, one a quiet and peaceful man, the other angry and violent, the judge must not refuse to mete out justice, so that the stronger may not have a pretext to persecute the weaker one.

The witnesses should know for whom they are testifying and the judges must always remember that they are standing before God. A judge must never act as an advocate. He must be severely impartial. A case involving a farthing must be handled as carefully as a case involving a million dollars. A judge should not listen to the litigants in chamber but to each one in the presence of the other. Jew and gentile are equal in the eye of Hebrew law.

"Thou shalt pursue only justice," the Bible states, meaning, in the interpretation of the Talmudical essayists, both in accordance with the law and in accordance with the rules of equity. For example, suppose two boats meet in a narrow body of water. If they both wish to pass at the same time they will collide. But if one follows behind the other they will pass unharmed. The same is true when two camels meet at a narrow mountain pass. A way must be found so that no one will suffer.

It is a virtue in the eyes of God to find the road to compromise. This is the kind of verdict which will bring peace with it.

Jerusalem was destroyed because the strict interpretation of the law was applied instead of the rules of common sense and equity.

When the judge issues a verdict which the poor man is unable to carry out and the judge pays for him, he thereby accomplishes two things: He renders a just verdict and gives charity at the same time. He recompenses the one and gives aid to the other. This was the way of King David.

What methods did the Sanhedrin adopt in order to prevent errors in judgment?

In the first place, we have already seen the principles of publicity and freedom operating. Even the evidence of the witnesses and the prosecutors had to be given in public. In addition, the accused was free from every possible personal investigation. The accused was not tormented with questioning and interrogation, and no one sought to trip him up in his testimony.

The entire responsibility fell upon the witnesses, and their testimony had to agree in every detail. The High Priest swore in every witness with the most severe oaths and forced him to look at the accused while he was giving testimony. In questioning the witness the judges would scrutinize him and watch his every word and grimace. The smallest discrepancy in the evidence would be sufficient to disqualify a witness. Generally, the judges would always attempt to weaken the accusation and to minimize the importance and value of the evidence against the accused.

During the period of the Second Temple, and also later, an accused who did not confess was never sentenced. The following story is told in the Gemara (Sanhedrin, 37b): Rabbi Simon ben Shetah one day saw someone being chased into a ruined building. Upon arriving at the ruin Rabbi Simon found that the one chased was lying dead with chaser standing over him with a bloody sword in his hand. Rabbi Simon then said to the murderer: "You evil one, who killed him, you or I? And what can I do to you since I am the only witness?"

Two witnesses were indispensable, and without two witnesses no one could be convicted even if he had confessed. Furthermore, the accused had to be warned first. The witnesses first had to warn the murderer that the punishment for murder is death, and the accused had to answer that he knows about it and is prepared for it (Sanhedrin, 40b).

The Sanhedrin worked out so many limitations and hedges in procedure that it was practically impossible to convict an innocent person. To try a person without a previous thorough investigation whether there are sufficient motives and evidence for trial was a great sin and was called a perversion of justice. This rule was applied to criminal cases as well as to financial matters. In financial cases either the prosecutor or defendant could testify first, but in criminal cases the defendant and his witnesses had to testify first. In financial cases a majority of one was enough for conviction, whereas in criminal cases a majority of one was sufficient to free and majority of at least two was required to convict. In financial cases the sentence could be changed to be made more severe or more lenient, whereas in criminal cases the sentence could be changed only in favor of the accused. In financial cases anyone could give evidence in favor of the defendant or accuser, whereas in criminal cases evidence from the public was allowed only in favor of the accused.

In criminal cases the court never gave its decision in the same day as the trial unless it was in favor of the accused. In case of an unfavorable decision at least twenty-four hours had to elapse before a decision was rendered, so that if even the slightest possibility existed for some evidence in favor of the defendant were to be unearthed it may still be given (Sanhedrin, chapter V, Mishna 1).

Trials could take place only during the day and never on the Sabbath or on a holiday. The law even specified a certain diet for the judges, so that they may be healthy and energetic and be able to carry on the trial with a clear mind and in a calm mood. If the trial had to be continued the next day the judges had to be up the entire night searching for some mitigating evidence for the defendant. That night they were not supposed to eat too much, nor drink strong beverages.

Even when the accused was finally sentenced to death, efforts still had to be made to save him. The place of execution was at a distance from the court and the passage thereto was utilized for this purpose. One attendant stood at the door of the court with a handkerchief in his hand, and another attendant stood at the furthest point from the court, but still within its vision and held his eyes directed to the attendant at the court. If anyone came to the court at the last minute with some new evidence in favor of the accused the attendant at the court waved his handkerchief and the other attendant riding upon a swift horse overtook the accused and returned him to the court. Even if the accused himself on his way to the execution declared that he had some new evidence he was returned to the court (Sanhedrin, chapter VI, Mishna I).

There was no executioner to carry out the death sentence. The entire people carried out the sentence and the witnesses against the accused had to be the first to throw stones at him. If, during the period between sentencing and the execution of the sentence one of the witnesses against the defendant lost an arm, the sentence was thereby made null and void.

The Sanhedrin, generally speaking, conducted itself in accordance with such humanitarian concepts and principles as are difficult to find nowadays even in the most liberal countries. Even the precepts and rules which developed under the influence of ancient traditions are imbued with the spirit of justice.

The Torah prescribes death for a considerable number of offenses. Nevertheless, the Jews in their entire history so interpreted the law as practically to negate these laws. Thus Rabbi Akiba states that if he would be a member of the Sanhedrin the death sentence would never be issued. The Talmud characterized a Sanhedrin which even once in seventy years pronounced the death sentence as a murderous Sanhedrin.

With the destruction of the Temple (70 C.E.) the power and the dignity of the Sanhedrin also declined. Rabbi Jochanan ben Zakkai created a new Sanhedrin in Jabne, but for a long time this new Sanhedrin did not exert great influence. Apparently, it was difficult for Rabbi Jochanan to convince the Jews that it was not the place nor the Temple that lent importance and significance to the institution of the Sanhedrin. It was only later, when the Jews began to realize that the Jewish religion is not something static and can be transferred from one place to another and adapt itself to new conditions and new needs, did the newly established Sanhedrin begin to gain in importance.

That is why, apparently, Rabbi Jochanan did not dare to adopt the title of Nasi and did not assume the dignity and importance of a chairman of the Sanhedrin.

The Sanhedrin established in Jabne did not remain there long. It was soon transferred to Usha, from there to Cyprus and finally to Tiberius, where its juridical power was at a minimum.

The importance of the Sanhedrin fluctuated greatly, but it never regained the dignity and power that it once possessed, except perhaps during the brief period of the reign of Rabbi Judah. The cause may perhaps be found in the fact that in Babylonia and in other countries where Jews lived in compact masses new spiritual centers arose. In Babylonia, for example, the Exilarch was the recognized leader of the Jewish people and had the power of pronouncing a death sentence.

Under the reign of the Moslem caliphs the power of the Exilarch became even greater, and the importance of the Palestine Sanhedrin consequently declined. After Rabbi Judah the Sanhedrin deteriorated rapidly and by 425 C.E. it became completely extinct.

The process of Jewish spiritual creativity did not cease; it merely assumed new shape and form and was transferred to new lands and continents where it flourished anew with greater vigor and potentiality. The act of transition was as usual systematic, natural and continuous, without changing or losing its vitality and essence in the slightest degree.

CHAPTER FOURTEEN

AFTER THE CLOSE OF THE TALMUD

THE SUPPLEMENTATION OF THE SABORAIM. THE NOURISHMENT UPON THE AGADA. THE CREATIVE SPIRIT. THE ACCOMPLISHMENTS OF THE GEONIM AND EXILARCHS.

THE TALMUD WAS CLOSED AT THE END OF THE FIFTH CENTURY of our era. It must be made clear, however, that by that time it had not yet been completely finished and was far from being the accepted authority among all Jews. The process of compiling was still continuing, and was completing and supplementing the Oral Law.

As always, serious problems arose in day-to-day existence which demanded solution and decision. The same answer, of course, could not equally serve all countries in which the Jews were dispersed at that time. Conditions naturally differed and any decision therefore could not be binding upon everyone irrespective of where he lived. That is why gradually differences of opinion arose among the Amoraim.

It therefore became necessary to achieve absolute consistency in the practical rules and regulations, and thus it became necessary to reinterpret the existing laws in accordance with previously established methods and regulations.

This task the Saboraim who inherited the work of the Amoraim undertook. However, they did not succeed very well. Conditions were unpropitious then: persecutions increased, economic insecurity and poverty were not conducive to learning, and as a consequence it was most difficult to continue the work of extending the compass of the Law. At this time, therefore, the Jewish spirit was nourished upon the Agada, and the most important homilies and homiletical commentaries arose in that period.

This period lasted approximately 150 years. Nevertheless, even these difficult years were not altogether unfruitful. Even under the most unfavorable conditions the Saboraim succeeded in editing and in closing many books of the Talmud and in gathering and compiling a good deal of the Agada.

The word Saboraim stems from Sebara, which means opinion or thought. The Saboraim no longer had the authority to change the Law and they therefore contented themselves with expressing their opinions and explaining and interpreting the Laws that had been adopted in previous generations. Wherever the Amoraim failed to establish a given Law unanimously, the Saboraim fulfilled this task and thus brought the Talmudic Law to completion.

Rabbi Jose was the last head of the Pumbaditha Yeshiva. This was during the time of Rabina, the last head of the Yeshiva in Sura and the last of the Amoraim. The latter lived a number of years after the close of the Talmud.

According to a tradition established by Joshua ben Joseph Halevi, all passages in the Talmud which begin with the following phrase: "Whoever objects to this—let him concretize his objection" in other words, why ask a question when the answer is so clear?—have been added by the Saboraim. It is also plausible that many other passages in the Gemara, which begin with some peculiar expressions often repeated were the additions made by the Saboraim.

How long the Saboraim epoch lasted and who were its most outstanding personalities is not known accurately, and Jewish historians differ greatly concerning these matters. Sherira Gaon asserts that Rabbi Simuna was the very last of the Saboraim and died in the year 540 of our era.

The creative spirit of the Saboraim during this entire epoch expressed itself in the development of the Midrashim. Conditions in the East were then very hard. Under Byzantine as well as under Persian rule severe persecutions began, which prevented the further development of the Law. Although a methodology had already been fully worked out by previous generations of scholars, the task of continuing the development of the Law in the manner of the Amoraim now became exceedingly difficult. In order, therefore, to strengthen the will to live of the oppressed Jews, the Saboraim neglected the Law and devoted themselves to the creation of a world of homiletical literature.

This change in the direction of the creative spirit is described in the Midrash Shir Ha'shirim Rabba:

"In previous times, in the days of the Tanaim and Amoraim, when the Jews lived more or less in peace and prosperity, people were devoted to the Law. But now, when sufferings have weakened many and poverty reigns, people only wish to hear the consolation and solace of the Agada."

Unfortunately, however, even this creative process soon declined, and by the middle of the seventh century it had dried up entirely. It took another century for the creative spirit to become revivified and for the compilation of the Talmud in its broader aspects to be continued. This fruitful period began under the rule of the Arabs and continued to about the middle of the eleventh century. It is one of the most important periods in the history of Jewish culture and is known as the period of the Geonim.

Babylonia, formerly known as Mesopotamia and at present as Iraq, has, with the single exception of Palestine itself, had the deepest impact upon the development of Jewish culture. The most ancient historical traditions of our people are closely bound up with Babylonia; Abraham came to Canaan from Ur of the Chaldees. It was in Babylonia that Ezekiel created his prophetic and poetic masterpieces. It was in Babylonia, too, that our greatest work, the Babylonian Talmud, was formed, a work that has had a most direct and most important influence upon Jewish life.

Jewish creativity came to fruition in Babylonia, because it became almost a new Jewish homeland. For hundreds of years the most compact Jewish community in the world continued to exist in Babylonia. Entire cities were populated almost exclusively by Jews, most of them land owners or agricultural workers. The Jews in Babylonia had the greatest religious and cultural autonomy. They were well organized into communities, and at the head of the entire Jewish settlement in Babylonia was the Exilarch, who derived his lineage from the House of David. While Jews in other countries of the Diaspora spoke the language of the countries in which they resided, first Greek and then Latin, the Jews in Babylonia continued to speak Aramaic, which was close to Hebrew.

Furthermore, during the course of centuries the Jews modified the Aramaic language, introducing into it many Hebrew words and idiomatic expressions.

After Moslem rule had become firmly established in Babylonia and after the friction and quarrels between the Jews and the adherents of the new religion subsided, the creative process among the Jews was renewed and a strong desire once more stimulated learning among the people. Central yeshivas arose in Pumbaditha and Sura, where the study of the Jewish Law was seriously undertaken.

At the head of these yeshivas were the Geonim, and it was due to their enormous energy that they soon succeeded in assuming the spiritual leadership of world Jewry.

Babylonia was famed for its yeshivas even in the days of the Talmud. The chief creation of the Amoraim, the Babylonian Talmud, far surpassed both in scope and in substance the Jerusalem Talmud. Nevertheless, in a previous period it was Palestine that held spiritual sway and the yeshivas in Palestine were the religious authorities of world Jewry. But the authority of Babylonian Jewry grew apace and Babylonia soon became the recognized spiritual center of the Jews.

The caliphs that ruled the Mohammedan countries gave the Jews full autonomy and upheld the power of the Exilarchs and the Gaonim. The Exilarch held in his hands chief administrative power, as well as some religious functions. If the Exilarch happened to be a scholar, which was quite often, he would deliver a scholarly address during the ceremony of assuming his exalted position. If he was not, such an address was made by the Gaon, i.e. the head of the yeshiva in Sura.

The Exilarch maintained his own supreme court, headed

by the "Judges of the gate," nominated by him. The Exilarch also had the right to appoint judges for some Jewish communities in Babylonia, and occasionally even in other parts of Asia. In addition, the Exilarch was the highest representative of the Jewish people and held an eminent position among the many judges and lords at the caliph's court.

Next to the Exilarch the Gaon was the highest authority in the religious sphere. Just as in the period of the Talmud, the yeshivas would hold twice a year, during the months of Elul and Adar, a public gathering of all the scholars throughout the country. Upon the dais sat the head of the yeshiva; in the first row sat ten of the greatest scholars, seven with the title "heads of the academy," and three with the title "fellow"; one of the heads of the academy was the chief justice and was called "Judge of the gate." In the next six rows sat sixty scholars, ten in a row. It was these seventy scholars together with the head of the yeshiva who represented the ancient Sanhedrin of Palestine.

At these public gatherings questions of religion that had been submitted by the various Jewish communities throughout the world within the last six months would be discussed. And upon the basis of the discussion that took place the head of the yeshiva submitted the judgment.

From the very beginning the head of the yeshiva in Sura bore the title Gaon, but in approximately the tenth century of our era the head of the Pumbaditha yeshiva gained more prestige and the title, together with all its prerogatives and dignity, remained with the head of this yeshiva until its decline.

Unfortunately the documents of the Geonim have not always been kept. Of about 80 Geonim beginning with Shishna Gaon at the end of the seventh century and ending with the death of Hai Gaon in 1038, the questions and answers, the Responsa, of only some 20-odd Geonim have survived.

But many questions and answers had been saved because of the system that was later developed of sending and copying the correspondence to other Jewish communities. The Jewish community in ancient Cairo, Egypt, was such a communicating center between the Jews of Africa and southern Europe on the one hand and the Gaonim and other religious authorities in Babylonia on the other hand.

Of the letters sent to Egypt a copy would first be made and only then would they be sent on to the proper address in Babylonia. Thus, in the library of Cairo a mass of materials survived which would otherwise be lost for history.

The position of Gaon was as a rule transmitted from father to son. In the course of 277 years, from the period of the Karaimic Schism in 761 until the death of Hai Gaon in 1038, the posterity of Budai Gaon held the position of Gaon for 102 years. All the Geonim in Sura for a period of 200 years came from but three families.

The other positions in the yeshivas, such as the judges of the gate, the heads of the academies, deacons and others, were also transmitted by heritage, most of them to relatives of the Gaon.

Although the jurisdictions of the Exilarch and the Gaon respectively were defined in detail and marked out in the course of many generations, conflicts and arguments between these two leaders nevertheless broke out from time to time.

When the Exilarch died without issue, in the second half of the 12th century, the Gaon Samuel Ben Ilai took over both offices. The prestige and the influence of the new leader then fell markedly because independent cultural centers arose in Europe and in North Africa.

Samuel ben Ilai was truly a very energetic man and great scholar, but his influence and sway were maintained only in those places where he was backed by the power of the government. And even in these countries he was obliged to make a show of great determination and severely punish any transgressors.

The famous Jewish voyager of the time, Petachiah of Regensburg, wrote as follows in his memoirs:

In all of Syria, Damascus, Persia and Midai Samuel ben Ilai is the unquestioned Jewish ruler. All judges are appointed by him, and all rabbis must be ordained by him. He is feared by everyone, because every transgression and sin is punished by severe lashings. He dresses in kingly style in clothes woven with gold, and the rooms of his palace are decorated with silks and satins. His chief virtue is that he is a great scholar and also well learned in secular sciences. Whenever he delivered a lecture in the yeshiva he sat upon a high throne, and only those who exhibited extra-ordinary knowledge were allowed in to the lecture.

The legislative activity of the Geonim was far more extensive than that of the Sanhedrin in previous years. It is to this creative period that we owe the final determination of the laws, the forms of private and public prayers, and the numerous regulations concerning procedure in the court, taking oaths, etc. The prayer books of only four Geonim survived: Natronai,

Zemah, Amram and Saadia. The most popular prayer book is that of Amram Gaon.

By virtue of the fact that the Geonim decided cases coming to them from countries throughout the world, the scope of the Talmudic Law was thereby extended and accommodated to the specific conditions obtaining at the time. The Geonim, however, made their own regulations required in this period in accordance with the changes in the political, economic, and cultural situation. Thus, every man who took to himself a second wife was required to divorce his first wife if she demanded it. A woman who forced her husband to grant her a divorce was also entitled to her dowry. A woman was entitled to collect her dowry and a creditor his loan not only from real estate but also from personal property.

In formulating new regulations the Geonim were, of course, careful not to change the letter of the law as written down in the Talmud. Thus, for instance, if the Talmud prescribed that if anyone grants another person certain rights, he must include in the contract a specification that he allows the grantee four feet of his property, the Geonim interpreted this regulation in such a way as to cover even those who do not own any property. The justification was that any Jew anywhere owns at least four feet of ground in Palestine, because Palestine belongs to all the Jewish people and every Jew consequently has some property there.

The achievements of the Geonim are of great national and historical importance, because they took place during the time of a complete transformation in Jewish life. It was the Geonim who completed the Talmud and raised it to the high level of the Scriptures themselves.

It was then that the Oral Law became an integral part of the Written Law and it has since taken its place at the very pinnacle of Jewish life throughout the world. On the basis of the Talmudic law and the decisions of the Geonim the first complete codex was elaborated in the year 900, the Great Laws, Halachoth Gedoloth, of Simon Kayyara, who for the first time attempted to list all "613 Commandments" (Mitzvoth).

The long period of the Geonim left an indelible mark upon Jewish culture. The traditions of the Jewish people are full of the splendor and brilliance of the Geonim epoch. In the memory of the people is forever enshrined the proud fact that even in the Diaspora the Jews maintained their cultural autonomy for a thousand years. Even to this day on every Sabbath Day we recite with great awe in the prayer "Yekum Purkon" the leaders of the then flourishing Jewish center in Babylonia: "To the heads of the Academy, to the heads of the Exile, to the heads of the Yeshiva and to the Judges of the Gate."

The epoch of the Geonim begins, according to many authorities, with Rabbi Hanan de Asikia, the head of the Pumbaditha Yeshiva, in 589. The Yeshivas of Sura and Pumbaditha maintained their existence during the entire Geonim epoch. In 890 the Pumbaditha yeshiva was transferred to Bagdad, and since then it became the more outstanding educational center. One hundred years later the yeshiva of Sura was also transferred to Bagdad, then the capital of the Caliphate. In this later period the Jewish population was greatly impoverished and the yeshivas often led a precarious existence.

But it was precisely during this period of material difficulties that there were such outstanding personalities among the Geonim as Saadia Gaon, Sherira Gaon and his son Hai Gaon.

Saadia Gaon (905-942) maintained his steadfast faith that Judaism can be completely harmonized with philosophy. He stood firmly upon the Talmudic Law and energetically fought against every attempt to deviate from it.

Hai Gaon was the greatest authority on Halacha and Talmudic law. He was also distinguished in several other fields, such as the Masora, the Midrash, liturgical poetry, and grammar. If the 300 years of the Amoraim epoch created the Babylonian and Jerusalem Talmud and a magnificent Midrash literature, the Geonim epoch produced a splendid exegetical literature. This was the Responsa, the written answers to legal and ritual questions which were sent to the various Jewish communities in Asia, Africa, and southern Europe.

The Geonim, for reasons incomprehensible, were not particularly concerned that their decisions should remain to posterity. Hai Gaon says concerning this: "We do not remember what we wrote, nor what our father wrote, but we say whatever pleases us and what we think should be done" (Shaarei Zedek). With such an attitude it is no wonder that the complete literature of the Geonim epoch has not come down to us. But although we may not have sufficient material to shed light upon this epoch, the period of Hai Gaon's life is one of the most glorious in the creative process that has contributed so much to the study of the Halacha.

In the Responsa, the Geonim, whose epoch lasted approximately 450 years, laid the basis for all laws and regulations and also prepared the materials which were later used by the expounders, commentators and codifiers. This task was necessary to perform because the Talmud, whose methods are logic, argumentation, and debate, did not lay down any definitive set of laws. The editors of the Talmud, who usually complete the treatment of this or that law, merely tie together the ends of the discussion concerning this or that problem, but do not define the law itself and do not therefore determine the correct interpretation of any given law. Whoever is acquainted with the Talmud knows how difficult it is to determine the laws from the text, because the Talmud is not an ordinary law book in which the laws are clearly and definitively promulgated without any equivocation or debate so that anyone may know what the law is. The Talmud is rather an encyclopedia of law, in which have been included the various opinions concerning a given law and its determination, and which therefore includes all the pros and cons of any argument together with the evidence for these arguments.

In this period instruction to students was usually given orally. Even after permission had been granted to compile the Talmud in book form, there was still a great dearth in books, the printing process not yet having been invented. The students thus studied everything orally, and relying upon their memory they would write up after their classroom study everything they had learned in their own style. This in itself was sufficient cause for all kinds of errors and emendations to creep in in the original text of the Talmud. It is therefore no wonder that even after the close of the Talmud the Jews did not as yet possess a corrected and fully annotated code of laws, rules, and regulations. The Geonim recognized this difficulty and attempted to compile books in which the laws would be set down clearly and definitively, without the various opinions and discussions. Thus it is that they created the great edifice of Rabbinic laws. All "Shealoth Tluyoth," doubtful questions, were decided upon in the yeshivas of the Geonim, in their Responsa contained in the tractate Sopherim, and to a very large degree in the works of Hai Gaon and in his decisions, a large part of which, about 2,000 in number, have come down to us. Although there must have been a far greater number, those that have been preserved represent a splendid heritage of great value for the study of the Law and an inexhaustible source for the history of that period.

Hai Gaon was born in the year 940 in Pumbaditha. In his youth he received a secular as well as a traditional Talmudic education. Besides the Talmud he also studied the various sciences of that time, knew the Hebrew language thoroughly and was also well acquainted with the literature of the world. Because of his wide knowledge he often entered into debates with the Mohammedean scholars and always came out on top. He read much in philosophy and knew many languages. Besides the vernacular of Babylonia, which was an Aramaic-Persian-Chaldaic dialect, he knew Arabic and Greek, which were useful to him in the scientific study of the Talmud.

Already in his youth he had gained the esteem of many of his generation. His father, Sherira Gaon, respected him for his great knowledge and profound erudition.

In the year 967 he was appointed dean of the Pumbaditha yeshiva, and together with his father he had charge of all matters relating to the yeshiva and of interest to Judaism. He also devoted himself to social work, applying himself particularly to the reform of the Jewish communities, introducing order and discipline. Because of this work he was always in correspondence with many near and distant communities. From all corners of the world came students to study in his yeshiva, and his name became known throughout the Jewish world. Rabbenu Gershom, the "light of the Diaspora," greatly respected Hai Gaon and had the highest opinion of him. Rabbi Nathan ben Jechiel of Rome, who compiled the first Talmudic encyclopedic dictionary, the "Aruch," utilized the interpretations of Hai Gaon for this work. Abraham Ibn Daud (known as the first "Rabad") in his book "Safer Ha'kabbala" says concerning Hai Gaon that "he spread the Torah among the Jews more than any other of the Geonim . . . and his equal among the Geonim cannot be found." The famous Talmudic mystic and commentator, the Ramban, gives Hai Gaon a new and important title: "the father of Jews." From every land inquiries concerning the Torah were sent to him. Among those who sought his advice were such great Jewish personalities as Rabbi Samuel Hanagid, Rabbi Abraham Eta, and others. Hai Gaon was at that time not only the recognized authority in religious matters, but also the highest Judge, and his decision was final in religious questions as well as in civil.

The advice of Hai Gaon was often sought on questions, the answers to which were quite well established merely out of curiosity to see how his nimble mind would explain the law, what logic, what originality, what erudition and keenness he would bring to bear upon his polished and well organized replies. Hai Gaon was also one of the greatest arbitrators of his time. Whenever a quarrel arose it was immediately referred to him for adjudication, and he had the gift of finding the principle upon which to unite and satisfy the warring sides.

In addition to his Teshuvoth, which are devoted primarily to juridical problems arising among the Jews, Shealoth of law and rights have come down to us. One is the "Mishpatei Shevuoth," Laws Concerning Oaths, which deals with all questions concerning oaths among Jews, and which was translated from the Arabic into Hebrew by an unknown translator. The other work is "Mekach Umemkar," Buying and Selling, translated into Hebrew by Rabbi Isaac ben Reuben of Barcelona 40 years after the death of Hai Gaon. This last work is an attempt to introduce a new method in dealing with Talmudic law.

The method which he used both in instruction and in his determination of the laws was the method of synthesis, of drawing singular propositions together under general rules of deduction and generalization. That is why his works in this sphere, both in form and in preparation, are so dissimilar to the works of other scholars who have written upon Talmudic jurisprudence.

In the Mishna and the Gemara the inductive, or analytic method, which derives singular propositions from general laws, is always predominant over the synthetic or theoretical method, which seeks to subsume everything under general laws. The usual explication of the laws and regulations in the Talmud takes the form of an example derived from reality, of single facts and cases. As a rule, the Mishna always tries to avoid the expression of general principles. This is also true concerning the Gemara, and the same tradition is also followed by the codifiers, who arranged the laws in accordance with the single cases and ordinary laws which came up daily before the judges. To this date our scholars have not adequately answered the questions why Jewish jurisprudence is not based upon the same synthetic method as Roman jurisprudence.

One of the non-Jewish scholars seeks to solve this puzzle by saying that the character of jurisprudence is always determined by the character of the people. There are people, he says, who are capable of creating general concepts and are thus able to express ordinary laws in simple and scientific form. And on the other hand, he continues, there are people who express their laws only in individual, day-to-day cases. It is possible, Professor Chernowitz (Rav Tzair) asserts in his book "Toldoth Halacha" (The History of the Halacha) that herein is expressed a historical truth concerning the qualities of the Jewish people.

Jewish thought, even when it is abstract and theoretical in the highest degree, is conceptual and concrete. Even the most absolute and abstract thoughts in Judaism received expression in concrete terms. Jewish thinkers never philosophized concerning the essence of justice and right. They never asked, as did the Greek thinkers, what is justice and what is kindness. The essence of these concepts becomes clear in concrete, day-to-day activity. Even the Talmudic disputations, this method of learning and thinking which has no counterpart among any other nation, although highly abstract and theoretical, are nevertheless concrete and specific. The final result of the disputations is always to return to the concrete and specific principle which is based upon acts. Thus our laws and regulations were created and to the extent that they are an expression of the national psychology and national spirit, they always developed in the direction of the inner essence of the Jewish people, adapting themselves to the historical character of the people, whose genius runs more to the concrete than to the abstract.

From this viewpoint it is therefore clear why Jewish jurisprudence has never ceased to be practical, and has always borne in mind the purpose of the law, which issues in some act or some activity.

But an exception to this rule was the great genius of Hai Gaon, who created a new method in Jewish jurisprudence, laying in his works the foundation for abstract reasoning and synthetic explanation of law and justice, and who bases his laws not upon concrete, day-to-day acts, but upon general principles, exhibiting in this sphere his immense power of generalization. That is why he has always been unique in his epoch, unique in his deductive method, unique in his logical thinking, unique in his scientific description. Very justly he is considered as the most original thinker and creator of Jewish jurisprudence. No one of the Geonim could compare with him in this field. He surpassed all the other Geonim not only in his secular education, but primarily in the knowledge of laws and decisions. His book "Buying and Selling" is still considered one of the greatest and most important works of Talmudic law.

Hai Gaon also wrote poetry. Most of it consists of prayers, penitentials, and elegies, and are printed in many prayer books. One liturgical poem called "Shema Kolli" (Hearken to My Voice) is still recited by the Sephardic Jews on the night of Yom Kippur. In addition to the elegies and penitentials he also wrote poems on secular subjects under the name "Mussar Haskel" (Wise Instructions). In these poems he attempts to show that Jewry is not opposed to knowledge and inquiry. He counsels everyone to study science, and advises the children and youth to study besides the Torah also arithmetic and the Arabian language:

"Acquire knowledge and not gold and silver;
Study science even when it is difficult;
Study arithmetic and have some knowledge of medicine,
Then you will grasp the movement of the stars
And understand the four seasons of the year."

And just as he tried to teach his wisdom to others, so with great modesty and humility he learned from others, without reluctance willing to ask the meaning of a word or phrase even from a non-Jewish scholar.

Rab Samuel Hanagid relates that when Rabbi Matzliah of Sicily returned from Bagdad he sent him a letter describing the life of Hai Gaon and his great qualities. Among other things he wrote that at one time a great debate raged in the Pumbaditha yeshiva concerning the correct interpretation of a phrase. Hai Gaon then asked Rabbi Matzliah to visit a Catholic scholar and ask him the correct meaning of the phrase. And when Hai Gaon perceived that Rabbi Matzliah did not greatly relish this task, he was angered and told him that the fathers and the holy men did not cavil at getting the correct meaning of words even from scholars of other nations. Only then did Rabbi Matzliah visit the Catholic scholar and the latter gave him the correct meaning in the Syrian translation.

Hai Gaon also wrote commentaries on the Torah, on Sedarim Zeraim and Teharoth, and on various parts of the Gemara. He also wrote a book against the Karaites. In his time he was known as one of the strongest opponents of the Karaites and in this work he defends Judaism against them.

Hai Gaon died at the ripe age of 99, in the year 1039. He left no sons or successors.

Samuel Hanagid thus eulogizes him:

"And although he died without children,
And the Torah has no heirs in his own house,
He left behind students, spiritual children,
Whom he educated in the hundreds in all Arab lands."

Hai's contemporaries praised him as pure of body, holy of heart, whose brightness may be compared to that of Moses himself.

The youthful Ibn Gabirol in a poem of lamentation writes:

"Who is fitting to take over the leadership,
And who should sit upon the judge's chair,
And who will take the part of justice for the oppressed,
And who will now be able by his wisdom
To still my spiritual thirst,
And where can we find a rabbi to take the place of Hai?"

Hai Gaon was the last, if not the greatest, produced by Babylonian Jewry during the Geonim epoch. With his death the Jewish center in Babylonia, and with it the glorious Babylonian period, ceased to exist and was transferred to Spain. But his influence did not cease. Many hundreds of years after his death his books still served as an important source for writers and codifiers engaged in the study of Talmudic law. Until the fourteenth century Hai was known as *"The Gaon,"* and whenever this title was mentioned it referred to Hai. The first commentators after the Geonim epoch, and the codifiers after them, based their work wholly or in part upon the interpretations of Hai Gaon.

And if his father, Sherira Gaon, was the first historian among the Jewish people, having written the history of the Tanaim, Amoraim and of the Saboraim, the "Iggereth Sherira Gaon"

(The Epistle of the Gaon Sherira), his son was the first to lay a firm systematic and scientific foundation for Jewish jurisprudence, which later commentators, codifiers and rabbis built upon and completed as the splendid edifice of Jewish law and justice.

CHAPTER FIFTEEN

THE TRANSFERENCE OF JEWISH CENTERS OF LEARNING

THE SPIRITUAL REAWAKENING IN NORTH AFRICA, SPAIN, FRANCE, ITALY AND GERMANY. THE APPEARANCE OF JEWISH SCIENTISTS AND LITERARY MEN. THE THEORETICAL AND PRACTICAL SCHOOLS. RASHI AND THE TOSEFOTH. ALFASI AND JOSEPH CARO.

THE END OF THE GAONIM EPOCH MARKED THE TRANSFERENCE of centers of Jewish spiritual life to North Africa, Egypt, Spain, France, Italy and Germany. At this time persecution and oppression of Jews in these countries were relatively mild and the Jews were able to continue their religious life and customs as heretofore. The creative process, too, found an outlet and a great effort was made, despite many hindrances, to strengthen the Talmudic Law and traditional customs.

Under the Fatimite dynasty in North Africa, particularly in Kairawan, there was ample opportunity to weld once more the golden chain that had been broken by the persecutions in Babylonia. Chananel ben Hoshiel at the beginning of the eleventh century was the first to replace Saadia Gaon's leadership in Jewish religious philosophy. He too sought to discover the plain and direct meaning of the Torah, and his commentary upon the Talmud follows a definite pattern, a pattern which links him directly to the last of the Gaonim. His commentary, we might add, made the study of the Talmud considerably easier.

But this spiritual reawakening in North Africa did not last long. Soon new rulers began to persecute all non-Moslems, and more particularly the Jews. The Jewish creative process was thus permanently stopped in North Africa.

By divine intervention, however, just at the time that the sun declined in Babylonia and North Africa it reappeared in fulsome brilliance in Spain.

A small number of Jews were in Spain even as early as the first century. In the course of many years the number of Jews gradually increased, planting the seeds of a Judaism based upon the Oral Torah. Until the end of the seventh century all intellectual creation was based solely upon the Talmud. The aim was to achieve a closer acquaintanceship with all the sources of the Law and to adapt it to daily life.

With the beginning of the eighth century a spiritual renaissance arose among the Jews of Arab Spain. At first they drew their spiritual nourishment directly from the Gaonim in Babylonia, recognizing them as the highest authority. But a short two hundred years later all the cultural treasures from Babylonia, Italy, and France had been transferred to Spain.

In the tenth century Arab Spain was permeated by a liberal atmosphere and Jewish culture flourished. Under the patronizing influence of the caliphs Arab culture, too, reached its highest peak. The capital, Cordoba, became a city of art, science, and culture. Seventeen great universities and seventy fine libraries helped to nourish an extensive cultural life.

It is inevitable that all this should have had a great influence upon the Jewish people. They devoted themselves to the cultivation of the intellect with great zeal and energy. Soon Jewish scientists and literary men appeared, occupying a prominent place in the development of Jewish culture. The first of these was Menachem ben Saruk, who was secretary to the great Jewish statesman and leader, Chasdai ibn Shaprut. He was a great linguist, specializing in Hebrew, and his most enduring achievement was in the field of grammar and lexicography. His dictionary, Machbereth, is the first such work in Hebrew which defined every word contained in the Torah. He also enriched Hebrew grammatical terminology and the words "dikduk" and "medakdek" are his inventions. For hundreds of years his Hebrew dictionary was the only one used by scholars in France and Germany.

As a philologist he was sharply criticized by Dunash ibn Labrat (Adomin Ha-Levi), who was a devoted disciple of Rabbi Saadia Gaon. Like Menachem ben Saruk, he too was supported financially by Chasdai ibn Shaprut. In his work "Teshuboth de Dunash" he not only criticized his contemporary, Menachem, but even his rabbi, Saadia Gaon. But he was not merely a critic correcting others' errors. He also made important contributions of his own to grammar and its terminology.

While the Babylonian Gaonim exerted great influence upon the Jewish communities in the Moslem countries, the Palestinian Gaonim maintained contacts with the Jews in the Christian countries. Thus, wherever there were large Jewish communities a network of yeshivas developed, which became the centers of Talmudic study and research. Even those who devoted themselves to the secular study of the Hebrew language, to the development of poetry, and religious philosophy, at the same time emphasized the necessity of fostering the study of the Talmud and spreading its influence.

Beginning with the second half of the tenth century France and Germany, especially the cities clustered about the Rhine, became centers of Jewish culture. The first great yeshiva, which drew hundreds of students from virtually all of Europe, was established by Rabbenu Gershom ben Judah, who is known as the "Meor Hagolah," the light of the Diaspora. His influence in Europe was exceedingly great. His decisions and judgments were speedily accepted as valid for all time. His most important reform was the prohibition of polygamy. Others of his edicts were: no woman may be divorced against her will; letters of other people may not be opened; apostates who return to Judaism must not be derided. All these decrees he bolstered by providing the severe punishment of excommunication for those who violated them.

Rabbenu Gershom was also creative in the field of the study of the Scriptures and the Talmud, and his commentaries were later included in every good edition of the latter work. His commentaries are in reality the work of two generations of scholars, who labored under his tutelage in the Mayence Yeshiva. When Rabbenu Gershom read the Gemara, expounding the more difficult passages, his pupils took notes avidly. These notes, or "Kuntresim" as they are called in Hebrew, were edited at the beginning of the twelfth century by Rabbi Eliakim ben Meshullam, who published them under the title of "Rabbeunu Gershom," the founder of the yeshivas in France and Germany.

It was in this period that the development of the Talmud and Talmudic studies took two different directions. One was practical, the other theoretical. The practical school aimed at the continuation of the development of Talmudic Law and at broadening its contents and scope. The theoretical school aimed at a more profound understanding of its essence and meaning, at probing its spiritual significance. This, naturally, included the study of the Hebrew language and its grammatical foundation.

The practical school had its locus in the middle European countries, particularly in northern France. The center of the theoretical school, on the other hand, was in Spain, where the system which sought to bring about harmony between faith and philosophy blossomed forth in this period.

There was another distinction between the two schools, in addition to the one sketched above. In the middle European countries the Talmud and the entire exegetical literature became a dire necessity, because they affected daily life, regulating and adjusting the existence of every Jew. All the commentaries were therefore directed to facilitating the understanding of the Talmud by the non-scholar. In Spain, on the other hand, the Talmud at this time was a work meant only for the scholars and the intellectual elite who were interested only in studying its contents and structure.

The development of the practical school in northern France reached its culmination with the rise of Rashi (Rabbi Solomon ben Isaac, 1040-1105), who apparently had been selected by

God to become the greatest and most beloved of all commentators.

In interpreting the Torah and the Talmud, Rashi chose the golden middle road between the ordinary meaning of the word and its symbolic explanation. First, he gave the common-sense meaning of a passage and then he utilized symbolism to give it color and attractiveness. Whenever he could not offer a satisfactory explanation he was humble enough to admit it, and whenever he endowed a passage with symbolic meaning he stated so and did not try to pass it off as the ordinary meaning.

With the commentaries of Rashi the Talmud became an open book to everyone and the intellectual energy of the scholars was now channeled into an entirely different direction. Rashi's work was continued by his own children, his most devoted and gifted students. His three scholarly daughters (he had no sons) married men of high ability and the offspring resulting from these felicitous marriages continued the work of interpretation.

Rashi's grandchildren studied his exegetical writings and made many improvements and additions. These additions made in the course of more than two hundred years are known under the collective name of *Tosefoth*.

The greatest and most prominent of the writers of *Tosefoth* was Rabbenu Tam, also known as Rabbi Jacob the Perfect. He was the very soul and incarnation of this entire group of writers. He possessed a striking personality and evoked great admiration and respect. His work was accepted as the dictum of the greatest authority and his decisions as the very law itself.

His chief work is the *Sepher Ha-Yasher*, The Book of the Righteous, which contains his supplements to thirty-three tractates of the Talmud. Here he exhibits great brilliance of mind and illuminates the most abstruse passages in the Halacha. His method is keenly analytical and he does not omit from his dissection the least hypothesis, opinion, or assertion.

The three crusades, which virtually destroyed Jewish life, suppressed and almost entirely put a stop to the Jewish creative process in the middle European countries. Thus, towards the end of the thirteenth century the main role in the further development of the Talmud passed to Spanish Jewry. Well established yeshivas had been in existence in Spain long before and it was through these institutions that Jewish culture burgeoned.

The *Alfas* of Isaac Alfasi (1013-1103) is a codification of Talmudic Law. It soon became the most authoritative work in Jewish religious life. Rabbi Isaac became the foremost and final authority on the subject and almost put into shade the authority of the Gaonim.

Already in the days of the Gaonim the need for codification of all the laws contained in the Talmud was keenly felt. The seven *Minor Tractates* were perhaps an attempt at least partly to satisfy this need by compiling several books of the Law in a more concrete and orderly fashion than in their original form. The "*Shimushei Rabba,*" written by the Gaonim, is also such a volume, and it is clear that many other books codifying the Law in specific subjects must have existed which were subsequently lost.

That this need for codification of all the laws became increasingly pressing may be seen in the fact that the *Responsa* in the Gaonim period arrived in great numbers from all parts of the world. Needless to say, the *Responsa* is also a part of the literature of codification.

In the second half of the eighth century the very first of the minor codifiers appeared: Rabbi Achai Gaon (748-760), Judai Gaon (756-770), and Simon de Cairo.

Rabbi Achai Gaon was one of the heads of the yeshiva in Pumbeditha. Because the Exilarch did not appoint him as Gaon he left Babylonia and settled in Palestine. It is not known for certain in which of these countries he wrote his codex *Sheilatoth*. If one examines its contents one is led to the belief that this work is a compilation of lectures which he delivered in the yeshiva. The *Sheilatoth* is arranged according to the sections of the Torah and is based upon the order of the Mitzvoth enumerated therein. The purpose is to explicate these Mitzvoth according to the interpretation given them by the Talmud and other books of Halacha.

Judai Gaon composed the *Halachoth Pesukoth*, which is also known as *Halachoth Ketuoth* and *Halachoth Ketzuboth.* These additional names were given it because Judai Gaon did not give the sources for his laws.

The third book of codification, the "*Halachoth Gdoloth*" by Simon de Cairo, partly follows the *Sheilatoth* in method. However, it is more of a Talmudic codification giving for the first time a detailed list of the 613 Mitzvoth.

There most certainly must have existed many other minor codexes in various countries of the world. Many of them, however, were entirely lost and of many others we have merely fragments. The *Alfas* is the first important codex which has come down to us in its complete and authorized form.

The *Alfas* is a work written with great talent and even greater erudition. Immense knowledge and keenness of mind were necessary to establish laws which should be firmly based upon authorities and capable of acceptance for all times. Alfasi was an independent thinker and often even dared to differ from the Gaonim.

Alfasi also established a great number of methodological rules for the interpretation of the Talmud. Not only does he give the law in accordance with his judgment, but he also cites the relevant passage in the Gemara dealing directly or indirectly with the subject at hand. In time many commentaries were written upon the *Alfas*; to such an extent that this work itself became the center and the subject of a vast literature.

Nevertheless, even the *Alfas* was not quite sufficient. It could serve as a sufficient basis for the Law, but it could not serve as a compendium of the Law for all times and for all subjects dealing with practical life. A work which shall encompass every conceivable subject was still lacking, until the rise of the Rambam (Rabbenu Moses ben Maimon, 1135-1204), a man of genius, of unlimited knowledge and talent. He it was who created a complete codex of Hebrew Law, which is authoritative as well as scientific. His *Mishna Torah* or *Yad-Ha-Chazakah* ever since its publication has made it considerably easier for students to wander through the labyrinths of the Talmudic Halacha.

The codex compiled by the Rambam (Maimonides) is distinguished by its order and logic. It gives the law in clear and comprehensible form, without any burdensome aides or references, without sources or citations. It is really far more than a legislative codex. It is a work which deals with every subject contained in the Law. Although the Rambam's codex immediately evoked great admiration and became widely known throughout the world, the Rambam himself was later severely criticized and called forth a great deal of opposition. His most redoubtable opponent was Rabbi Abraham ben David (1125-1198), who objected to many of the Rambam's decisions. Opposition to the Rambam was based primarily upon the fear that the *Mishna Torah* would tend to weaken the study of the Talmud itself. History, however, has proved otherwise. The Rambam's work stimulated further study of the Law and the study of Talmud was thus not weakened but, on the contrary, considerably strengthened.

The most important codex following that of the Rambam's were the "*Turim*" (The Four Rows) composed by Rabbenu Jacob ben Asher (1280-1340). This new codex introduced perfect order and harmony into the codification of the Law and stimulated a new movement in Jewish scholarly life.

The *Turim* consist of four separate parts: *Orach Chaim*—"The Way of Life"—containing laws concerning holidays, prayers and customs; *Yoreh Deah*—"Guide of Knowledge"—containing laws concerning Kashruth, slaughter, inspection, charity, mourning, etc.; *Eben Haezer*—"The Stone of Help"—containing laws concerning marriage and divorce; *Choshen Hamishpat*—"The Breastplate of Judgment"—containing laws concerning civil life.

In the fifteenth century particularly violent persecutions of Jews began in most European countries and especially in Spain, and it seemed as if the religious animosity of the Christians would entirely destroy the Jewish nation. At such a time it was inevitable that the creative process should suffer a decline.

Towards the middle of the century the Jewish communities in Palestine were recognized by the Turkish government and many Hebrew scholars in Spain fled to Palestine. Palestine thus became a small Jewish oasis for a period of several hundred years.

The vast accumulated and scattered literature of the Halacha then received its final codification in the work of Rabbi Joseph Caro (1488-1575). Already in his early years he had written the *Beth Joseph* ("The House of Joseph"), a commentary upon the *Arbah Turim* (The Four Rows), in which he cited all the relevant sources. Twenty years he had labored upon this project, and at the end remained dissatisfied. He continued his studies for another twelve years until he felt confident that the laws as formulated by him were consistent and authentic. But then he came to the realization that all hitherto existing codifications and their commentaries can not be used as handbooks for the ordinary Jew. He therefore condensed the *Arbah Turim* and his own *Beth Joseph* into one book. In order to emphasize its simplicity and practicableness he called the new work *Shulchan Aruch* ("The Prepared Table"). This work is now accepted throughout the Jewish world and historians compare his achievement with that of the Rambam in the *Mishna Torah.*

After the publication of the *Beth Joseph* a new Jewish center arose in Eastern Europe, where the Jewish creative spirit continued in an unbroken line.

CHAPTER SIXTEEN

THE JUDICIAL SYSTEM

CAPITAL PUNISHMENT. JUSTICE IN THE MIDDLE AGES. PHYSICAL DAMAGE AND MONETARY COMPENSATION. HUMANE LAWS IN TIME OF WAR.

AS EARLY AS IN THE INITIAL PHASE OF HUMAN DEVELOPMENT, barely with the appearance of the initial signs of civilization, inauguration of a judicial system became imperative.

And the great lawgiver and student of men, Moses, likewise realized the need of a judicial system and code of law, to permeate the life of the individual and the community.

The basic idea which made possible the establishment of a Jewish Nation was—deliverance, aspiration towards personal freedom and human equality; this fundamental concept is interwoven in the structure of all our laws and court procedure.

Placed on the highest level has been the untouchability of the human person and his personal freedom. "For has not one's fellowman been created in the womb of a woman, as I?"

Of course, the Torah realized the need for a judicial system, for laws and punishment; how different, though, from the laws prevailing among other nations!

Generally speaking, jurisprudence is not an exact science, and Talmudic jurisprudence is even less so. The Law of the

Torah, both oral and written, is quite elastic and can be, without too much straining and sophistry, interpreted in many different ways. And it is upon this very elasticity of the Torah that the gigantic and splendid edifice of the Talmud has been erected.

Talmudic Law is thus always humane and considerate. Superficially it may seem to be severe and rigorous, but in essence it is always liberal and democratic, practical and idealistic, human and divine.

Let us take as an example the command "Thou shalt not steal." The Pentateuch is quite explicit and clear on the matter: Stealing is prohibited. But then the Talmud mitigates the harshness of the law by adding the following precept: Thou shalt not embarrass anyone who steals in order to satisfy his hunger.

No other nation has such a humane law, and it is not seldom that we hear of a judge sentencing someone who stole a bottle of milk for his baby.

Some of our enemies consider themselves scholars and they will often point out passages in the Talmud which, in their opinion, should be condemned. Nevertheless, in citing these passages they forget that there is also a great Talmudic literature which may interpret these passages in a different fashion.

Those who are against capital punishment seemingly have the strongest argument against the Torah. They stress the literal meaning of the Torah, as the Sadducees and Karaites used to do. The adherents of capital punishment on the other hand, likewise base themselves upon the literal meaning of the Torah and thus absolve themselves of their own responsibility.

It is quite true that the Written Torah prescribes capital punishment for a large number of transgressions, including many of a purely religious character. But it is also true that the Jews, even in their early history, have given these as well as many other rigorous laws, a liberal interpretation which virtually entirely negatived their effect.

Theoretically, capital punishment was never abolished, since the Torah is very explicit concerning this matter and the Torah is, after all, the constitution of the Jewish people handed down by God Himself. Now, a constitution cannot be abrogated, but it can be interpreted and amended.

In the early history there were four kinds of capital punishment: stoning, burning, killing and strangulation. The Torah considers the death punishment in principle not as revenge by the state, but as a warning and as a means of preventing other transgressions of the law. That punishment is for the purpose of making the people "hear and fear" is repeated many times in the Torah. The severity of the law is especially emphasized in the case of a rebellious son and of witnesses convicted of false evidence. However the severity of the law is lightened even for murderers who killed with intent and who must therefore be dragged away to justice even from the altar.

"If the wicked man will turn aside from his sins he will live. Do I then desire the death of any wicked man? Do I not rather desire that he should eschew his sinful path and remain alive?" In Proverbs (Chapter 24, 11-13) it is specifically stated that it is a duty to save those who are about to be sentenced to death.

It is interesting to observe that those who are always pointing to the brutality of the maxim "an eye for an eye and a life for life" concede that society has a right to use capital punishment. In the New Testament this right is repeated no less than five times (Matthew, XV, 4; XXVI, 52; John, XIX, 10-11; Acts, XXV, 11; Romans XIII, 35). The Apocryphal and Apocalyptic writings cite death as an absolutely necessary punishment.

With the beginning of the Christian Era the Jewish attitude towards the death penalty became more liberal and progressive. The Mishna (Sanhedrin, chapter VI, Mishna V) states that God is pained when the wicked man is put to death. Later the Talmudic scholars began to look with horror upon the death penalty and tried to avoid it by all sorts of means.

In the first place, two witnesses had to testify that they saw the murder with their own eyes. Circumstantial evidence was not accepted. The witnesses who saw the murder first had to warn the accused. If he was not warned beforehand the death penalty could not be imposed.

Anyone was able to defend the accused and the number of defenders could not be limited. Even after the defendant had already been sentenced, advocates could still appear in his behalf. The defendant himself could appeal to the court before sentence was actually carried out if he had any new evidence to adduce.

We recall vividly a trial of one Louis Williams accused of murdering his brother-in-law. In attempting to save him from the death penalty, the defense attorney argued that his client was deranged. Basing himself upon this declaration of the defense attorney, the judge henceforth no longer allowed any evidence which would go outside the limits of the insanity plea. No other arguments in favor of the defendant could be used. If the defense adopted the wrong course, the court asserted, it is to the gain of the prosecution.

An illustration of this principle may be the following parable: A man found himself in a burning house and kind people attempted to save him. At first it was thought that the best thing for him to do is to jump out of the window. But on more mature reflection it was seen that jumping would be dangerous and that it would be better for him to go up to the roof and from there get on to a neighboring house. But according to the ruling of the court, which incidentally is in consonance with accepted traditions of American jurisprudence, the unfortunate man should be left to be consumed by the flames because a wrong course was first chosen.

Our own judges of more than two thousand years ago were in this respect true humanitarians and took the greatest pains to absolve the accused from guilt. Once a judge, for instance, expressed a favorable opinion about the accused he could no longer change it. He was able, however, to change an unfavorable opinion.

Non-Jewish justice, even in our own times, is not as humane. In the Middle Ages, for instance, even small children were punished with the death penalty. In France and in Germany, even as late as the eighteenth century, the death penalty was imposed for trivial offenses. In 1770 in France two thieves were sentenced to die by being trampled under by a heavy wagon. One had stolen a shirt and another a piece of cheese. In 1873 in Great Britain a nine-year old child was sentenced to death because he accidentally broke a window pane valued at two pence.

Death in practically all countries was by hanging, decapitating, quartering, tearing out the heart, opening the arteries, burying alive, stoning, burning, drowning, choking, throwing among wild animals, exiling to an uninhabited island, placing in a leaking boat, trampling underneath a heavy wagon, or throwing into a cauldron of boiling lead.

An ancient codex of Lithuanians prescribes the following mode of procedure for executing the death penalty: First the guilty person should be led through the market place and his flesh be torn with pincers. Then he should be placed in a leather bag together with a dog, cat, and snake, and the bag thrown into the lake.

By the time that Christ appeared and advocated compassion and humaneness and strongly objected to the precept of "an eye for an eye, tooth for tooth and life for life," the Jews had long ago given up this harsh maxim. In fact, all his humanitarian and moral precepts are to be found in the Talmud expressed in far more beautiful prose and exhibiting a far deeper conception of human worth.

At the time of Simon ben Shetah, when complete victory had been gained over the Sadducees and their strict interpretation of the Torah, it was established definitively for the first time that the maxim "an eye for an eye" merely means divine compensation for physical injury (Baba Kamma, 83b; Mechilta Mishpatim, Section V).

Compensation for physical damage was prevalent even among the Romans, but it would be a mistake to think that the Talmudic scholars simply included the knowledge they possessed of Roman jurisprudence. Conceptions of justice and equity are determined by the general level of morality among a people, and this level itself changes with the times, ascending higher as the people reach a higher stage of civilization.

Every law passes through various transformations. A people that has risen to a higher stage of civilization will naturally have a more humane conception of justice than a people of a lower civilization.

When the Pharisees interpreted the maxim "an eye for an eye" to mean simply monetary compensation it was not necessary for them to adopt this interpretation from the Romans or anyone else. In the first place, the Jews have always been original in their legislation, and furthermore they stood as high as the Romans in the scale of civilization and their laws were dictated by their own conceptions of justice and equity.

The Oral Law as well as the Written Torah attempted to lay down humane and civilized rules and regulations in time of war, even in a case of a just war, when the Jews were attacked and had to defend themselves. If it was impossible to be entirely humane, the attempt was at least made to diminish brutality. Here are some of these rules:

If not absolutely necessary, do not cut down a fruit tree when you besiege the enemy's city. You eat of the tree, it is your provider.

Before you go to war, make every effort to maintain peace.

Do not begin any war, even with the Amalekites, before you sincerely try to create a basis for peace.

If the enemy surrenders, do not kill him.

Always leave open one side of a besieged city so that the enemy may have a chance of escape if he wants to.

One of King David's strongest desires was to build the Temple. He prepared all the necessary materials and devoted himself to the task with the greatest zeal and energy. Nevertheless, God told him: "You have spilled too much blood and conducted great wars. You will not build this house for Me." David's wars were all necessary and forced upon him. And nevertheless God did not look kindly upon them.

Whenever a king wished to undertake a war of aggrandizement he first had to get permission from the Sanhedrin, and even then he could not force his soldiers to fight with sword in hand.

CHAPTER SEVENTEEN

SERVITUDE AND SLAVERY IN THE TORAH AND IN TALMUDIC LAW

SLAVERY IN EGYPT, GREECE AND ROME. FREEDOM AND SERFDOM. THE JEWISH SLAVE AND THE GENTILE SLAVE. THE RELIGIOUS AND SOCIAL ATTITUDE.

THE FIRST TO INTRODUCE SLAVERY EXTENSIVELY WERE THE Egyptians. They were the originators of this evil system. Greece and Rome were merely the followers. Slavery in Egypt was brutal and degrading. According to the Jewish Agada, Hebrew infants were immured in the walls.

The institution of slavery in Greece and Rome was not much more humane. Families would be torn asunder and sold into slavery. The Merchants made quite a considerable trade of it, and the people as well as the rulers considered it with pride.

In Greece the slaves were beaten and tortured, starved, or even put to death on the caprice of the owner. The slaves had no names, were not grouped together according to their tribe or country of origin, could not bring suit against a freeman, and were generally outside the pale of the law. The slave was considered as a cow would be considered; fed while she is giving milk and killed when she ceases to give milk. When a slave became old his owner simply drove him off his property. In his work *"What is Property"* Prudhon calls the slaves "the labor of machines." Like cattle, the slaves were branded with hot irons. Even an intellectual giant like Aristotle considered slavery a natural thing. The Athenian philosophers generally classified property on a two-fold basis: dead and living instruments; the slaves were the living instruments.

Until the time of Hadrian, the Romans had the power of life and death over their slaves. Until the rule of Claudius, the old and weak slaves were taken to an island and there allowed to perish. The slaves were kept in dark and dank prisons and, when they were taken to work, were put in chains. Many of them bore chains even while at work. Later, when Rome became a republic and created the famous Roman Civil Code, which became the foundation of modern jurisprudence in many countries throughout the world, the slave nevertheless remained outside the law. Physical injury, the Roman law states, is primarily an injury to one's personal dignity, and a slave is a creature without any personality and dignity; he can therefore be physically injured without injuring his personality or dignity.

Rav left the bathhouse, got dressed, sat down, and began to busy himself with communal affairs. His slave handed him a cup of wine, but Rav was too occupied to take notice and paid no attention to him. In the meanwhile the slave dozed off and when Rav perceived it, he remarked: "King Solomon expressed it very well when he said that the slave works hard and that is why he sleeps well. But we who are concerned with community affairs are not allowed to sleep."

"The greater the number of slaves, the greater the number of robberies. The greater the number of maid servants, the greater the licentiousness. Slaves are libertines" (Aboth II, 8).

"A slave seeks advice after the deed is done" (Gittin, 13a).

"The slave of a scholar is like the scholar himself" (Mechilta Exodus).

"When the Almighty sent forth the Israelites from Egypt and delivered them from bondage into freedom, He said: "The Jews are the servants of God. Therefore, they must not be sold as slaves to slaves" (Kiddushin, 22b).

"Rabbi Jacob ben Zebid says: Why is a slave liberated when he loses an eye or a tooth as a result of a beating at the hands of his master? Because Ham, the son of Noah, was cursed to become a slave as a result of sinning against his father with his eyes and teeth, (that is with his vision and his speech). Therefore the slave is freed of the curse of servitude when his master knocks his eye or tooth out."

"When your brother becomes impoverished and sells himself to you for a servant (Leviticus XXV:39), Even when you employ him as your servant he is still your brother. You must not enslave him and insult him. You must not give him unnecessary labor just to keep him busy. You must not think that you can fool everyone. God surely cannot be fooled and you must fear Him" (Mechilta Leviticus).

"The Biblical phrase: 'because he is well with thee' (Deuteronomy XV:16), the Talmudical sages interpret thus: The master must not eat white bread while the servant eats black bread. The master must not drink aged wine and the servant new wine. The master must not sleep upon featherbeds while the servant sleeps upon a straw sack. The scholars deduce from the above maxim that purchasing a slave is like purchasing a master" (Kiddushin, 20a).

"Rabbi Jose's wife quarrelled with her maid one day and Rabbi Jose gave the right to the maid. He said that she is a human being just as we are and, furthermore, we must have greater consideration for her because she is unprotected."

"Rabbi Gamaliel had a very fine and wise servant by the name of Tabi. One day he unwittingly hit him in the eye and then joyously freed him."

The Gemara (Baba Metzia, 60b) tells the following characteristic story: A gentile slave, old in years, dyed his hair and beard in order to conceal his age and came to the Amora, Rabba, requesting that the Rabbi indenture him permanently in his household. Rabba refused him because he did not wish any slaves on principle. The slave then went to Rabbi Papa and the latter acquiesced in the slave's request. Once Rabbi Papa asked the slave to bring him a glass of water. The slave removed the dye from his beard and head and said to Rabbi Papa: "Look, I'm older than you are, why then should I serve you?"

Even from this enigmatic story we are able to understand that there is no trace in the Torah of the Egyptian, Greek, or Roman slave system. Moreover, it is difficult to find in Judaism even the concept of the slave. Servitude and slavery mean the annihilation of individual freedom and the transformation of the human being into a chattel or animal. According to the Torah, therefore, no man may be robbed of his freedom. Already while they were at Mt. Sinai the Hebrews heard the first admonition: "I am the Lord, thy Lord, Who brought you out of the land of Egypt, out of the House of Bondage." The

Talmud (Baba Kamma 116b), comments as follows upon this: "The children of Israel are slaves to Me; they are My slaves, and not slaves of slaves."

According to the Torah and the Talmud no slavery exists among Jews. There are only several categories of workers. "Ebed," translated by our teachers as "servant," but by perverse translators as "slave," simply means someone who hires himself out for a period to perform all kinds of labor. This is in contrast to the "Poel" and "Sachir," who hire themselves out only for the day. At any rate, all these words signify a man who hires himself out voluntarily to do some work; not someone who is captured and, against his will sold into slavery for the rest of his life. The Torah specifies death as the punishment for capturing a man and selling him into slavery. The slave is without any protection and always dependent upon the least whim of his master. But an Ebed among the Jews is protected by law. He is considered a human being and the attitude towards him is thoroughly humane and kind. This is written down in many laws and regulations. "And all the regulations which we have discussed thoroughly in the law concerning servants are humane; compassion and kindness must be shown to the poor" (The Guide for the Perplexed, Part III, chapter XXXIX).

The Torah specifies: "And if thy brother becomes poor and sells himself unto thee, thou shalt not compel him to work as a bond-servant. But as a hired laborer, as a sojourner, shall he be with thee; until the year of the Jubilee shall he serve with thee. And he shall depart from thee, he and his children with him; and he shall return unto his own family, and unto the possession of his fathers shall he return. For my servants are they, I brought forth out of the land of Egypt; they shall not be sold as bond-men are sold. Thou shalt not rule over him with rigour; but thou shalt have fear of thy God. And over your brethern the Children of Israel, one over the other, ye shall not rule with rigour" (Leviticus XXV, 39-43).

Hard work, the Rambam declares in his *"Halachoth Abadim"* (Laws of Servitude), is likewise the kind of work which is not absolutely necessary for the owner, although the work may be as light as, for instance, warming or cooling a drink. If the master, for example, tells his servant to plow the orchard until he gets home, this is considered hard work and is strictly prohibited. The intent obviously was not to make the servant feel in any way whatsoever that he is a servant. The owner must likewise never ask his servant to follow him with a pillow, remove his shoes, carry him upon a litter or canopy, etc. because all these chores have the character of slavery and are prohibited in the Torah (Siphre B'har).

The hired Jewish laborer is no servant and most certainly no slave. The owner must not make fun of him, must not call him servant and must not exhibit any traces of "bossism." The laborer may work only during daytime, not at night. If he is a skilled laborer the owner may not put him to unskilled tasks. If the laborer is unskilled and has no trade the owner must not teach him a trade simply in order to take advantage of his labor. The owner must likewise never ask the servant to do work below his dignity, nor agricultural labor in the field or in the orchard (Mechilta Mishpatim; Siphre B'har).

Whoever hires a Hebrew servant is obligated to feed not only the servant, but his wife and children as well (Kiddushin, 20a). The owner may not eat white bread while the servant eats black bread; nor must he drink aged wine while he gives his servant new wine; he must not sleep upon feather mattresses while his servant sleeps upon straw (Siphre B'har). If the owner possesses only one pillow he must give it to the servant (Tosephoth Kiddushin, 20a). Wherever the owner dwells and sleeps, there his hired laborer must dwell and sleep. If he goes on vacation, winter or summer, he must take his servant with him. The owner also must not wear any better or cleaner clothes than his servant.

To summarize, the word "Ebed" does not mean slavery. It stems from "abodah," which means to labor, and the word "Ebed" simply means worker.

In its humanity and justice to the working classes the Talmud went to such extremes that a witticism has it that whoever hires a Jewish laborer hires a master over himself (Kiddushin, 20a).

A Jew could not indenture himself for his entire life. If he was stubborn and insisted on remaining a servant the Torah commanded that his ear should be pierced. The Talmud justifies this punishment in the following manner: the ear heard God's assertion that the Hebrews are His slaves alone and not slaves of slaves, and since the servant has voluntarily submitted himself to eternal servitude, his ear should be pierced as a permanent token of ignominy (Kiddushin, 22b).

A Jew may hire himself out when he becomes impoverished, or the court may let him out for hire for a theft which he must return. But in no case must he be robbed of his personal freedom. He must likewise never sell himself in order to enrich himself or to buy cattle or furniture.

Every Jewish servant is manumitted at the end of six years. "Six years he shall work and upon the seventh he shall be set free without any money payment" (Exodus, XXI, 2). Even if the servant had cost the owner a large sum of money he must be freed at the end of the seventh year. The owner does not have to give him any token of liberation since this is a matter of course. Even if the laborer had been sick for three years, he must still receive full payment for six years and be unconditionally released (Kiddushin, 17a). If the laborer had been sick the entire six years, he must be liberated but will not receive any compensation. If the owner has given him money for medical services he must not deduct it from the servant's compensation (Kiddushin, 17a).

The Jewish servant must also be liberated in the jubilee year, as it is stated in the Torah (Leviticus, XXV, 10): "And thou shalt keep holy the jubilee year, and thou shalt announce the liberation of all the citizens in the country, everyone shall return to his own soil, to his own family." Rabbi Jochanan ben Broka says: "Upon Rosh Hashanah the laborer would quit his work, but would not yet quit the house of his owner. He would do nothing, eat, drink, and be merry, and adorn his head with laurel wreaths. But upon Yom Kippur, when the sound of the trumpet was heard for the jubilee, they all went home" (Torath Kohanim B'har).

The Torah (Deuteronomy, XV, 13) also commanded the owner not to liberate the servant without some provisions. "Thou shalt give him of your sheep and of your granary and of your wine-press." Even if the owner did not make any profit from the servant he must nevertheless still give him these gratuities. Rabbi Meir says that these gratuities must amount to not less than 15 Selaim; Rabbi Judah says 30, Rabbi Simon—50 (Kiddushin, 17a).

As a general rule the hired servant could also buy his freedom at any time by paying the owner for the remaining time that he still had to serve. A servant girl can also get her freedom when she reaches puberty, or the age of twelve years. A servant girl must not be sold by her owner to someone else, and the Torah virtually forces him to take her for his wife so that she may not feel as a servant girl in the house (Exodus, XXI, 7-11).

The Jewish attitude even towards the Canaanite servant was equally considerate and humane. The Torah severely prohibits the killing of a slave. If the owner mistreats the non-Jewish slave and knocks out one of his teeth, the slave is automatically freed. A Jew was allowed to have non-Jewish slaves, but only from those who were already slaves; in other words, a free gentile could not be captured and enslaved.

From many passages in the Talmud it is clear that the scholars were opposed to the institution of slavery altogether. In the first place, the Talmud declared that capital punishment must be imposed for killing a slave; that is to say, if the owner kills his slave he must himself be killed. Furthermore, the Talmud extended the bases upon which a slave might be freed; thus, a slave was liberated not only when his owner knocked out one of his teeth or an eye, but when he damaged any of twenty-four other organs of the body. If the owner damaged more than one organ he was forced, in addition to freeing the slave, also to give him compensation for the damage.

The Rambam (Halachoth Abadim) says: The precepts of ethics and religion dictate that we have sympathy with the gentile servant as well as with the Jewish servant. The ancient Jews gave the non-Jewish servant the same food they ate themselves. The servant was fed first and his owner afterwards. The slave was always supposed to be treated with justice; he could not be insulted physically or verbally; he could not be treated with anger or irritation; he could not be overworked. Cruelty and insolence toward slaves are to be seen among all the peoples of the world, but not among the children of Abraham, Isaac, and Jacob.

The general rule in the Talmud concerning the slaves was: When a slave is bought, only his labor is purchased, not his body and soul.

When a gentile slave allowed himself to be circumcised voluntarily in the course of a year he could no longer be sold to another gentile. If, despite this prohibition, a Jew nevertheless did sell him or hired him out to a gentile, the slave was automatically freed and the Jewish owner was required to ransom him even if he had to pay ten times as much as the slave originally cost. If a slave was sold to an owner residing abroad he was likewise liberated. If a Jewish owner wished to leave Palestine he could not force his slaves to accompany him. If the owner gave the slave a freewoman for wife, forced him to wear philacteries, read three sentences from the Torah, or do other things which only a freeman is required to do, the slave was automatically liberated and the owner was required to sign a document to that effect.

The Gemara (Aboda Zara, 17b) relates: The Roman government arrested and tried Rabbi Eliezer ben Perata, because he had freed his slave. According to Roman law this was an offense punished by death. Rashi interprets this as follows: The Romans forbade the liberation of slaves, because the Jewish religion required their liberation.

In the epoch of Ezra and Nehemiah gentile slaves returned to Palestine as free men.

The Gemara (Erubin, 47a; Kethuboth, 57a; Moed Katon, 11a) states: A Jew may attend a fair of gentiles, although he is forbidden to visit a place indulging in pagan orgies, in order to buy gentile slaves there, because by that act the Jew will save them from brutal owners. In fact, the Jew is obligated to do this because the gentile slave is his brother (Baba Kamma, 4a).

After the second destruction of the Temple slavery was entirely abolished. The Talmudic scholars reasoned that since the Torah enjoins the owner to liberate a slave in the jubilee year, therefore since the destruction did away with the jubilee year it at the same time did away with slavery.

CHAPTER EIGHTEEN

THE ATTITUDE TOWARDS LABOR

THE BIBLICAL AND TALMUDIC ATTITUDE. COLLECTIVE AND PRIVATE OWNERSHIP. THE SABBATICAL AND JUBILEE INSTITUTION. LABOR AND AVODAH. JEWISH AND NON-JEWISH WAGE-EARNERS.

MOST OF THOSE WHO BATTLE, IN THE NAME OF MARXISM, to inaugurate a better social order, have, unfortunately, taken up, along with the social struggle the fight against religion.

It is almost axiomatic that labor's struggle inevitably leads to the belief that religion is the opiate of the masses. Playing a vital role in the social struggle, labor has, perhaps more than any other group, become suspicious of church and synagogue.

Superficially, a cardinal contrast *possibly* prevails between religion and Socialism. The Marxist interpretation of history is materialistic. All that transpires in the world, all cultural phenomena, are linked with materialism. Religion, on the other hand, seeks to transform the material into spiritual.

It is outside the pale of this analysis to dwell upon the possibility of a synthetic link between the material and the spiritual. Our presentation concerns itself mainly with the Jewish attitude and position in this respect, with the Talmudic stand on progressive movements designed to improve man's lot and raise labor's social level.

As every other religion, the Jewish faith has designated Godliness as life's loftiest aim. This aspiration is basic throughout the Pentateuch, the Prophets and the Talmud.

Judaism's uniqueness may be attributed to the fact that its morals and ethics are realistic throughout. At its very inception, the Jewish faith has greatly cherished human life and, consequently, has not remained impassive to the process of labor and the workingman.

True, not always has Judaism elevated itself to the high level of religious teachings. As early as in the era of the Prophets, wealth had already been acquired by unjust means. In reality, though, Judaism has remained linked with its Torah and faith.

Rabbi Judah the Nasi has even honored the rich, but that was in a period when the wealthy acquired their wealth by means of international trade and were, for the most part, Talmudic scholars with a zeal for justice and righteousness. Even then the Talmud despised the unjust capitalist: "The wealthy of Babylon will descend into Hell." And when, in the Middle Ages, the fine type of benefactor—donator to charitable causes—entered the picture, he was highly honored. When, however, he became the "Rosh Hakahal," the head of the community and "take-what-you-can" character, he was greatly despised.

The Jewish faith doesn't desire antagonistic classes and, at all times, despises him who ignores the commandments that bear upon the relationships of man to man. The Talmud is well aware of labor's great value in society and maintains that while the worker gives his all, his very soul, the capitalist gives not even his body. The Jewish faith nurtures boundless love for the worker, as for the impoverished generally, warning that he who labors be not oppressed, that he be even aided by means of non-interest loans, and be protected against oppression. No other faith maintains the attitude toward labor that is held by the Jewish religion. Rabbi Samuel David Luzatto asserts that the Torah has injected compassion into legal matters.

The Jewish faith doesn't desire seeing a growing capitalist society. In the days to come, says the Gemara, "mine" and "thine" will be obliterated.

The earliest Jewish labor legislation will be found in the Bible. In the very first chapter we may discover the broad humanitarian principles in which this legislation was conceived. It proclaims the dignity of man, that the man was fashioned in the image of God and that in every human being is to be found the breath of the Divine Spirit. Man is, therefore, a child of God, and may not be mistreated.

This principle was incorporated in the Ten Commandments: Six days shalt thou labor and do all thy work; but the seventh day is a sabbath unto the Lord thy God, in it thou shalt not do any manner of work, thou . . . nor thy man-servant, nor thy maid-servant . . . nor thy stranger that is within thy gates; that thy man-servant and maid-servant may rest as well as thou (Deuteronomy V, 13-15).

From the very outset, the Jewish social structure has been built upon collective land ownership, and even much later, in the era of the Judges and Kings, definite traces of the collective form still remained. Linked with this was also the tradition of confining ownership within the sphere of one's own family. When one was compelled to sell a parcel of land, the purchaser had to be a member of his own family.

An iron-clad tradition, this; and it was upheld even in the gravest hour of need and misfortune. Hanameel approached his cousin, Jeremiah, demanding: "Purchase from me my field, located in Anathoth, for according to the law of redemption, you are obligated so to do." And while in jail, Jeremiah purchased the field from him (Jeremiah XXXII, 7-9).

Subsequently, when the last vestige of collective ownership vanished, private ownership became sanctified and remained the dominant form of ownership. The Torah says: "Desire not your friend's wife, nor his slave, nor his child, nor his ass—nor anything that belongs to your friend." Michah the Prophet cried out: "Woe to those who seek the fields and rob them, who seek the homes and pillage them, who ravish the master and his abode, the man and his fortune" (Michah II, 2).

Having exercised the greatest influence upon the future development of the social movement among Jews, the Prophets were the first to publicly appear in opposition to those elements oppressing the masses. They would deliver addresses in the Temple's courtyard and at Jerusalem's gates—certainly the very first public political and revolutionary assemblages of the citizenry.

The Torah is progressive and humane in its entire makeup, in contents as well as in character. The social laws go far beyond the liberal reforms prevailing in a democratic system;

they are the planks of a definite social program, a design for living in a just and righteous society. The Talmud even contains laws symptomatic of an extremely idealistic social order.

The Sabbatical and Jubilee institution is basically religious-ethical in nature; in consequence, however, it is a far-reaching progressive reform. Repeated every half-century, the Jubilee annuls all transactions of immobile chattels which had been transacted in the interim; the original owner's property is returned to him without formality and without payment.

"The land is all God's" is the prevailing religious-ethical motive. This motive does not diminish the social content. It bars concentration of land into the hands of a few individuals. The late Rabbi Kook once said: "Should the laws of the Torah be adopted in the rebuilding of Eretz Israel, an unjust social system would never be possible."

One's very being in Israel became dependent upon the observance of the commandment "That they inaugurate in the land the just and righteous laws of the Torah."

Jewish life during the long years of exile differed considerably from the life of ancient Judaism as expressed in the Torah, Talmud and the entire Rabbinical literature.

While in exile, the Jew could not be the master of his own situation, which was determined, for the most part, by foreign, hostile forces.

The Torah's social laws, interpreted and widened by the Talmud, are not alone exemplary from the historical point of view, but are also highly progressive, even if the strictly socialistic measuring stick is applied.

Labor is held on a higher plane than is the principle of doing honor to one's parents, and the worker occupies a more honored place than the pious. When God brought Adam into Paradise, He did so with the object of having Adam cultivate it. According to the Jewish concept, Paradise is not a place where one is freed of labor; rather, it is a place where one labors.

Upon having heard God's decree: "Thou shalt eat the grass from thy field," Adam burst into sobs: "Do I and my ass have to eat out of the same trough?" However, when the Almighty subsequently said: "By the sweat of thy brow shalt thou eat thy bread," Adam calmed himself and realized that man is on a much higher plane than cow and animal, and that man heightens his worth by securing his food through hard labor (Pesachim 118a).

Labor is termed in Hebrew: "Avodah"; however, the word also means "religious observance," and indicates that labor is held on the same plane as prayer.

Similarly, the ideal woman, the virtuous woman, who is lauded in chant by every pious Jew, is one who "does not eat the bread she had not earned."

Even the Holy One, blessed be He, did not cause His Shechinah to alight upon Israel until they had done work; as it is said, "Let them make for Me a sanctuary that I may dwell among them" (Exodus XXV, 8).

This attitude became reinforced in the Talmudic literature. The Rabbis concerned themselves mainly with safeguarding the rights of labor. Talmudic legislation was favorable to labor because the legislators themselves were largely drawn from the laboring class.

No other people can pride itself with so many scholastics who were, at the same time, plain workers. Hillel was a woodcutter; Shamai—a mason; Rabbi Joseph—a flower-grinder; Rabbi Jose ben Chalafta—a tanner; Rabbis Joshua and Isaac—blacksmiths; Rabbis Jochanan, Chanina and Oshaya—shoemakers; Rabbi Abbina—a carpenter; Rabbis Abba Bar Zminah, Daniel, Chanan and Yehudah—tailors; Rabbi Adda—a shepherd; Rabbi Judah—a baker; Rabbi Nechunia—a digger; Rabbi Shesheth—a porter.

The Bible states: "God will bless you in everything you do." This means that when a man works, does something useful, he will be blessed. Achievement does not come out of the clear sky. A man must not say, I will eat and drink, and be merry, but will not work. God will help me. That is why the Bible says that a man must labor by the sweat of his brow and God will then bless him (Tosephta Kiddushin).

Here is a parable illustrating this point. A Gentile once owned a horse, a donkey, and a pig. The donkey and the horse he fed rather sparingly. But the hog he stuffed daily. The horse then said to the donkey: "Observe what the fool, our boss, does. We work for him and he feeds us stingily. The hog does nothing and he is fed right royally."

"Just wait a bit," replied the donkey, "and you will understand why he is fed so well."

When a festival came around, the owner slaughtered the pig and prepared him for a festive meal. The young donkey was then given some corn to eat, but it refused in fear of being slaughtered. The mother then said: "Do not be frightened, my child. It is not the food that is the cause of the slaughter, but idleness." (Tanchuma Vayetze)

Idleness causes stupidity and monotony.

"When ye will arrive in Israel, ye shall plant," says the Bible. Even if you find there abundance, ye must work and plant for your children, as others have planted for ye.

If man prepares not before the Sabbath, what shall he eat on the Sabbath? If man plows not, threshes not, and harvests not during the summer, what shall he eat during the winter?

Only thorns grow by themselves, without labor. In order to get wheat out of the earth work must be done (Bereshith Rabba, chapter 44).

Labor gives man warmth, labor gives man dignity (Nedarim, 49b).

A man must learn a trade during his life. There were seven lean years, but hunger never crossed the threshold of the artisan.

Rabbi Joshua said: "If a man studies only two chapters of the Law in the morning and two in the evening and devotes himself the rest of the day to his work it is considered as though he had fulfilled the Torah in its entirety." (Tanchuma Beshallach).

Whoever works for a living is considered greater than a God-fearing man. Because it is said concerning a God-fearing man that he shall be blessed and happy in the other world. But whoever eats of the fruits of his labor shall be happy and prosperous both in this world and the next (Berachoth, 8a).

Blessed is the man who bears a burden from his youth

onwards. The burden of the Torah, the burden of his family, and the burden of his trade.

Rabbi Judah says: "If a man fails to teach his son a trade, it is the same as if he taught him robbery." (Tosephta Kiddushin).

Rabbi Meir says: "A father should always teach his son a clean and easy trade and pray to Him who owns all the wealth and treasures in the world, because wealth depends upon the labor of people." (Kiddushin, 82b)

"God made everything good in its time." That also means that God created some suitable occupation for everyone (Berachoth, 43b).

A man should hire himself out for some work, even work that is unpleasant, in order not to depend upon other people. As Rav said to Rabbi Kahana: "skin a carcass in the marketplace and take money for it, and don't say I am a priest, I am privileged, it is undignified for me to do such work" (Yebamoth, 63a).

Labor is above intercession of ancestors. The intercession of his ancestors was enough for Jacob to save his possessions from Laban. But his labor was necessary to save human beings from Laban's grasping hands.

The Torah says: "Thou shalt not withhold the wages of a hired man, of the poor and needy . . . On the same day shalt thou give him his wages . . . for his soul longeth for it." (*Deuteronomy* XXIV, 14-15). The poor laborer risks his life in his work, climbing upon tall buildings or trees, because he needs his day's wages to feed his family. That is why if the man who hired him keeps back his wages without paying him the same day it is considered as if he took his very soul, his very life away. He transgresses thereby the five 'Don'ts' in the Torah." (Baba Metziah, 111a).

The following story illustrates this point. A man went on a trip with his donkey following him. The man bought a bundle of feed for his donkey and carried it upon his back. The hungry donkey hoped that soon the man would stop to feed him. Finally, the man put the donkey in the stable without giving him food. Such a man is a wicked man. The same is true of the man who withholds wages from the man who worked for him.

Rabbi Jochanan asked his son to hire some laborers. The son thereupon made a contract with them not stipulating the amount and kind of food they were to get. When he told his father, the latter said: "My son, even if you will prepare for them a feast in King's Solomon style you will not have done enough. Go and tell them that you will give them only bread and vegetables."

The Midrash relates: Simon Sibna, a well-digger and cave-worker, once halted a great Tanai, Rabbi Jochanan ben Zakkai, and said unto him: "Rabbi, I am as great as you." Whereupon Rabbi Jochanan replied: "What do you mean thereby? Why, I am the Head of the Academy!" Maintaining his bearings, the worker countered: "And I, Rabbi, am an ordinary laborer, and for that reason I am just as important, for I am engaged in fulfilling man's needs."

The teachers of the Jabne Yeshiva, headed by Rabbi Jochanan ben Zakkai, have, indeed, taught the principle that "I am God's creature and so is my neighbor; my occupation is in the city and his—in the village; I go to work early and he—to his job; just as he cannot surpass me in my field, so can I not surpass him in his; it matters not whether one does big things or little things; the reward will be the same—provided his heart is directed to God."

Rabba, the great teacher of his generation, commanded his countless number of students to remain at home during certain seasons of the year, suspend study and teaching and occupy themselves solely with farming (Kiddushin 29a).

The Wise Men also taught this: "Study and learning unaccompanied by physical labor, leads to naught and nets only sin" (Aboth II, 2).

The worker's wage must be paid him the selfsame day, and the worker is privileged to leave his place of employment at any time, without incurring any loss, while the employer may not enjoy this privilege under any circumstances. The worker may even change his mind in mid-day (Baba Metzia 77a).

The employer must also disclose, verbally, what he will serve the worker as food, for the worker is a privileged character. Our Rabbis taught this: "Thou ought treat thy employees as well as thou treat thyself; thou must not eat cake while he eats bread; thou must not drink aged wine while he drinks fresh wine; thou ought not sleep upon soft pillows while he sleeps upon a straw sack."

He who engages workmen and orders them to start early or continue late, in a place where they have the custom not to start early or continue late, is not permitted to compel them to exceed the usual hours of labour. Where it is the custom to feed the workmen he must feed them; where it is the custom to supply them with a dessert after the meal, he must do so; all should be according to the practice of the district (Baba Metziah, chapter VII, Mishna 1).

The porters engaged by Rabba bar Bar Chanah broke a cask of wine belonging to him, and as a penalty he took their coats from them. They went and complained to Rab who ordered him to restore their garments. He asked, "Is that the law?" Rab replied, "It is, for it is written (Proverbs II, 20), 'That thou mayest walk in the way of good men.' " He gave them back their coats. The porters then said, "We are poor and have toiled throughout the day and are hungry; we are destitute." Rab said to him, "Go and pay their wages." He asked, "Is that the law?" He replied, "Yes, for it is written (Proverbs II, 20), 'And keep the paths of the righteous' " (Baba Metziah 83a).

In order to guard the workers against a money-greedy employer, the Talmud established the hard-and-fast rule of "Priority Right" for the laborer, which vests in him tremendous power, in the eyes of the Judges. The prevailing principle is: "In controversies with his employer, the worker must have the upper hand."

Displaying prejudice against the worker is prohibited. "For he is a poor man and, for his wages, he 'risks his life.' " As the Gemara says (Baba Metziah, 113b): "Why, if not for wages, does the worker climb upon a high ladder to build a house, or upon a tree to collect the fruit—in the face of danger of his falling and losing his life?"

The Laborer engaged by the day collects his wages during the night that ensues; if engaged by the night he collects them during the day that ensues; if engaged by the hour he collects them during the ensuing day or night; if engaged by the week or month or year or period of seven years, he collects his wages during the day of his discharge. Should his term end in the daytime or during the night, he collects the very day of his discharge (Baba Metziah, chapter IX, Mishna 10).

The worker's wages and the prompt payment thereof are here formulated with the greatest clarity. This decree embraces, too, another vital point: no differentiation is made between the Jewish and the non-Jewish wage-earner. The working class is here, in solidarity, a complete entity.

And the Torah decrees: "Thou shalt not rob a wage earner, an impoverished man amongst your brothers, or an outsider who is in your land and within your borders. Don't hold up his wages; he should receive his wage on time, at the end of his day's toil. He has hired himself out to you and this—because he is poor; see to it, therefore, that he not have to protest against you to God; if he does, the sin will then be yours."

CHAPTER NINETEEN

THE PERSECUTIONS OF THE TALMUD

ENEMIES WITHIN AND ENEMIES WITHOUT. THE ROLE OF THE APOSTATES AND INFORMERS. THE TRIALS AND PUBLIC BURNINGS. THE CHRISTIAN DEFENDERS AND JEWISH PERSEVERANCE.

PERSECUTIONS OF THE TALMUD BEGAN LONG BEFORE IT HAD been fully completed. Its first and most bitter enemy was undoubtedly Antiochus Epiphanes, who lived approximately in the second century before our era. Since then the Talmud has had to contend against enemies both from within and from without, all of them seeking to smother the spiritual creative development of the Jewish people. This is as true of the Sadducees, as it is of the Hellenists and the Apostates.

Since Antiochus Epiphanes, the Jews have had no respite and the persecutions against the Talmud—and this, of course, means against the Jews—have been ever more severe and frequent.

No sooner did he ascend the throne than the Roman emperor Hadrian (117-138 of our era) decreed that anyone receiving or giving ordination was to be executed. His successor, Antoninus Pius (138-161), at first renewed this injunction and only later, after a long and courageous intervention by the Nasi Simon ben Gamaliel and two Tanaim, Rabbi Simon ben Jochai and Rabbi Jose, was it somewhat lifted. In the third century the Roman emperors Constantine the First and Constantinus Chlorus issued harsh decrees which destroyed the yeshivas and drove from the land many of the Jewish scholars.

These persecutions in fact took place even during the first phase of the creation of the Talmud, when it was still being created, discussed, and studied orally. But the real troubles which have virtually continued down to our own day, began during the epoch of the Saboraim, when they sealed the Talmud and declared it immutable. In the year 553 Justinian prohibited the observance of the Jewish traditional Law and its interpretation, which was in fact a prohibition of the study of the Talmud.

In the Eastern countries, under Persian rule, the Talmud was also severely persecuted. Jews revolted frequently, actually fighting with weapons in their hands, and it took a long century of such struggles to enable the Jews to continue the web of the Talmud in all its intellectual brilliance.

The Talmud had its enemies inside the gate ever since the establishment of the Karaites in the second half of the eighth century. Their hatred for the Talmud was so violent that it concerned them not at all that because of their struggle Jews were forced to leave their own people and join the camp of their enemies.

Persecutions in the Middle Ages began in Germany, at the beginning of the eleventh century, when Wecelinus, a relative of the Holy Roman Emperor and the bishop of Duke Conrad, embraced the Jewish faith and condemned the Christian religion in writing.

The first public burning of the Talmud took place at the end of the year 1233. This case is particularly interesting, because it was caused by the quarrel between the adherents and the opponents of the Rambam (Maimonides). Solomon of Montpelier sought to condemn the Rambam's chief work, "The Guide to the Perplexed," as heretical, and in order to achieve his end he accepted the aid of the Dominican friars who had great power because of the Inquisition. The friars quite easily obtained an order from the resident Cardinal to search every Jewish home for copies of the Rambam's works. The search, whether fruitful or not, resulted in a public burning in Paris of 12,000 religious books.

In 1239 Pope Gregory IX issued a decree to confiscate the Talmud. A year later the stringency of the decree was increased, it was circulated to all the bishops of France, England, Castile, Aragon, and Portugal, and it at the same time censured them for their laxity in carrying out the original decree. Many countries and provinces ignored the decree, but in France, where the weak-minded Louis IX then reigned, it was carried out with the utmost severity, the penalty of disobedience sometimes being as high as death.

This particular persecution began, as usual, through the denunciations of an apostate Jew. In 1225 a Jew by the name of Donin, who lived in La Rochelle, France, began to oppose the authority of the Talmud. As a consequence, the Parisian rabbi and chief of the local yeshiva, Rabbi Jehiel ben Joseph, excommunicated him. For ten years Donin thus remained excommunicated, but nevertheless considered himself a part of the Jewish community. Suddenly, however, he embraced Christianity and became a friar of the Franciscan Order, changing his name to Nicholas de Rupella. He soon began to incite the crusaders against the Jews living in Britany, and as a result of his activities 3,000 Jews perished and more than 500 forsook Judaism. In 1238 he visited Rome and there made a written denunciation of the Talmud to Pope Gregory IX. This piece of infamous literature contained thirty-five citations from the Talmud purportedly hostile to the Christian religion, as interpreted and misinterpreted by Donin.

The French Jews realized that this incident was the beginning of a series of persecutions and therefore decided to defend themselves. They demanded an open trial and the French king willingly granted their request.

On the 25th of June, 1240 an open trial took place in the king's palace. The Jews were represented by their greatest scholars, the authors of the Tosaphoth, Rabbi Jehiel ben Joseph, Rabbi Moses of Kusi, Rabbi Samuel ben Solomon, and Rabbi Judah ben David. The Christians were represented by a large number of learned bishops headed by the apostate Jew and informer. The trial was conducted by the king, Louis IX, and the Queen-mother, Blanche. Both were pious Catholics, but the queen was apparently honest and sincere and never allowed the apostate Donin to treat the Jewish scholars with disrespect.

The chroniclers of the trials have given us a vivid picture of the event, of which two dramatic incidents stand out especially. The first incident took place when Rabbi Jehiel refused to take an oath. The informer seized upon this and tried to argue that this signifies that Jews do not intend to tell the truth. But Rabbi Jehiel asserted that a Jew following the precepts of the Torah would never on any account tell a lie. The Queen liked this courageous and proud stand and she therefore absolved Rabbi Jehiel from taking an oath.

The second incident took place when the informer attempted to prove that the Talmud forbids help to a Christian and specified that he must be treated as a lower being. Rabbi Jehiel then opened the Gemara (Gittin 61a) and read the famous precept: "Needy gentiles are to be fed, along with needy Jews; sick gentiles are to be visited, along with sick Jews; and dead gentiles are to be buried, along with dead Jews."

Rabbi Jehiel thus achieved a great victory for the defense, but it goes without saying that the judgment had already been made and determined upon beforehand. Two years later the Talmud was publicly burned and the study of the Talmud was completely prohibited.

Only Rabbi Jehiel was questioned at the trial. The other rabbis were kept in solitary confinement so that they would not be able to communicate with each other. Several questions were put to Rabbi Judah of Melun, but since he gave the same answers as Rabbi Jehiel his interrogation soon ceased. It is interesting to observe that the local archbishop, Walter Cornutus of Sena, strongly interceded in behalf of the Jews and at first stayed the burning of the Talmud. But he soon died and the enemies of the Jews got the upper hand. They convinced the king that the archbishop's death was God's punishment and the king then renewed his edict to burn the books.

For many years afterwards the French Jews continued to observe the day upon which the Talmud was burned as a general fast day. In commemoration of this tragic day the Maharam,

Rabbi Meir of Rothenburg, composed the well known threnody, "Ask ye who have been burned in fire."

Once a beginning had been made in burning books this barbarism was soon repeated often afterwards. Only two years later a new pope, Innocent IV, gave permission to burn the Talmud anew. Thus in May, 1244, 12,000 religious books were again gathered in a heap and burned publicly.

It is apparent, however, that the Jewish people were not entirely frightened by these events and always managed to conceal a large number of books. This became evident three years later, after a most thorough search. Gemaras were then found hidden in wells, in the ground, in trees. Many of these books were partly burned, evidently having been snatched right out of the fire.

On August 12, 1247, the pope asked 40 Christian scholars to study the Jewish religious books for the purpose of determining whether they contained any hostility to Christians or the Christian religion. One year later, Albertus Magnus, the head of this scholarly commission, reported that the Talmud is full of insults to Christianity. Thereupon twenty wagon loads of books were once more publicly burned.

In 1255 Pope Innocent IV again decreed the burning of the Talmud and severely prohibited the study of the Talmud, even orally. It is interesting to notice that just then Rabbi Samuel ben Solomon of Falaise edited and published the Tosephoth. He did not have the Talmud before him, but he was a genius for memorizing and was able to quote all the pertinent parts of the Talmud from memory. At this time too there was a clandestine yeshiva in Paris with about 300 students, and Rabbi Ezekiel taught them the Talmud orally. Later Rabbi

Ezekiel was harshly persecuted and had to flee to Palestine in great poverty.

In August, 1263 the king of Aragon decreed that the Jews must delete from the Talmud all objectionable passages or to allow a censorship appointed by him to do it.

In 1264, another apostate Jew, Pablo Christiani of Montpelier, induced Pope Clement IV to confiscate the Talmud and allow a commission of Franciscans and Dominicans to study it and render judgment. Pablo Christiani himself delivered this decree to the Spanish and Portuguese kings, which they carried out religiously. The Bishop of Barcelona thus became the permanent head of a commission to censor the Talmud and make the necessary alterations.

But the apostate Pablo Christiani was still dissatisfied, and he managed to arrange a debate between himself and the Ramban, Rabbi Moses ben Nachman (Nachmanides), under the supervision of King James. The Ramban induced the king to allow him to speak freely. When the apostate began to bombard him with excerpts from the Scriptures purporting to show that Jesus is the Messiah, the Ramban refuted them clearly and cogently. Furthermore, the Ramban pointed out that the question at issue is not whether Jesus is the Messiah but whether he is God or God's only begotten son. And turning to the king he said:—

"My lord king, you were born a Christian and educated under the tutelage of the Church. It is therefore most natural that you should imbibe the faith of your parents and teachers and sincerely believe in the divinity of Jesus. Moreover, because of this education it is pleasing to your ears to hear your priests speak about this. Your faith, however, cannot be accepted on a rational basis, since it goes against human nature. It is impossible for me to conceive that God, the creator of everything, should enter the belly of a Jewish maiden, lie there for nine months and then be born again as a small child. This child then grows up, is handed over to his prosecutors, sentenced to death, crucified, resurrected, and ascends to heaven whence he came."

The Ramban himself described this debate in his "Milchamoth Chobah" (War of Duty), and gives all the questions put to him and his answers in detail. The king was rather pleased with these bold answers and even gave him a gift of 300 gold pieces. Nevertheless he ordered some books to be burned and others to be revised. The Pope, on the other hand, ordered all Jews in Aragon to hand over their books to the Inquisition.

In 1299 and again in 1309 the Talmud was burned publicly in France. The then reigning king, Philip the Fair, did not content himself merely with burning the books but granted the right to the Inquisition to destroy the Talmud once and for all.

Louis, the son of Philip the Fair, allowed in 1315 the exiled Jews to return to France, but the Talmud was nevertheless still prohibited. Encouraged by this continued prohibition, the Inquisition again made house to house searches and succeeded in ferreting out two wagon loads of religious books which it proceeded to burn.

In 1322, on the order of Pope John XII, a public burning of all religious books took place. This was accompanied by a massacre in which thousands of Jews perished.

In 1380 another apostate Jew appeared upon the historical scene, Pedro Alphonso by name, who induced Charles II of Navarre to cause to prohibit the reciting of the benediction "Blessed be Thou that ye have not made me an unbelieving and paganistic gentile" from the Hebrew prayer book, or to reply with the refrain "blessed be He and blessed be His name, amen." Punishment for anyone saying these prayers was to be one hundred lashes. The king also ordered certain parts of the Talmud and other Hebrew books to be deleted.

Another apostate, Geronimo de Santa Fe, who was the personal physician of Benedict XIII, induced the succeeding Pope Martin V to burn the Talmud and prohibit the Jews from studying it.

In 1442 the pope deprived the Jews of all their rights and prohibited all Hebrew books except the Bible. In 1490 the chief inquisitor Torquemada even burned the Bible itself.

These constant persecutions evoked an intense interest on the part of many Christian scholars to study the Talmud and Hebrew lore. Among the Christians, particularly among the clergy there were many great scholars who knew Hebrew thoroughly, as well as Aramaic and Chaldaic. In the course of years an entire class of scholars arose who studied Hebrew literature from original sources. Nevertheless, the Jews did not derive any comfort or any lessening of persecutions from this study. On the contrary, it only brought more and greater persecutions.

A thousand years passed until a Christian arose who became a sincere defender of the Jews, a Christian who was himself severely persecuted for his beliefs, but never flinched. This

Christian was Johannes Reuchlin who lived in an age (1455-1522) when Humanism was spreading throughout Europe.

Germany in this period was split up into hundreds of small states, all of them ruled by despotism and tyranny. The masses of the people were extremely backward and under the influence of a superstitious church. Under such conditions the situation of the Jews was unbearable, and every day brought new harsh decrees and persecutions.

It was at this time that the apostate Jew, John Pfefferkorn, a butcher in a small town in Moravia, who had been imprisoned for some time because of some thefts, appears upon the historical scene. There has been conjecture that he became a Christian simply in order to get out of jail. He immediately applied for the protection of the Dominicans and began to publish attacks and libels against the Jews and Judaism.

The clergy, of course, supported these attacks, since they were hoping thus to strengthen their hold upon the people, a hold which was beginning to weaken. In Cologne there existed at this time a tribunal of the Inquisition and its chief, Jacob Von Hoogstraten, was bent on making a public burning of the Talmud. The clergy as a whole wished to force the Jews to adopt Christianity or be driven out of the country.

Pfefferkorn wrote a number of libelous books against the Jews. His first work "Das Judenspiegel" (The Jewish Mirror), was published in 1507, obviously for the purpose of inducing the government to establish local inquisitions under the supervision of the Dominicans. At first his writings, as well as those of the Dominicans, achieved little success. Later however the sister of the Emperor Maximillian induced the government to grant permission to Pfefferkorn to search Jewish homes and to confiscate Hebrew books. The decree provided that a priest and two members of the magistracy must be present at every visitation. It was easy enough to get members of the Magistracy, but it was far more difficult to induce priests to participate in these house to house raids. One possible reason for this is that the Archbishop of Mayance, probably because of envy, specifically forbade the clergy to participate. Although Pfefferkorn and his gang did not achieve universal success, he nevertheless managed to create a good deal of trouble for the Jews and to confiscate many Hebrew books.

The Jews protested vehemently and used all their influence to reach the Emperor and the highest Imperial courts with their protestations. As a result a priest, John Reuchlin, was appointed to study the confiscated volumes in order to find out whether they really contained insults to Christians and Christianity. Reuchlin was then in his ripe years and was already well known for his erudition in Hebrew. He had even published a book on Hebrew grammar, as well as a eulogy of the study of Hebrew, written in the form of an argument. In the latter book, incidentally, he criticized the Vulgate translation of the Bible, pointing out many errors and mistranslations.

On October 10th, 1510, Reuchlin published his report, a warm defense of the Hebrew books. He specifically denied that the Talmud was harmful to Christianity. On the contrary, he said, the Talmud, Zohar, and other Hebrew books have a great theological and scientific use. The only book which he recommended burning was an anonymous scroll. "The Birth of Jesus," which had circulated among the Jews at the beginning of the Middle Ages. On the other hand, he recommended the burning of all Christian books and pamphlets against the established Church.

Reuchlin's report evoked the stern anger of the Dominicans and they began to persecute him. The Chief Inquisitor, Hoogstraten, put Reuchlin on trial and would undoubtedly have executed him if not for the intervention of the Archbishop Urial von Gemingen, who annulled the judgment of the Inquisition.

The Humanist Reuchlin was at that time also supported by the scholars of the "New Learning," Luther, Ulrich von Hutten, Melanchton, Erasmus, and Franz von Sickingen. It is noteworthy that in 1520 Pope Leo X allowed the inventor and printer Leo Bomberg of Venice to publish and distribute the Talmud. In the same year Reuchlin also published an important work on the Cabala, and again emphasized the essential sanity of Jewish wisdom and knowledge.

Nevertheless, the enemies of the Jewish people did not rest and despite many failures they finally induced the new Pope, Julius III, to renew an old edict requiring the destruction of the Talmud. On September 9th, 1553, a public burning took place in Rome of untold numbers of Hebrew books collected in Barcelona, Venice, Romagna, and Pesaro. On May 29th, 1554, another public burning of Hebrew religious books took place in Rome and in Ancona. In 1557 a public burning took place in all the papal states. These public burnings became an annual event until 1559, when Pope Pius IV established a press in the Vatican and himself published a complete edition of the Talmud with all the exegetical writings. But despite that fact, in the very same year confiscations and public burnings took place in many countries and provinces. In 1569

Cardinal Carlo Borromeo destroyed the Hebrew library in Cremona, burning its entire contents, about 12,000 volumes.

In 1581, with the permission of Pope Gregory XIII a new edition of the Talmud containing a number of changes made by apostate Jews was published in Basle. In 1592 a new Pope, Clement VII, again issued an edict prohibiting the possession of any Hebrew books with the exception of the Bible and a Hebrew grammar.

In 1613 the head of the Inquisition permitted the possession of Rabbinical books in libraries under condition that they be kept separately and marked as prohibited literature. In 1618 Pope Sixtus V allowed the publication of the Talmud under a strict censorship. But one year later, after the death of this pope, the Inquisition declared the Talmud a harmful and useless work.

On February 25th, 1693, Pope Clement VII again renewed all the harsh decrees against the Jews in the papal states of Ancona and Avignon. The Jews were banished entirely from the other papal states, but found a shelter in the Duchy of Tuscany, ruled by Ferdinand, who allowed them to live in Pisa and to possess prohibited books. Nevertheless, the censors were mostly apostates and they succeeded in making things hard for the Jews.

With the beginning of the 18th century public burnings of the Talmud ceased, but confiscations still took place from time to time. Sometimes the Jews succeeded in reacquiring the books, but this cost much effort and money. The very last great burning took place in Poland on October 14, 1757, perpetrated by the Bishop Dembowski. This day has been commemorated among the Polish Jews as a general fast day.

The persecutions of the Talmud did not always result from alleged calumnies against Christianity contained therein; they did not even always take place because of hatred to the Jew or to the Jewish religion. Most of the time they were simply due to a need of despoiling the Jews of their wealth. But whatever the reasons, the Talmud, the greatest intellectual achievement of the Jewish people, shared the same fate as its creator. Both the Jew and the Talmud have always been persecuted and oppressed in a world of evil and violence; but both also possess immense spiritual strength which assures them an eternal future.

CHAPTER TWENTY

THE TALMUDIC CONCEPT OF ETHICS

THE SCHOOLS OF PHILOSOPHY. THE BIBLICAL CONCEPT. FAITH AND MORALITY. THE TRUE JUDAISTIC CONCEPTION.

ETHICS IS THE SCIENCE OF MORAL AND RIGHT BEHAVIOR, THE art of so regulating human conduct as to ensure happiness to all mankind, the system of thought which attempts to change the factors determining our manners and to introduce harmony and clarity in them.

Ethics is the compass for the individual and the group. The individual as well as the group must build his life on the foundation of human justice. No one can or should be judged by his strength, or physical vigor, riches or education, power or social position. The individual or the group is only as strong as the excellence of its system of ethics.

Ethics is essentially the teaching of human justice, the teaching of precepts that bind the individual to obligations that are not enforceable by law. Ethical obligations are not under the jurisdiction of a court, and no one can be punished for violating them. The individual himself is responsible for adhering to them, and they are entrusted to him alone.

It is almost superfluous to observe that concepts of ethics have not always been the same and have differed among various nations and times. What is right and moral among cannibals may be a most terrible crime in more civilized groups. In ancient Sparta it was a social duty to kill sick children and old people. Today this is accounted a crime in that country. Carnivals in ancient Rome were notorious for their licentious orgies, which were then considered perfectly moral and religious. Slavery, and the feudal system later, were both justified on religious and philosophical grounds.

Even in our own time there are deeds which in one country are considered moral and in another a crime. In Japan even to this date the "geishas," high-class prostitutes, are considered respectable members of society.

The various schools of philosophy believe, however, that ethical concepts are not completely arbitrary, and although they may often change they remain essentially the same. The Naturalist, the Intuitive, and the Hedonistic Schools all hold that beliefs are inborn in human nature and that it is by intuition that man knows what is right and what is wrong.

The ethical beliefs of Judaism are totally different. They are immutable and are independent of human will or intuition. The laws of right and wrong are universal, because they are determined by the will of God.

Every fact of Jewish history, the entire Jewish system of beliefs and traditions, the very mode of living of the Jew the world over is evidence of a positive Jewish system of ethics on a high level.

Even from the purely human viewpoint, in the light of everyday experience, the Bible and the Talmud are the greatest and most glorious works of ethics; this is true as regards their prismatic clarity, as well as their historical significance, their many humanitarian laws, and their great influence.

When the foundations were being laid for the future world city of Rome on the hills of the Tiber, the prophets of Israel had already been prophesying about the fate and future of nations. At the present time, when we are in possession of the ancient literatures of the Egyptians, the Assyrians, and the Babylonians, we are able to judge that the truth of the Bible has no equal; and that the most magnificent and splendid works of other peoples were created under the influence of Jewish ethics.

In their spiritual rise the Jews apprehended three fundamental truths: The belief in one God, the belief in a moral and ethical life, and the hope for the salvation and liberation of all mankind.

The Jewish faith in God is impregnated with spirituality and profound understanding, but is divorced from reason. The Rambam asserts that we can apprehend divinity only by negation: God is not limited, He has no beginning nor end, He is not corporeal nor has He any resemblance to a body.

Although it is impossible for us to apprehend the Divinity with our ordinary senses, our senses nevertheless are inspired and influenced by our belief and faith in God. All our concepts are imbued with the thought of God. In the Jew reason and feeling are not antagonistic forces, but flow both from the same source.

The great poet Solomon Ibn Gabirol clearly expresses this synthesis which is the strength of Judaism, and he expressed this synthesis and clarity in his philosophic work "Mekor

Chaim" (The Fountain of Life) which was utilized by the great philosophers of the Middle Ages, Albertus Magnus and St. Thomas of Aquinas; strangely enough, or perhaps not so strangely, Ibn Gabirol expressed this synthesis in the poetic rhythms of his immortal poem "Kether Malchuth" (Kingdom's Crown).

It is the belief in a monotheistic God which is the source that has given purpose and sense to Jewish existence. The illimitability and infinity of the Divinity have raised us above the momentary and accidental and have linked us to eternity and to the infinite universe.

Faith is for the Jew obligatory and absolutely binding. Without faith there is no Divinity and the bond between God and man is sundered. Reason and logic, system and doctrines will not help without faith, because reason, system, doctrine are not positive. Logical proofs can always be controverted by other equally logical proofs.

The Jew submits himself as the slave of God, and it is precisely because of this bondage that he becomes the freest of all men. By his belief that God's will reigns above everyone and everything, that God is the supreme ruler, and that His undivided guardianship protects each one of us at every moment of our existence, the Jew is freed from all the dark and sinister forces which hover about him.

Faith in God demands of the Jew a disciplined moral life, regulated by the precepts concerning the relations between man and God and man and man. Only the transgressions against God can be forgiven, but not the transgressions against man. The duty subsisting between man and man is absolute and must be observed absolutely, because this duty flows from the very faith in Divinity.

Faith and morality, belief and good deeds are all closely bound together. According to the Talmud morality without faith is an impossibility. This is clearly expressed in the Psalms (X, 4): "The wicked man says in his heart: There is no God, therefore do we commit wicked deeds."

The moral duty considered from the purely human standpoint therefore is, according to this concept not sufficiently strong to prevent men from doing evil, because the tendency to do evil is far stronger than the tendency towards social responsibility. When man is sole master over himself he will seldom choose the righteous path. The desire to satisfy the immediate want will always conquer the desire to serve the community. Often men will doubt altogether whether it is really necessary to sacrifice himself for some principle of social responsibility.

The Jews could not accept the ideal god of the Greek philosopher Aristotle, a god who is bound like a slave to his own creation and is incapable of changing anything. The essence of our life is not complete harmony in the present, but continuous creation and recreation.

The foundation of Greek philosophy is the belief that everything is determined by unalterable law and has existed from the beginning of time. Such a belief admits no longing for Divinity. Even the God of reason desiccates our life and leaves us without feeling, without heart, without passion, without longing, without faith.

The covenant made with Abraham was not a rational and logical covenant with God, but one that grew out of sentiment and emotion. A rational pact may change as soon as reason tells us that we are not obliged to keep it. Reason would have told Abraham not to make the covenant, because God had originally shown him the difficult path which his children would have to traverse. But Abraham made the pact, because it was dictated by the unity of magnetic forces which he could not withstand, forces which desired and longed to become merged.

In Judaism it was not the Aristotelian concept of the deity that held sway, nor even the philosophy of the Rambam, which very brilliantly attempted to achieve a reconciliation between Jewish religion and the philosophy of Aristotle. In Judaism it was the philosophy behind the covenant of Abraham that finally conquered and maintained its supremacy, and this covenant is joined by all those who feel the presence of the Divinity, although they may not be able to perceive it with their reason.

Our modern scholars, such as Ahad Haam, Klausner, and Newmark attempt to link up ethics with various philosophical and scientific systems, and they have succeeded in creating a system which is strictly scientific and logical, but without soul, without heart, without feeling. One of them wishes to reconcile ethics with Spencer's philosophy; Klausner does so with Kant; Newmark with the Bible critics. In addition, they are, perhaps against their better intentions, very dogmatic and wish authoritatively to lay down the foundations of morality. But what they all lack is the mystical, the poetical, the purely religious element. Their morality is a morality for its own sake. But where is the prophetic element which demands ethical justice even from society?

This is undoubtedly the inevitable error of all philosophers and metaphysicians. To them reason is the highest degree of perfection; abstract reason, but reason nevertheless. Perhaps even the Rambam committed the same error in his conception of God, when he said: "He is knowledge, he is the knower, and the One Who is known about." Everything thus revolves around reason and knowledge.

The true Judaistic conception is that of the Rabbi from Ladi: "The essence of God is that insomuch as He is above corporeality, He is at the same time above spirituality."

The concepts of democracy, freedom, equality, and fraternity are found first in the Torah. If there is such a thing as ethics, they are rooted in Jewish life, in its very innermost being and essence. Jewish ethics, in their immense scope and vast conception, were the first to burgeon upon our earth, they were the very first foundation of civilized life.

It was the Talmud which gave Jewish ethics their breadth and depth of conception. The Jews derived their views upon morality and individual responsibility, their ideas concerning their relations to man and society, Jew and non-Jew, from the Talmud. The main foundations have always been universal. Love and justice for all of humanity. This is best expressed in the maxim: love thy neighbor as thyself.

The Christian religion, too, proclaimed this ethical principle. But there this principle was never so deeply rooted nor so universally carried out. It remained merely an abstraction which had very little to do with actual life.

The concepts of man and the universe, their attributes and ends, were never the same among the other nations as in the Jewish religion. On the contrary, their concepts were always in contradiction to each other, and perhaps that accounts for their virulent hatred of the Jews.

In his "*Humanity as Religion*" Samuel Hirsch states: "The term 'man,' as it is comprehended by the Jews is entirely unknown to the world. Even the Greeks, next to the Jews the greatest creative nation in the world, had but a hazy idea of what the Jews included under the term man and humanity. The Greeks, who bequeathed to the world the science of esthetics, divided mankind into pleasure seekers and vulgar barbarians, whom it was a virtue to enslave. The Jews were the first and only people to develop clearly and comprehensively the idealistic view of man and mankind. The Jews were the first to regard labor as sacred, to put aside a day of rest, to proclaim complete freedom and equality, and to pray for peace among nations."

The above quotation makes crystal clear the battle of ideas which the Talmud so bitterly conducted aganst Hellenism, never allowing any compromise between Mt. Sinai and Mt. Olympus.

According to the Talmud, the belief in God and in His so-called attributes is the foundation and edifice containing the entire Jewish spiritual lore. The apprehension of the Divinity does not grow out of human ethical concepts, but because human sentiments are an integral part of the Divinity and are fundamentally rooted, in and linked with, human consciousness.

The Jewish concept is that ethics are the divine spirituality, the mark of God with which man was created. In distinction to that is the Greek concept that ethics are a result of purely human rationalism. Judaism demands spirituality, while Hellenism demands pure reason. Judaism believes in a world of deeds, while Hellenism believes in a world of thought. Judaism is soul and sentiment, Hellenism is mind and reason. Judaism emphasizes cleanliness, Hellenism emphasizes beauty. Judaism teaches morality, Hellenism teaches art. Judaism is holiness, Hellenism is lust. Judaism is ethics, Hellenism is esthetics.

The first face-to-face encounter with Greek thought took place about two thousand years ago when Jews were still living on their own soil and stubbornly fighting for the existence of their own culture and way of life. It was at this time that Simon the Just, the High Priest (according to other sources it was Onias), met Alexander the Great, the first Greek who attempted to spread his sovereignty and culture throughout other dominions. At this encounter the High Priest was completely victorious. The Jewish spirit conquered Greek power. Nevertheless, a spark of Hellenism remained within the aristocracy of the people. With the rise of the Hasmoneans, however, these remnants were rapidly erased.

But Hellenism left a deep impress upon the further course of history. Its belief that morality and ethics are completely divorced from faith and are not a consequence of a belief in God placed the main emphasis upon man and prepared the soil for an uncontrolled individualism.

In the idealistic systems of philosophy man became the creator of world, the foundation and the source of being. The universe exists only through man and with man. The universe is an image of man and only as an idea of man does it have a place in universal creation. Even political absolutism fed upon these idealistic systems of philosophy.

The totalitarian governments are also an extension of this concept of the absolute ego—a morality which serves only man and his own materialistic and physical aims.

Completely different is the Judaic ethical concept. Not man but God is the central point of existence. It is not man's will which prevails, but the will of God. Not man's justified or unjustified passions and caprices must be fulfilled, but the eternal ethical laws of God, the laws of morality and justice, of truth and equity, peace and brotherhood.

It is the passion to achieve divine perfection which is so often heard in the voice of our consciousness. It is the part given to us by God which creates the Jewish personality and molds his essence.

Jewish ethics draw their nourishment solely from the sphere of faith and are based exclusively upon religion. The basis of Jewish morality is the attribute of a perfect and integrated Divinity.

The Hebrew God is not merely a judge and a king above kings Who possesses the qualities of justice and pity, but also a guide in the life of every individual.

The great prophets of Israel, those giants of ethics and morality, never speak in their own name, but in the name of God: "Thus saith God." This leitmotif does not cease with the prophets. It runs through the Talmud and the Midrashim, finds its perfection in the later religious literature, and is revived in the Chassidic literature.

The Talmud apparently believed that without religious influence morality and ethics are divested of their fundamental basis. The Talmud also believed that no logical theory is capable of inducing an individual or group to do that which may be against their own immediate interests.

The modern world reduces the value of moral laws to the level of mutual defense and aid, as for instance the laws concerning street traffic. But the prophets and the Talmud consider it far too dangerous for man to observe ethical precepts merely because they are for the good of the community. It is far easier for man to enjoy that which is immediately available than to think of the welfare and security of the group. This is seen in the observance of the same traffic laws. Automobile drivers pay little regard to speed limits and rush as if they were pursued by demons.

Jewish religion is far more practical and realistic. It seeks its nourishment not from the source of good and evil, of security and danger. According to the Jewish religion observance of ethical laws is necessary solely for the perfection of human character and the uplifting of the spirit. Jews have always based their ethics not upon reason and logic, but upon divine authority and divine perfection.

But Judaism is not merely ethics, nor social betterment, nor even a politico-national feeling, nor a religious philosophy, but all of these taken together as a whole. All these are included in Judaism as integral and necessary elements, because all of these are attributes of the Divinity and are influenced and illuminated by the infinite glory of God Himself.

According to the Talmud the desire to acquire ethical standards of conduct comes not from man, but from the portion of the Divinity that is found within man. The desire comes from its primeval source, which is the Power of Creation and the Power of Domination. Without God ethics are without essence and foundation, without influence and reality, without system and permanence.

The Talmudic concept is in sharp contradiction to the old and new religions and therefore the consequences are also quite different. Every religion had consequences of world import, but these led to negative attitudes to life itself. The majority of the world's religions deal primarily with life in heaven and with the salvation of the sinful soul. The consequences are therefore on the one hand resignation and on the other—animalism and brutality. The entire world process cannot be understood unless we take into consideration the influence upon life of the teaching concerning the attributes of the gods. The Jews are unique in the world in this respect. The attributes of God are clearly and in detail listed in the Torah, in the Talmud, and in Jewish philosophic literature. God is infinite, sacred, and without analogy. God is not a part of nature and is not corporeal. God is full of pity and kindness. Man has been created in God's image, and as God is full of pity, so must man be. "You must be as God."

It is this which has created Jewish optimism, Jewish drive and energy, and which has given aim and purpose in life: to achieve divine perfection.

The central metaphysical principle of Christianity is that God sent His son down to the sinful world in order to save mankind. Jesus was crucified because the world is evil and wicked and the soul has been destined to suffer in hell. The entire Christian religion revolves around the assumption that man is wicked and depraved.

That is the apparent reason why the Christian world denies the force of Jewish ethics. Dominated by the belief that only Jesus can save the universe and mankind, it finds it difficult or it is unwilling to understand that Judaism is pure ethics. Others are willing to compromise a little and admit that Judaism does have a spark of ethics, but that spark is applicable to Jews only. Indeed, such people argue, the Jewish religion places upon the Jew an obligation not to apply his ethical principles to a non-Jew.

Jewish ethics may be seen clearly expressed in the law, as it was taught in the courts of law from Moses right until Hofetz Haim. This law, as embodied in both the Written and Unwritten Torah, represents a system of just laws which in their humanitarianism surpass anything existing in the legislation and procedure of any other nation.

Needless to say, Jewish law was never so soft and self-abnegating as the sickly and sentimental Christian maxim of giving the left cheek when one is slapped on the right. Whenever necessary, the Jewish law said: "Let the law cleave a mountain." But even in its rigidity the Law was always human. Because of the desire to preserve the Jewish ethical principles the Law was surrounded with a network of barriers and restrictions which introduced mitigation even in the harshest laws. Very often these mitigations entirely nullified the law itself.

The Talmud places emphasis upon the justness of the law. The Gemara (Sanhedrin, 7a) states: "Every judge who does not issue verdicts in accordance with the true law causes the Divinity to leave the Jews." And commenting on the Biblical passage: "Judges and officers shalt thou appoint unto thyself," the Midrash says: "God says, when you observe justice and the law I become uplifted."

In *Aboth* (I, 18) Rabbi Simon ben Gamaliel says: "The world is based upon three elements: Truth, justice and peace." And the Gemara interprets this as follows: "All three elements are merely one. When justice is done, then we also have truth and peace."

In connection with love of mankind the *Pesikto* states: "If one hates a man, whoever he may be and to what nation he may belong, it is as if he hated God Himself."

APPENDIX

THE COURSE OF TRADITION

	Jewish calendar	Civil calendar
Moses receives the Torah on Mount Sinai	2448	1313 B.C.E.
Joshua and Elazar	2488	1273 B.C.E.
Pinchas and the Elders	2516	1245 B.C.E.
Othniel	2566	1195 B.C.E.
Ehud	2636	1125 B.C.E.
Shamgar	2636	1125 B.C.E.
Barak-Deborah	2676	1085 B.C.E.
Gideon and son	2719	1042 B.C.E.
Tola	2742	1021 B.C.E.
Yair	2764	999 B.C.E.
Jephtah	2787	976 B.C.E.
Avtzan (Boaz)	2793	970 B.C.E.
Eilon	2803	960 B.C.E.
Abdon	2811	952 B.C.E.
Samson	2830	933 B.C.E.
Eli and his Beth Din	2830	933 B.C.E.
Samuel and his Beth Din	2870	893 B.C.E.
David and his Beth Din	2884	879 B.C.E.
Achiya of Shiloh and his Beth Din	2924	839 B.C.E.
Elijah the Prophet	2962	801 B.C.E.
Elisha the Prophet	3047	716 B.C.E.
Yehoyoda the Priest	3055	708 B.C.E.
Zechariah, his son	3070	693 B.C.E.
Hoshea ben Beeri	3090	673 B.C.E.
Amos	3110	653 B.C.E.
Isaiah	3140	623 B.C.E.
Michah	3160	603 B.C.E.
Joel	3190	573 B.C.E.

	Jewish calendar	Civil calendar
Nahum	3240	523 B.C.E.
Habakuk	3254	509 B.C.E.
Zephaniah	3280	483 B.C.E.
Jeremiah	3316	447 B.C.E.
Baruch ben Neriah	3350	413 B.C.E.
Ezra and his Beth Din	3370	393 B.C.E.
Simon the Just	3400	363 B.C.E.
Antignos of Socho	3460	303 B.C.E.
Jose ben Joezer and Jose ben Jochanan	3500	263 B.C.E.
Joshua ben Perachya and Nitai the Arbelite	3560	203 B.C.E.
Judah ben Tabbai and Simon ben Shetah	3621	142 B.C.E.
Shemaiah and Abtalion	3722	41 B.C.E.
Hillel and Shamai	3728	35 B.C.E.
Rabban Simon and Rabbi Jochanan ben Zakkai	3768	5 C.E.
Rabban Gamaliel	3800	37 C.E.
Rabban Simon ben Gamaliel	3810	47 C.E.
Rabban Gamaliel	3828	65 C.E.
Rabban Simon ben Gamaliel	3881	108 C.E.
Rabbi Judah Hanasi	3910	137 C.E.
Rav, Mar Samuel and R. Jochanan	3979	206 C.E.
R. Huna, R. Judah, R. Nachman and R. Kahana	4010	237 C.E.
Rabba and R. Joseph	4060	287 C.E.
Abaye and Rabba	4085	312 C.E.
Rav Ashi and Rabina	4127	354 C.E.
Compilation of Talmud	4260	387 C.E.

THE TANAIM

LIST OF TEACHERS QUOTED OR REFERRED TO IN THE TEXT OF THE MISHNA

PRE-TANAITIC (from circa 200 B.C. to circa 10 C.E.):

Abtalion
Admon
Akabya ben Mehalaleel
Antigonus of Socho
Baba ben Buta
Ben Bag-Bag (Jochanan)
Ben-He-He
Chanan the Egyptian
*Hillel the Elder
Jochanan the High Priest
Jose ben Joezer
Jose ben Jochanan
Joshua ben Parachya
Judah ben Tabbai
Measha
Menachem
Nittai of Arbela
Onias the Circle-maker
Shamai the Elder
Shemaiah
Simeon ben Shetah
Simeon the Just.

FIRST GENERATION (circa 10 C.E. to circa 80 C.E.):

Ben Bukri
Dositheus of Kefar Yatma

* Indicates members of the Hillel dynasty who were presidents of the Sanhedrin.

Eleazar ben Dolai, Abba
*Gamaliel the Elder (Rabban)
Chananian ben Hezekiah
Chanina the Perfect
Jochana ben Gudgada
Jochanan ben Ha-Horani
Jochanan ben Zakkai
Joezer of the Birah
Jose Holi Kufri, Abba
Judah ben Bathyra
Menachem ben Signai
Nachum the Mede
Nachum the Scrivener
Nechunia ben Gudgada
School of Hillel
School of Shamai
*Simeon ben Gamaliel I
Simeon of Mizpah
Zechariah ben Ha-Kazzab
Zechariah ben Kabutal

SECOND GENERATION (circa 80 C.E. to circa 120 C.E.):

Ben Bathyra
Dosa ben Harkinas
Eleazar ben Arach
Eleazar ben Azariah
Eleazar ben Diglai
Eliezer ben Hyrcanus
Eliezer ben Jacob I
Eliezer ben Zadok I
*Gamaliel II
Chalafta
Chanina ben Dosa
Chanina ben Gamaliel
Hyrcanus of Kefar Etam
Jeshebab
Jose ben Chamin, Abba
Jose ben Meshullam

Jose ben Onias
Jose son of the Damascene
Jose the Priest
Joshua ben Bathyra
Joshua ben Chananiah
Joshua ben Hyrcanus
Nechunia ben Elimatham
Nechunia ben Ha-Kamah
Papias
Samuel the Younger
Saul ben Bathnith
Simeon ben Bathyra
Simeon ben Nathaniel
Simeon brother of Azariah
Simeon of Shezur
Simeon of Teman
Simeon son of the Perfect
Yakim of Haddar
Zadok

THIRD GENERATION (circa 120 C.E. to circa 140 C.E.):

Abtolemos
Akiba
Ben Azzai
Ben Nanos
Ben Zoma
Eleazar ben Hisma
Eleazar ben Judah
Eleazar ben Perata
Eleazar of Modiim
Elisha ben Abuyah
Chananiah ben Akashya
Chananiah ben Hakinai
Chananiah ben Teradion
Chanina ben Antigonus
Ilai
Ishmael ben Elisha
Jochanan ben Baroka

Jochanan ben Joshua
Jochanan ben Matthias
Jochanan ben Nuri
Jose ben Kisma
Jose the Galilean
Joshua ben Matthias
Judah ben Baba
Judah the Priest
Levitas of Jabneh
Mattithiah ben Cheresh
Nechemiah of Beth Deli
Simeon ben Akashya
Simeon ben Azzai
Simeon ben Nanos
Simeon ben Zoma
Tarfon

FOURTH GENERATION (circa 140 C.E. to circa 165 C.E.):

Abba Saul
Eleazar
Eleazar ben Jose
Eleazar ben Mattai
Eleazar ben Pilai
Eleazar ben Shammua
Eliezer ben Jacob II
Eliezer ben Zadok II
Chalafta ben Dosa
Chananiah ben Akabya
Chananiah of Ono
Ishmael ben Jochanan
Jacob
Jochanan the Sandalmaker
Jonathan
Joshua ben Karcha
Jose ben Ha-Hotef
Jose ben Chalafta
Judah ben Ilai
Meir

Menachem
Nehemiah
*Simeon ben Gamaliel II
Simeon ben Jochai

FIFTH GENERATION (circa 165 C.E. to circa 200 C.E.):
Abba Gorion
Dositheus ben Janai
Eleazar ben Simeon
Eleazar Ha-Kappar
Ishmael ben Jose
Yaddua the Babylonian
Jose ben Judah
Jose of Kefar Babli
*Judah Ha-Nasi
Judah ben Tema
Nathan the Babylonian
Nehorai
Phineas ben Yair
Simeon ben Eleazar
Simeon ben Chalafta
Simeon ben Menasya
Symmachos

SIXTH GENERATION (circa 200 C.E. to circa 220 C.E.):
Simeon ben Judah Ha-Nasi
*Gamaliel III

POST-TANAITIC (circa 240 C.E.):
Joshua ben Levi
Yannai

THE AMORAIM

LIST OF TEACHERS QUOTED OR REFERRED TO IN THE TEXT OF THE GEMARA

PALESTINIAN—

FIRST PERIOD (circa 219 C.E. to circa 279 C.E.):

Janai the Elder
Jonathan the Elder
Hoshaia the Elder
Levi bar Sisi
Chanina bar Chama
Hezekiah
Jochanan bar Nappecha
Simeon ben Lakish
Joshua ben Levi
Simlai

SECOND PERIOD (circa 279 C.E. to circa 320 C.E.):

Eleazar ben Pedat (Tiberias)
Ammi and Assi (Tiberias)
Chiyya bar Abba
Simeon bar Abba
Abbahu (Saesarea)
Zeira

THIRD PERIOD (circa 320 C.E. to circa 359 C.E.):

Jeremiah
Jonah (Tiberias)
Jose bar Zabda (Tiberias)

BABYLONIAN—

First Period (circa 219 C.E. to circa 257 C.E.):

Shila (Nehardea)
Abba Areca (Sura)
Mar Samuel (Nehardea)
Mar Ukba

Second Period (circa 257 C.E. to circa 320 C.E.):

Huna (Sura)
Judah ben Ezekiel (Pumbaditha)
Chisda (Sura)
Shesheth (Shilhi)
Nachman ben Jacob (Nehardea)
Rabba bar Bar-Chuna
Ulla ben Ishmael

Third Period (circa 320 C.E. to circa 375 C.E.):

Rabba bar Huna (Sura)
Rabba bar Nachmani (Pumbaditha)
Joseph bar Chiyya (Pumbaditha)
Abaye (Pumbaditha)
Rabba ben Joseph bar Chama (Mehuza)
Nachman ben Isaac (Pumbaditha)
Papa bar Chanan (Narash)

Fourth Period (circa 375 C.E. to circa 427 C.E.):

Ashi (Sura)
Amemar (Nehardea)
Zebid bar Oshaya (Pumbaditha)
Dimi bar Chanina (Pumbaditha)
Rafram I (Pumbaditha)
Kahana bar Tachlifa (Pumbaditha)
Mar Zutra (Pumbaditha)
Judah Mani ben Shalom
Eliezer ben Jose
Jose ben Abin
Tanchuma

Fifth Period (circa 427 C.E. to circa 468 C.E.):

Mar Yemar (Sura)
Ide bar Abin (Sura)
Mar bar Ashi (Sura)
Acha of Difta (Sura)
Rafram II (Pumbaditha)

Sixth Period (circa 468 C.E. to circa 500 C.E.):

Rabina bar Huna (Sura)
Jose (Pumbaditha)

CHRONOLOGICAL LIST OF THE GEONIM

SURA:

	Year
Mar R. ben Mar R. Huna	609
R. Hanina	—
Mar R. Huna	—
Mar R. Sheshua ben Tahlifa	—
Mar R. Hanina of Nehar Pekod	689
Mar R. Nehilai of Naresh	697
R. Jacob of Nehar Pekod	715
Mar R. Samuel (descendant of Amemar)	733
Mar R. Mari HaKohen of Nehar Pekod	751
Mar R. Aha	759
R. Yehudai ben Mar R. Nachman	760
R. Achunai Kahana ben Mar Papa	764
Mar R. Haninai Kahana ben Mar R. Huna	769
R. Mari HaLevi ben R. Mesharsheya	777
R. Bebai HaLevi ben Mar R. Abba	781
Mar R. Hilai ben Mar R. Mari	792
R. Jacob HaKohen ben Mar Mordecai	801
R. Abimai, brother of Mar R. Mordecai	815
Mar R. Zadok ben Mar R. Ashi	823
Mar R. Hilai ben Mar R. Hananiah	825
R. Kimoi ben Mar R. Ashi	829
R. Moses Kahana ben Mar Jacob	832
R. Kohen Zedek ben Mar Abimai	845
Mar R. Shalom ben Mar R. Boaz	849
R. Natronai ben Mar R. Hilai	853
Mar R. Amram ben Mar R. Sheshna	856
R. Nachshon ben Mar R. Zadok	874
R. Zemach ben Mar R. Chaim	882

SURA *(Continued)*:

	Year
Mar R. R. Malka	887
R. Hai ben Mar R. Nachshon	889
R. Hilai ben Natronai Gaon	896
R. Shalom ben Mar R. Mishael	904
R. Jacob ben Mar R. Natronai	911
R. Yom-Tob Kahana ben Mar R. Jacob	924
R. Saadia ben Mar Joseph	928
R. Joseph ben R. Jacob	942
R. Samuel HaKohen ben Hofni	died 1034

PUMBADITHA:

Mar ben R. Chanan of Isklya	589
Mar R. Mari ben Mar R. Dimi	609
Mar R. Chanina	—
Mar R. Chana	—
Mar R. Isaac	660
Mar R. Rabbah	—
Mar R. Bosai	—
Mar R. Huna Mari ben Mar R. Joseph	689
R. Chiyya of Meshan	—
Mar R. Rabya	—
Mar R. Natronai ben Mar Nehemiah	719
R. Judah	—
Mar R. Joseph Kitnai	739
Mar Samuel ben Mar R. Mar	748
R. Natroi Kahana ben Mar Achnai	—
Mar R. Abraham Kahana	—
R. Dodai ben Mar R. Nachman	761
R. Chanania ben R. Mesharsheya	767
R. Malka ben Mar R. Abba	771
Mar Rabba ben R. Dodai	773
R. Shinwai	—
R. Chaninai Kahana	782
Mar R. Huna ben Mar HaLevi	785
R. Manasseh ben Mar R. Joseph	788

PUMBADITHA *(Continued)*:

	Year
Mar R. Isaiah HaLevi	796
Mar R. Joseph ben Mar R. Shila	798
Mar R. Kahana ben Chaninai Gaon	804
Mar R. Abumai	810
Mar R. Joseph ben Mar R. Abba	814
Mar R. Abraham ben Mar R. Sherira	816
R. Joseph ben Mar R. Chiyya	828
Mar R. Isaac ben Mar Chanania	833
R. Joseph ben Mar R. Abba	839
R. Paltoi ben Mar R. Abaye	842
Mar R. Abbai Kahana ben R. Mar	858
R. Menachem ben Mar R. Joseph	859
R. Mattithiah ben Mar R. Rabbi	861
R. Abba ben Mar R. Ammi	869
Mar R. Zemach ben Mar Paltoi	872
Rab Hai ben R. Mar David	890
Mar R. Kimoi ben R. Achai	898
Yehudai ben Mar R. Samuel	906
R. Mebasser Kahana	918
R. Kohen Zedek Kahana	926
R. Zemach ben Mar R. Kafnai	935
Mar R. Chaniah ben Mar R. Yehudai	938
R. Aharon ben Mar R. Joseph	943
R. Nehemiah ben R. Kohen Zedek	961
R. Sherira	968
R. Hai	998

CHRONOLOGICAL LIST OF COMMENTATORS

SEFER MAFTEACH *(The Key-book)* by Nisim ben Jacob (died 1040).

RABBENU GERSHOM, by Gershom ben Judah (also called Gershom the Elder and The Light of the Diaspora). Born at Metz in 960, and died at Mayence in 1040.

RABBENU CHANANEL BEN HUSHIEL, Rabbi of Kairwan, Tunis, Africa. Born about 990; died in 1050. He wrote a commentary on the greater portion of the Talmud, and is often quoted as authority by later commentators.

HAI GAON BEN SHERIRA GAON (939-1038). His commentary is on the Mishna only.

RASHI, by Rabbenu Shlomoh Itzchaki (Solomon ben Isaac). Born at Troyes, France, in 1040; died there July 13, 1105. He wrote a commentary on almost the whole of the Talmud, which is printed in all editions thereof.

RASHBAM, by Rabbenu Samuel ben Meir (1085-1174).

RABBENU TAM, by Rabbi Jacob ben Meir Tam (1100-1171).

ISAAC BEN SAMUEL of Damperre; Tosaphoth to the treatise of Kiddushin.

JOSEPH IBN MIGASH; commentaries on the treatise of Shebuoth.

RAMBAM, by Rabbenu Moses ben Maimon (1194-1270); commentaries on the treatise of Rosh Hashanah.

ISAIAH DI TRANI; Tosaphoth to 21 treatises.

RAMBAN, by Rabbenu Moses ben Nachman (Nachmanides).

RASHBA, by Rabbenu Solomon ben Abraham of Spain (1235-1310).

MOSES BEN JACOB of Coucy, France; Tosaphoth (circa 1250).

ROSH, by Rabbenu Asher ben Jechiel (1250-1328).

RITBA, by Rabbenu Yom-Tov ben Abraham Ishbili (circa 1350).

CHOCHMATH SHLOMOH, by Solomon ben Jechiel Luria, head of the yeshiva at Lublin. Born at Brest-Litovsk in 1510; died at Lublin in 1573. His commentaries are appended to the later editions of the Talmud.

ATZMOTH JOSEPH, by Joseph Ibn Ezra (1591).

SHITAH M'KUBETZETH, by Bezalel Ashkenazi (1591).

MAHARSHA, by Samuel Edels of Lublin (1612).

MAGINEI SHLOMOH, by Joshua ben Solomon (1648).

MAHARAM SCHIFF, by Meir ben Jacob Schiff (1662).

MLECHETH YOM-TOV, by Yom-Tov Lipman Heller (1654).

PNAI YEHOSHUA, by Jacob Joshua ben Zvi-Hirsh of Cracow (1680-1756).

BETH JEHUDA, by Judah ben Nissan of Dassau (1698).

DIBREI SHMUEL, by Samuel Zerphathi of Amsterdam (1699).

ROSH YOSEPH, by Joseph ben Jacob of Amsterdam (1700).

EIN YAAKOV, by Jacob ben Joseph Rescher of Wilmersdorf (1729).

SHNOTH ELIYAHU, by Eliyahu ben Shlomoh, known as the Gaon of Vilno (1720-1797). He also wrote "Eliyahu Rabba," a commentary on the tractate of Teharoth, and "Hagahoth Hagra," a selection of glosses to the Talmud.

SHAAR YOSEPH, by Haim Joseph David Azulai (1756).

ROSH YOSEPH, by Joseph ben Meir Teumim (1756).

MISHNATH RABBI AKIBA EIGER, by Rabbi Akiba Eiger (1756).

AYELETH AHUVIM, by Aryeh Yehudah Loeb Teomin (1799).

SHEMEN ROKEACH, by Eleazar Low (1802).

CHIDUSHEI CHASM SOPHER, by Moishe Sofer (1822).

BETH YAAKOV, by Rabbi Jacob Lissa of Harubishov (1823).

CHIDUSHEI TUV GITTIN, by Zvi-Hirsh Heller (1829).

ORUCH L'NEIR, by Jacob Attlinger (1850).

CHIDUSHEI RAPHAEL, by Raphael Shlesinger (1877).

CHRONOLOGICAL LIST OF EXILARCHS (RESH GALUTHA)

Nahum Jochanan Shepot	140-170
Huna I	170-210
Uqba I	210-240
Huna II, his son	240-260
Nathan I, ben Huna	260-270
Nehemiah I	270-313
Mar Uqba II	313-337
Huna III, his brother	337-350
Abba Mari, his son	350-370
Nathan II	370-400
Chanan, son of Abba Mari	400-415
Huna IV	415-442
Mar Zutra I, son of Chanan	442-455
Chanan II	455-460
Huna V, son of Zutra	465-475
Huna VI, son of Chanan	484-508
Mar Zutra II (Achunai)	508-520
Huna Mar Chanan	520-560
Kafnai	560-580
Chanini	580-590
Bostanai	-660

THE TALMUD AT THE STAKE

Time	*Place*	*Persecutor*
1244	Paris	King Louis IX
1244	Rome	Pope Innocent IV
1248	Paris	Cardinal Legate Odo
1299	Paris	Philip the Fair
1309	Paris	Philip the Fair
1319	Toulouse	Lous
1322	Rome	Pope John XXII
1553	Rome	Pope Julius III
1553	Barcelona	Pope Julius III
1553	Venice	Pope Julius III
1553	Romagna	Pope Julius III
1553	Urbino	Pope Julius III
1553	Pesaro	Pope Julius III
1554	Ancona	Cardinal Carlo Borromeo
1554	Ferrara	Cardinal Carlo Borromeo
1554	Mantua	Cardinal Carlo Borromeo
1554	Padua	Cardinal Carlo Borromeo
1554	Candia	Cardinal Carlo Borromeo
1554	Ravenna	Cardinal Carlo Borromeo
1558	Rome	Cardinal Ghislieri
1559	Rome	Sextus Sinensis
1757	Poland	Bishop Dembowsky

THE MASECHTOTH OF THE BABYLONIAN TALMUD

In order to enable the reader to find at once in which of the 12 volumes of the Babylonian Talmud the different Masechtoth (treatises) of the Mishna are treated, we subjoin the following table:

Name of Masechta	*Volume*	*Order*	*No. of Masechta*
Aboth	IX	Nezikin	10
Aboda Zara	VIII	Nezikin	9
Baba Bathra	VIII	Nezikin	3
Baba Kamma	VIII	Nezikin	1
Baba Metzia	VIII	Nezikin	2
Bechoroth	X	Kodashim	4
Berachoth	I	Zeraim	1
Beza	III	Moed	7
Bikkurim	I	Zeraim	11
Chagiga	III	Moed	12
Challah	I	Zeraim	9
Chullin	XI	Kodashim	2
Demai	I	Zeraim	3
Eduoth	IX	Nezikin	7
Erachin	XI	Kodashim	5
Erubin	III	Moed	2
Gittin	VI	Nashim	4
Horayoth	IX	Nezikin	8
Kelim	XII	Teharoth	1
Kerithuth	XI	Kodashim	8
Kethuboth	V	Nashim	2
Kiddushin	V	Nashim	3

Name of Masechta	*Volume*	*Order*	*No. of Masechta*
Kilayim	I	Zeraim	4
Kinnim	XI	Kodashim	11
Maasroth	I	Zeraim	7
Maaser Sheni	I	Zeraim	8
Maccoth	IX	Nezikin	5
Machshirin	XII	Teharoth	9
Megilla	IV	Moed	10
Meilah	XI	Kodashim	7
Middoth	XI	Kodashim	10
Mikvaoth	XII	Teharoth	6
Menachoth	X	Kodashim	3
Moed Katon	III	Moed	11
Nazir	VI	Nashim	6
Nedarim	VI	Nashim	5
Negaim	XII	Teharoth	3
Nidda	XII	Teharoth	7
Ohaloth	XII	Teharoth	2
Orla	I	Zeraim	10
Parah	XII	Teharoth	4
Peah	I	Zeraim	2
Pesachim	III	Moed	3
Rosh Hashanah	IV	Moed	8
Sanhedrin	IX	Nezikin	4
Shabbath	II	Moed	1
Shekalim	IV	Moed	4
Shebiith	I	Zeraim	5
Shevuoth	IX	Nezikin	6
Sota	VI	Nashim	7
Succah	IV	Moed	6
Taanith	IV	Moed	9
Tamid	XI	Kodashim	9
Tebul Yom	XI	Teharoth	10
Temura	I	Kodashim	6
Terumoth	XII	Zeraim	6
Teharoth	XII	Teharoth	5

Name of Masechta	*Volume*	*Order*	*No. of Masechta*
Uzkin	XII	Teharoth	12
Yadaim	XII	Teharoth	11
Yebamoth	V	Nashim	1
Yoma	IV	Moed	5
Zabim	XII	Teharoth	9
Zebachim	X	Kodashim	1

MONEY, WEIGHTS AND MEASURES

A. MONEY:

Perutah ....the smallest copper coin current.
8 perutahs ....1 issar.
2 issars ....1 pondion.
2 pondions ....1 maah (the smallest silver coin current. Its weight is given as 16 barleycorns).
3 issars ....1 teresith.
12 pondions ....1 denar or zuz.
6 maahs ....1 denar or zuz.
5 Aspers ....1 denar or zuz.
2 Tropaics ....1 denar or zuz.
2 denars ....1 shekel.
2 shekels ....1 selah.
25 denars ....1 golden denar or zahub.
100 denars ....1 mina.

Roughly speaking a denar or zuz may be considered the equivalent of a shilling or 25 cents; and the selah approximately equivalent to a dollar.

B. WEIGHTS:

2 zuz ....1 common shekel.
2 shekels ....1 selah.
4 zuz ....1 shekel of the Sanctuary.
50 zuz ....1 tartimar.
160 zuz ....1 mina.
6000 zuz ....1 talent.

C. DISTANCE:

4 fingerbreadths	1 handbreadth.
2 handbreadths	1 sit. According to the Talmud, it is the distance between the tips of the outstretched thumb and index finger. According to Maimonides, it is the distance between the outstretched index and middle fingers.
3 handbreadths	1 span.
2 spans	1 cubit.
266–2/3 cubits	1 ris.
7½ ris	1 mil.
2000 cubits	1 Sabbath-day journey.

D. LIQUID AND DRY MEASURE:

64 kortabs	1 log (the contents of six eggs).
2 litras	1 log.
4 logs	1 kab.
3 kabs	1 hin.
6 kabs	1 seah.
3 seahs	1 ephah.
30 seahs	1 omer.

GLOSSARY OF UNTRANSLATED HEBREW TERMS

— A —

AB. The eleventh month of the Jewish calendar, counting from Tishre. It corresponds to the latter part of July and part of August.

AB BETH DIN. Chief of the House of Justice; Presiding Judge.

ABADIM. Servants; minor treatise in the Talmud.

ABODAH. Service; work; labor; ritualistic service in the Temple.

ABODAH ZARAH. Idolatry. Masechta of Nezikin.

ABOTH. Fathers. Masechta of Nezikin.

ADAR. The sixth month of the calendar, corresponding approximately to March. When the year is intercalated a month is inserted after Adar and before Nisan. This added month is known as Adar Sheni, "Second Adar."

AGADA (Pl. *Agadoth*). Literally "narration." The type of rabbinical interpretation and exposition of Scripture which aims at edification (as opposed to Halacha, which aims at defining or supporting legal usage). Agada is not frequently met with in the Mishna; but it is sometimes used as a conclusion to some of the tractates (cf. Peah, Yoma, Taanith, Sotah, Baba Kamma), and it is prominent in Aboth.

AM-HAARETZ (*"People of the Land"*). The name given to those Jews who were ignorant of the Law and who failed to observe the rules of cleanness and uncleanness and were not scrupulous in setting apart Tithes from the produce (namely, Heave-offering, First Tithe, Second Tithe, and Poorman's Tithe). Those Jews who, on the contrary, undertook to be faithful in observing the requirements of the Law are known as Chaberim (Associates).

AMORA (Pl. *Amoraim*). Speaker; interpreter; expounder. The teachers whose discussions, interpretations and decisions finally became embodied in the Gemara.

ARUCH. Literally: "prepared." Talmudic lexicon by Nathan ben Jechiel, of Rome, who flourished in the eleventh century. It is the oldest Lexicon for both Talmuds and the Midrashim, on which all later dictionaries are based.

ARUCH HASHALEM. Aruch completum, by Alexander Kohut, in which the original Aruch is corrected and considerably enlarged.

—B—

BABA. Gate; section; clause. A part of a Mishna paragraph referring to a separate case or proposition.

BABA BATHRA. The last gate. Masechta of Nezikin.

BABA KAMMA. The first gate. Masechta of Nezikin.

BABA METZIA. The middle gate. Masechta of Nezikin.

BERAITHA. Extraneous rabbinic tradition. Passages not included in the authorized Mishna of Rabbi Jehuda Hanasi.

BATH KOL. A divine voice.

BECHAROTH. First born. Masechta of Kodashim.

BERACHOTH. Benedictions. Masechta of Zeraim.

BETH DIN. Court house.

BETH HAKNESETH. House of assembly; synagogue.

BETH HAMIDRASH. House of study.

BETZA. Egg. Masechta of Moed.

BICCURIM. First fruits. Masechta of Zeraim.

BINYAN AB. Generalization of special laws.

—C—

CALLAH. Bride. A Minor Masechta added to the Babylonian Talmud.

CHAGIGA. Feast. Masechta of Moed.

CHALLA. Dough. Masechta of Zeraim.

CHARIPHOTH. Keenness; sharpness; brilliancy.

CHASSID (Pl. *Chassidim*). Pious.

CHEREM. Ban of excommunication.

CHOMER. Heaviness; that which is comparatively of great weight and importance.

CHOMETZ. Leavened bread.

CHULLIN. Profane. Masechta of Kadashim.

—D—

DARSHAN. Expounder.

DEMAI (or DAMMAI). Literally "dubious," i.e. produce not certainly tithed. The term is applied to produce bought from an Am-HaAretz and "dubious" in the sense that it cannot be assumed by an "Associate" (see Demai, 2b: one who undertakes to be scrupulous in his observance of the rules governing tithes and cleanness and uncleanness) who proposes to eat it, that heave-offering and tithes have been duly separated from it. Masechta of Zeraim.

DERASH. Search; investigate. A method by which a passage is interpreted in a more artificial way and deduction.

DERASHA. Interpretation; sermon; lecture.

DERECH ERETZ *(the conduct of life)*. Respect; reverence. Minor Masechta added to the Babylonian Talmud.

—E—

EBEL RABBATHI *(Great Mourning)*. Masechta added to the Babylonian Talmud.

EDUYOTH. Testimonies. Masechta of Nezikin.

ELUL. Twelfth month of the Jewish calendar, corresponding to August or September.

ERETZ YISRAEL. Land of Israel; Palestine.

ERUB. Literally "mixture," "amalgamation" or "combination." According to the Sabbath Law the movements of the people of a town are restricted on the Sabbath to 2000 cubits from the boundaries of the town. But if enough food for two meals is deposited in an accessible place on the eve of the Sabbath at the prescribed 2000 cubits distance, the spot counts as a man's temporary abode, thereby allowing him a range of 2000 cubits beyond the common Sabbath limit. Similarly Erub may be arranged as between the various domiciles within a courtyard; if all the occupants have a share in a deposit of food placed in a known place in the courtyard, they are all thereby given unrestricted access to the premises of the other occupants.

ERUBIN. Combinations. Masechta of Moed.

—G—

GALUTH. Exile; Diaspora.

GAON (Pl. *Geonim*). Majesty; grandeur; the illustrious one. Title of the head of the Babylonian academies at Sura and Pumbaditha.

GEMARA. Completion; supplement; teaching. The Gemara is the collection of commentaries and discussions of the Amoraim on the Mishna. Besides being a discursive commentary on the Mishna, the Gemara contains a vast amount of valuable material which does not always have any close connection with the Mishna text, as legal reports, historical and biographical information, religious and ethical maxims and homiletical remarks.

GENIZAH. Hidings; archives; discoveries.

GERIM. Strangers; apostates; a minor treatise.

GEZERA. Decree; decision.

GEZERA SHAVA. Analogy of expressions. In the Talmudic phraseology it denotes an analogy based on identical or similar words occurring in two different passages of Scripture.

GITTIN (Singular: *Get*). Divorces. Masechta of Nashim.

—H—

HABDALAH. Literally "division," "distinction." The ceremony which marks the end of a Sabbath or Festival-day and the entering in of an ordinary day.

HAGGADAH. See AGADA.

HALACHA (Pl. *Halachoth*). Literally "custom," "rule." An accepted decision in rabbinic law, usually, but not necessarily, derivable from Scripture. The term is also used for those parts of the Talmud concerned with legal matters in contrast to Agada. A usage dating from Moses as delivered from Sinai. A traditional law or traditional interpretation of a written law.

HECKESH. Analogy; comparison; syllogism. The analogy between two laws which rests on a biblical intimation (as Leviticus XIV:13) or on a principle common to both.

HORAYOTH. Decisions. Masechta of Nezikin.

—I—

IYAR. Eighth month of Jewish calendar, corresponding to May or June.

—K—

KAL. Light; minor. Easy to achieve.

KAL VE-CHOMER. Inference from major and minor. An inference from the less to the more important, and vice versa, from the more to the less important.

KETHUBOTH (Singular: *Kethubah*). Marriage contracts, containing, among other things, the settlement of a certain amount due to the wife on her husband's death or on being divorced. Masechta of Nashim.

KHELIM. Vessels. Masechta of Teharoth.

KHERITHOTH. Excisions. Masechta of Kadashim.

KHILAYIM. Mixtures. Masechta of Zeraim.

KIDDUSHIN. Sanctification; betrothals. Masechta of Nashim.

KINNIM. The bird's nests. Masechta of Kadashim.

KISLEV. Third month of Jewish calendar, corresponding to December.

KLAL. General rule or principle; community; generalization; statement by implication.

KLAL U-PRAT. Generalization and specification; interpretation based upon a general law followed by specification, or specification followed by generalization. When a law is once laid down in general, and in another place a specification is given (See: Leviticus VII:37), it is stated specifically not for its own sake alone, but as applicable to the whole class.

KNESETH. Assembly; parliament.

—M—

MAASEH. Deed, act, practice; report cited as proof.

MAASER. Tithe.

MAASER SHENI. Second tithe. Masechta of Zeraim.

MAASEROTH. Tithes. Masechta of Zeraim.

MARCHESHVAN. The second month of the calendar, corresponding approximately to November.

MACCOTH. Stripes. Masechta of Nezikin.

MACHSHIRIN. Preparations. Masechta of Teharoth.

MAR. Title for Babylonian teachers.

MASECHTA, or MESICHTA. Tractate; division of a Seder.

MASORA. Text by tradition.

MEGILLA. Scroll. Masechta of Moed.

MEILA. Sacrilege. Masechta of Kadashim.

MEMRA. A saying. A reported teaching, opinion or decision of the Amoraim.

MENACHOTH. Offerings. Masechta of Kadashim.

MESICHTA. See MASECHTA.

MIDDOTH. Measurements. Masechta of Kadashim.

MIDRASH: Exposition; interpretation of Scripture, originally in the sense of deducing an idea or rule from Scripture, in the manner of either Agada or Halacha. Homilies on the Scripture.

MISHNA. Teaching or repetition. The collection of legal traditions (explaining or supplementing the laws of the Pentateuch or derivable from the principles of those laws) in the form compiled by Rabbi Judah the Patriarch at the close of the second century C.E.

MISHNAYOTH. The six orders of the Mishna.

MOED. Festival. Seder of Mishna.

—N—

NASHIM. Women. Seder of Mishna.

NASI. Patriarch; prince. Title for the head of the Sanhedrin.

NAZIR. Abstainer; consecrated one. Masechta of Nashim.

NEDARIM. Vows. Masechta of Nashim.

NEGAIM. Leprosy. Masechta of Teharoth.

NEZIKIN. Damages. Seder of Mishna.

NIDDA. The menstruous. Masechta of Teharoth.

NISAN. The seventh month of the calendar, corresponding to the latter part of March and part of April.

—O—

OHALOTH. Tents. Masechta of Teharoth.

OMER. Literally "sheaf" (Leviticus XXIII:10). Before the new harvest could be reaped, a sheaf of barley must first be reaped and the flour offered as a meal-offering in the

Temple. Only after it had been offered was the produce of the new harvest permitted for the common use.

ORLA. Literally "foreskin," "uncircumcision" (Leviticus XIX:23). The fruit of the young trees was forbidden for common use during the first three years as being "the fruit of uncircumcision." In the fourth year the fruit could be "redeemed" (i.e. its equivalent in money set apart, plus a fifth of its value), and it was then free for common use. Fourth-year fruit must either be consumed in Jerusalem, or the money by which it was redeemed must be spent in Jerusalem. Orla is the name of the tenth tractate of Zeraim.

—P—

PARAH. The Heifer (Numbers XIX), whose ashes were used for the purification of the unclean. Masechta of Teharoth.

PARASHA (Pl. *Parashoth*). Separation; branching off. Section of the Torah. Weekly portion of the Law.

PEAH. Literally "the corner," section of the field that is being reaped. A portion of the crop of a field (and also of an olive tree) left by the reapers for the benefit of the poor (Leviticus XIX:9-10; Deuteronomy XXIV:19-21). Masechta of Zeraim.

PERAK (Pl. *Perakim*). A single division of a Masechta.

PESACHIM. Passovers. Masechta of Moed.

PESHAT. Plain meaning. A law or a passage in Scripture is explained in the most natural way according to the letter, the grammatical construction, and the spirit of the passage.

PILPUL. Disputation or debate displaying great dialectical acumen.

PROSBUL. A declaration made in court, before the execution of a loan, to the effect that the law of limitation by the entrance of the Sabbatical year shall not apply to the loan to be transacted.

—R—

RAB. Title for Babylonian teacher.

RABBAN. Literally "our master," "our lord." A title of honor given in the Mishna to most of the presidents of the Rabbinical Court after the time of Hillel.

RESH GALUTA. Head of the Jews in the Diaspora. Exilarch.

RESH METHIBTA. President of academy.

RESHA. Beginning case.

ROSH HASHANA. Beginning of the year. Masechta of Moed.

—S—

SABBATH. Masechta of Moed.

SABORAIM. Literally "ponderers." Babylonian teachers after the Amoraim.

SANHEDRIN. The courts. Masechta of Nezikin.

SEDARIM. Orders of. Series of Mishna.

SEDER. Section. Division of Mishna.

SEFER TORAH. The scroll of law. A minor treatise.

SHEBAT. The fifth month of the Jewish calendar, corresponding to February.

SEPHA. End of case.

SHEBIITH. The Sabbatical year (Exodus XXIII:11; Leviticus XXV:2-7; Deuteronomy XV:1-11). Masechta of Zeraim.

SHEBUOTH. Oaths. Masechta of Nezikin.

SHEKALIM. The half shekel which every Jew had to pay as a temple tax (Exodus XXX:12-16).

SHULCHAN ARUCH. Literally "prepared table." Annotations and commentaries by Rabbi Joseph Caro.

SIMANIM. Mnemonical signs. Paragraphs.

SIPHRA. Literally "the book." A collection of traditional interpretations of the whole book of Leviticus, introduced by an exposition of R. Ishmael's 13 hermeneutic rules.

SIPHRE. The books of the school of Rab, comprising the traditional interpretations of the book of Numbers, beginning with chapter V, and of the whole book of Deuteronomy.

SIVAN. The ninth month of the Jewish calendar, corresponding to June or July.

SOPHERIM. Scribes. Contributors to oral law.

SOTA. A woman suspected of adultery (Numbers V:12-31). Masechta of Nashim.

SUCCAH. Tabernacle. Masechta of Moed.

—T—

TAAM. Reason of law.

TAANITH. Fasts. Masechta of Moed.

TAKANA (Pl. *Takanoth*). Religious enactment promulgated by individuals or corporate bodies that exercised authority at the particular time.

TALMUD. Literally "learning." The general sense of the word is "study" of the Law. It is more common in the narrower sense of the comments and discussions (the "Gemara," literally "completion") on the text of the Mishna by Palestinian and Babylonian scholars from the third to the fifth century C.E., which constitute the Palestinian Talmud (Talmud Yerushalmi) and the Babylonian Talmud (Talmud Babli).

TAMID. The daily morning and evening offering in the Temple (Exodus XXIX:4; Numbers XXVIII:2-8). Masechta of Kadashim.

TAMMUZ. The fourth month of the calendar, corresponding with the latter part of June and part of July.

TANA (Pl. *Tanaim*). A teacher of the oral law, applied to those mentioned in the Mishna and Beraitha. The period of Tanaim is generally divided into five or six minor sections or generations.

TEBETH. The fourth month of the calendar, corresponding approximately with January.

TEBUL YOM. Immersed at day time. Masechta of Teharoth.

TEFILLAH. Prayer.

TEHAROTH. Purification. Sixth Seder of Mishna.

TEPHILLIN. Phylacteries tied on arm and head. A Minor Treatise.

TEREFAH. Literally "torn by wild beasts." Originally the term signified the flesh of clean beasts which had been mauled or killed by beasts of prey and so rendered unfit for food. It is more common in the Talmud as (a) the flesh of a beast that had received a fatal injury, such that it could not continue alive for another 12 months, or that suffered from some defect or abnormality; or (b) the flesh of an animal slaughtered unskilfully although in valid fashion, as distinct from Nebelah (carrion, animal carcase), a clean beast that has either suffered a violent death, or that was slaughtered not in a valid and regular fashion.

TERUMAH. Removal. Heave-offering; dedicated object; contribution for the sanctuary. The portion of the yield of their harvests which Jews must give to the priests (Numbers XVII:8ff; Deuteronomy XVIII:4). Heave-offering of tithe, which is given to the priests by the Levites out of the tithe they have received from the Israelites (Numbers XVIII:25ff).

THEMURA. Exchange. Sanctified things having been exchanged (Leviticus XXVII:10-27). Masechta of Kadashim.

TISHRE. The first month of the Jewish calendar, corresponding to September or October.

TORATH KOHANIM. See SIPHRA.

TOSAPHISTS. Authors of Tosaphoth, flourished during the twelfth and thirteenth centuries in France and Germany.

TOSAPHOTH. Additions. A collection of annotations printed in all Talmud editions on the exterior margin of the page.

TOSEPHTA. Supplement. The Tosephta contains mainly the remnants of the earlier compilations not adopted in the Mishna.

TURIM. Rows; tiers. An annotation of Halacha by R. Jacob ben Asher. The work is divided in four rows of laws: Tur Orach Chaim, Tur Yore Dea, Tur Eben Ha-ezer and Tur Choshen Mishpat.

—U—

UKTZIN. Stalks of Fruit. Stalks and shells of fruit in regard to conveying ritual uncleanness. Masechta of Teharoth.

—Y—

YADAYIM. Hands. The ritual on cleanliness of hands. Masechta of Teharoth.

YEBAMOTH. Levirate marriage (Deuteronomy XXV:5-10). Masechta of Nashim.

YOMA. The Day of Atonement (Leviticus XVI:3-34). Masechta of Moed.

—Z—

ZABIM. Persons suffering of running issues (Leviticus XV: 2-18). Masechta of Teharoth.

ZEBACHIM. Sacrifices (Leviticus I:1ff). Masechta of Kadashim.

ZERAIM. Seeds. First Seder of Mishna.

ZIZITH. Fringes. A Minor Treatise.

ZUGOTH. Pairs. Heads of Sanhedrin.

GENERAL BIBLIOGRAPHY

ABRAHAMS, I.—Studies in Pharisaism and the Gospels. Cambridge, 1917.

ABRAHAMS, I.—Chapters on Jewish Literature. Philadelphia, 1889.

ABRAHAMS, I.—A Book of Delight. Philadelphia, 1889.

ABRAHAMS, I.—Jewish Life in the Middle Ages. London, 1932.

ALBECK, CH.—Untersuchungen ueber die Halachischen Midrashim. Berlin, 1927.

ALLON, G.—Tehuman shel Hilkoth Toharoth. Tabriz, 1938.

AMRAM, D. W.—The Jewish Law of Divorce. Philadelphia, 1896.

BACHER, W.—Die Agada der Tannaiten. Strasburg, 1884.

BACHER, W.—Die Agada der Babylonischen Amoraer. Strasburg, 1887.

BACHER, W.—Die Agada der Palestinischen Amoraer. Strasburg, 1891.

BACHER, W.—Tradition und Tradenten in den Schulen Palestinas und Babyloniens. Leipzig, 1914.

BADER, G.—Our Spiritual Heroes. New York, 1935.

BAECK, L.—Die Pharisaer. Berlin, 1927.

BAER, S.—Abodath Yisrael. Redelheim, 1868.

BAMBERGER, S.—Die Sadduzaer. Frankfurt-am-Main, 1907.

BARON, S. W.—Social and Religious History of the Jews. New York, 1937.

BARON, S. W.—Freedom and Reason. Glencoe, Ill., 1950.

BENNY, P. B.—The Criminal Code of the Jews. London, 1880.

BENTWICH, N.—Philo. Philadelphia, 1912.

BENTWICH, N.—Hellenism. Philadelphia, 1919.

BERLINER, A.—Migdal Hannanel. Berlin, 1878.

BERNFELD, S.—The Foundations of Jewish Ethics. New York, 1929.

BERNFELD, S.—Der Talmud. Berlin, 1900.

BEVAN, E. R.—Jewish Parties and the Law. Cambridge, 1932.

BILDERSEE, A.—Jewish Post-Biblical History. Cincinnati, 1918.

BIRNBAUM, PH.—Pirke Aboth. New York, 1950.

BLOCH, M.—Die Ethik der Halacha. Budapest, 1886.

BOKSER, B.—Pharisaic Judaism in Transition. New York, 1935.

BOKSER, B.—The Legacy of Maimonides. New York, 1950.

BOUSSET, D. W.—Die Judische Apokalyptic. Berlin, 1903.

BOX, G. H.—Judaism in the Greek Period. Oxford, 1932.

BRANSCOMB, B. H.—Jesus and the Law of Moses. New York, 1930.

BRAUNSCHWEIGER, M.—Die Lehrer der Mishnah. Frankfurt-Am-Main, 1903.

BRAV, S. R.—Marriage and the Jewish Tradition. New York, 1951.

BREUER, J.—Fundamentals of Judaism. New York, 1950.

BRULL, J.—Mebo Hamishnah. Frankfurt, 1876.

BUBER, S.—Midrash Tanchuma. Wilna, 1913.

BUBER, S.—Eicha Rabba. Wilna, 1899.

BUBER, S.—Pesikta de R. Kahana. Lyck, 1868.

BUBER, S.—Midrash Shemuel. Cracow, 1893.

BUBER, S.—Midrash Tehillim. Wilna, 1891.

BUECHLER, A.—Das Sanhedrin in Jerusalem. Vienna, 1902.

CASSANOWICZ, I. M.—Non-Jewish Religious Ceremonies in the Talmud. New York, 1894.

CHARLES, R. H.—Apocrypha and Pseudepigrapha. Oxford, 1913.

CHARLES, R. H.—A Critical History of the Doctrine of a Future Life in Israel. London, 1899.

CHARLES, R. H.—Religious Development between the Old and New Testament. London, 1890.

CHWOLSON, D.—Das Letzte Passamahl. Leipzig, 1908.

CHWOLSON, D.—Beitrage zur Entwicklungsgeschichte des Judentums. Leipzig, 1910.
COHEN, A.—Jewish History in the First Century. London, 1920.
COHEN, A.—Everyman's Talmud. London, 1931.
COHEN, H.—Talmudic Sayings. Cincinnati, 1885.

DAICHES, S.—The Jews in Babylonia in the Time of Ezra and Nehemiah. London, 1910.
DARMESTETER, A.—The Talmud. Philadelphia, 1897.
DAVIDSON, I.—Parody in Jewish Literature. New York, 1907.
DAVIDSON, I.—Sefer Shashuyim. New York, 1907.
DEUTSCH, E.—The Talmud. Cincinnati, 1897.
DUBNOW, S.—The History of the Jews. Philadelphia, 1950.

EISENSTEIN, J. D.—Ozar Hamidrashim. New York, 1915.
ELBOGEN, I.—Studien zur Geschichte. Berlin, 1907.
ENELOW, H. G.—The Modern Reconstruction of the Pharisees. New York, 1908.
EPSTEIN, J. N.—Die Gaonasche Kommentar. Berlin, 1915.

FINKELSTEIN, L.—The Pharisees. Philadelphia, 1946.
FINKELSTEIN, L.—The Jews. Philadelphia, 1950.
FRANKEL, Z.—Darke Hamishnah. Leipzig, 1859.
FRIEDLANDER, G.—The Jewish Religion. London, 1915.
FRIEDLANDER, G.—Laws and Customs of Israel. London, 1915.
FRIEDMAN, M.—Pesikta Rabbati. Vienna, 1880.
FUNK, S.—Die Juden in Babylonien. Berlin, 1902.

GASTER, M.—The Samaritans. London, 1925.
GINSBURG, CH. D.—The Massorah. London, 1897.
GINZBERG, L.—Kebuzat Maamarim. Warsaw, 1910.
GINZBERG, L.—Gaonica. New York, 1909.
GINZBERG, L.—Ginze Schechter. New York, 1928.
GINZBERG, L.—Mekoma shel Halacha B'chochmat Yisrael. Jerusalem, 1931.
GINZBERG, L.—The Religion of the Pharisees. Philadelphia, 1928.

GINZBERG, L.—Legends of the Jews. Philadelphia, 1946.
GLAZER, S.—Guide of Judaism. New York, 1922.
GOLDMAN, S.—The Jew and the Universe. New York, 1936.
GOLDSTEIN, M.—Jesus in the Jewish Tradition. New York, 1950.
GOODMAN, P.—A History of the Jews. New York, 1919.
GOTTLOBER, B.—Bikoret L'toldoth Hakaraim.
GRAETZ, H.—History of the Jews. Philadelphia, 1922.
GREENSTONE, J. H.—The Messiah Idea in Jewish History. Philadelphia, 1906.
GREENWALD, L.—L'toldoth Hasanhedrin B'Yisrael. New York, 1950.
GRUENBAUM, E.—Die Sittenlehre des Judentums. Strasburg, 1878.
GUTTMAN, M.—Das Judentum und seine Umwelt. Berlin, 1927.
GUTTMAN, M.—Mafteach Ha-Talmud. Budapest, 1908.

HAHN, A.—The Rabbinical Dialectics. Cincinnati, 1879.
HALEVY, I.—Doroth Harishonim. Frankfurt, 1906.
HALPER, B.—Post-Biblical Hebrew Literature. Philadelphia, 1921.
HEILPRIN, J.—Seder Hadoroth. Carlsruhe, 1769.
HERFORD, R. T.—Pharisaism. New York, 1912.
HERFORD, R. T.—What the World Owes to Pharisees. London, 1919.
HERFORD, R. T.—The Significance of Pharisaism. London, 1924.
HERFORD, R. T.—The Truth about the Pharisees. New York, 1925.
HERFORD, R. T.—The Pharisees. London, 1924.
HERFORD, R. T.—Judaism in the New Testament Period. London, 1924.
HERSHON, P. A.—Talmudic Miscellany. London, 1880.
HERSHON, P. A.—Treasures of the Talmud. London, 1882.
HETZENAUER, M.—Vulgate. Rome, 1922.
HIGGER, M.—Intention in Talmudic Law. New York, 1927.

HIGGER, M.—Masechta Semahot. New York, 1931.
HIGGER, M.—Sheba Mesachtoth Ktanoth. New York, 1930.
HIGGER, M.—Masechta Derech Eretz. New York, 1935.
HILGENFELD, A.—Die Judische Apokalyptic. Berlin, 1857.
HOELSCHER, G.—Geschichte der Israelitischen Religion. Giessen, 1922.
HOFFMAN, D.—Die Erste Mishnah. Berlin, 1882.
HOFFMAN, D.—Zur Einleitung in die Halachischen Midrashim. Berlin, 1888.
HOFFMAN, D.—Midrash Tannaim. Berlin, 1908.
HOFFMAN, D.—Mechilta de R. Shimmon. Frankfurt, 1905.
HOLLMAN, H.—The Jewish Religion in Time of Jesus. London, 1909.
HYMAN, A.—Toldoth Tannaim. London, 1910.

ISAACS, I. S.—Stories from the Rabbis. New York, 1893.

JACKSON, F.—Our Lord and the Pharisees. Lancaster, 1910.
JELLINEK, A.—Der Talmud. Vienna, 1865.
JELLINEK, A.—Der Talmudjude. Vienna, 1882.
JELLINEK, A.—Kontres Ha-Kelaim. Vienna, 1878.
JELLINEK, A.—Kontres Hamafteach. Vienna, 1881.
JOSEPH, M.—Judaism as Creed and Life. New York, 1903.
JOSEPHUS, F.—Antiquities. London, 1926.
JOSEPHUS, F.—Complete Works. New York, 1902.
JOWETT, B.—The Dialogues of Plato. Oxford, 1924.

KAATZ, S.—Die Muendliche Lehre und ihr Dogma. Leipzig, 1922.
KAHANA, A.—Safruth ha-Historiah. Jerusalem, 1950.
KAMINKA, A.—Die Rabbinische Literatur und die Halacha.
KATZ, A.—Biographische Charakterbildungen aus der Judischen Geschichte und Sage. Berlin, 1905.
KAUFFMANN, E.—Toldoth Ha-Emunah Ha-Yisreelith. Jerusalem, 1937.
KITTEL, R.—Geschichte des Volkes Israel. Gotha, 1921.
KLAUSNER, J.—Historiah Yisraelith. Jerusalem, 1924.

KOHUT, A.—The Ethics of the Fathers. New York, 1885.
KRAUSS, S.—Talmudische Archaelogie. Leipzig.
KROCHMAL, N.—More Nebuche Hazman. Lemberg, 1863.
KRONBERG, N.—Rashi als Exeget. Halle, 1882.

LAUTERBACH, J. Z.—Midrash and Mishna. New York, 1916.
LAZARUS, M.—The Jewish Ethics. Philadelphia, 1900.
LESZYNSKY, R.—Die Pharisaer und Sadduzaer. Frankfurt, 1912.
LESZYNSKY, R.—Die Sadduzaer. Berlin, 1912.
LEVITAS, E.—Massoreth Ha-Massoreth. London, 1867.
LEWIN, B. M.—Ozar Ha-Geonim. Jerusalem, 1928.
LIBER, M.—Rashi. Philadelphia, 1906.
LIGHTLY, J. W.—Jewish Sects and Parties. London, 1925.
LUZZATTO, S. D.—Tal Oroth.
LUZZATTO, S. D.—Oheb Ger.

MAGNUS, L.—Outlines of Jewish History. Philadelphia, 1890.
MARGOLIS, M.—History of the Jewish People. Philadelphia, 1927.
MARMORSTEIN, A.—Perushim. (Ozar Yisrael, VIII). New York, 1912.
MARTI, K.—Geschichte der Israelitischen Religion. Strasburg, 1903.
MATHEWS, G.—The Jewish Apology. Chicago, 1910.
MENDELSOHN, S.—The Criminal Jurisprudence of the Ancient Hebrews. Baltimore, 1891.
MIELZINER, M.—Introduction to the Talmud. New York, 1925.
MIELZINER, M.—Legal Maxims and Fundamental Laws. Cincinnati, 1898.
MIELZINER, M.—The Jewish Law of Marriage and Divorce. Cincinnati, 1884.
MIELZINER, M.—The Rabbinical Law of Hereditary Succession. Cincinnati, 1900.
MONTGOMERY, J.—The Samaritans. Philadelphia, 1907.

MOORE, G. F.—Judaism in the First Centuries of the Christian Era. Cambridge, 1927.
MULLER, J.—Mafteach L'Teshuboth Ha-Geonim. Berlin, 1891.
MULLER, J.—Masechta Sopherim. Leipzig, 1878.

NAMIATH, R. M.—What Judaism Teaches. Los Angeles, 1940.
NEUMARK, D.—Toldoth Ha-Ikrim. Jerusalem, 1950.
NEUMARK, D.—Toldoth Ha-Philosophia B'Yisrael. Jerusalem, 1950.

OPPENHEIM, J.—Toldoth Ha-Mishnah. Jerusalem, 1950.
OSTERLEY, W. O.—The Religion and Worship of the Synagogue. London, 1911.
OSTERLEY, W. O.—Hebrew Religion. New York, 1930.
OSTERLEY, W. O.—Judaism and Christianity. New York, 1937.

PICK, B.—The Talmud. New York, 1887.
PINELES, F.—Darke shel Torah. Vienna, 1861.
POLANO, H.—The Talmud. London, 1876.

RAISIN, J. S.—Sect, Creed and Customs in Judaism. Philadelphia, 1907.
RAPOPORT, S. J.—Erech Millin.
RAPOPORT, S. J.—Rabbenu Nisim.
RAPOPORT, S. J.—Rabbenu Hannanel.
REICHLER, M.—What is the Talmud? Cincinnati.
REVEL, B.—The Karaite Halacha. Philadelphia, 1913.
RIDDLE, D. W.—Jesus and the Pharisees. Chicago, 1928.
RITTER, B.—Philo und die Halacha. Leipzig, 1897.
ROBERTSON, A. T.—The Pharisees and Jesus. New York, 1928.
RODKINSON, M. L.—What is the Talmud? Chicago, 1894.
RODKINSON, M. L.—The History of the Talmud. New York, 1903.
ROSIN, D.—Rabbi Samuel ben Meir.

ROSTOVZEFF, M.—A History of the Ancient World. Oxford, 1926.

RUDY, S.—Design for Living. New York, 1950.

SACHER, A. L.—A History of the Jews. New York, 1930.

SANDERS, F. K.—History of the Hebrews. New York, 1914.

SCHAEDER, H. H.—Ezra der Schreiber. Tuebingen, 1930.

SCHECHTER, S.—Documents of Jewish Sectaries. Cambridge, 1910.

SCHECHTER, S.—Fragments of A Zadokite Work. Cambridge, 1910.

SCHECHTER, S.—Some Aspects of Rabbinic Theology. New York, 1910.

SCHECHTER, S.—Studies in Judaism. Philadelphia, 1924.

SCHECHTER, S.—Aboth de Rabbi Nathan. Vienna, 1886.

SCHOEN, M.—The Man Jesus Was. New York, 1950.

SCHREIBER, E.—The Talmud. Denver, 1884.

SCHWARZ, A.—Die Controversen der Shammaiten und Hilleliten. Vienna, 1893.

SEKELES, S.—The Poetry of the Talmud. New York, 1880.

SHAW, G.—The Conflict of Jesus. Boston, 1916.

SHURER, E.—History of the Jewish People. Edinburgh, 1891.

SLIVKEN, H. S.—Ispaklaria Ha'Meirah. Warsaw, 1902.

SMITH, G. A.—Jerusalem from the Earliest Times. London, 1907.

STERN, I.—Die Frau im Talmud. Zurich, 1879.

STRACK, H. L.—Introduction to the Talmud and Midrash. Philadelphia, 1931.

SULZBERGER, M.—The Am-Ha-Aretz. Philadelphia, 1909.

SULZBERGER, M.—The Status of Labor in Ancient Israel.

TABENHAUS, G.—Echoes of Wisdom. New York, 1900.

TOY, C. H.—Judaism and Christianity. Boston, 1890.

TSCHERNOWITZ, CH.—Toldoth Halacha. New York, 1936.

TSERIKOWER, A.—Ha-Yehudim veha-Yevanim. Tel Aviv, 1931.

UNTERMAN, I.—Di Neviyim. Philadelphia, 1934.

UNTERMAN, I.—Rashi. Philadelphia, 1936.

VARGHA, J.—Defense in Criminal Cases with the Ancient Hebrews. Cincinnati, 1880.

VOGELSTEIN, H.—Die Landwirtschaft in Palestina zur Zeit der Mishna. Berlin, 1894.

WALDBERG, S.—Darke Hashinnuyim. Lemberg, 1870.

WAXMAN, M.—A History of the Jewish Literature. New York, 1930.

WEISS, I. H.—Dor Dor Ve'Dorshov. New York, 1924.

WELLENHAUSEN, J.—Die Pharisaer und die Sadducaer. Hanover, 1924.

WICKS, H. J.—The Doctrine of God in the Jewish Apocryphal and Apocalyptic Literature. London, 1915.

WRIGHT, D.—The Talmud. London, 1932.

YAWITZ, Z.—Toldoth Israel. Berlin, 1911.

ZAKUTO, A.—Sefer Yochasin. London, 1857.

ZEITLIN, S.—The History of the Second Jewish Commonwealth. Philadelphia, 1933.

ZEITLIN, S.—Megillath Taanith. Philadelphia, 1922.

ZIRNDORF, H.—Some Women in Israel. Philadelphia, 1892.

ZUCKERMANDEL, E.—Tosephta. Jerusalem, 1938.

BIBLICAL, MISHNAIC AND TALMUDIC REFERENCES

BIBLICAL

JERUSALEM TALMUD

MIDRASHIC

INDEX

INDEX TO SUBJECTS AND NAMES

References are to page numbers.

Key to Pronunciation:
All Hebrew terms in this index are spelled in accordance with the Sephardic pronunciation commonly used in Israel. Pronounce: "a," as in father; "o," as in more; "e," as in net; "u," as in put; "i," as in hit.